428
G56

BECOMING LITERATE IN ENGLISH AS A SECOND LANGUAGE

COGNITION AND LITERACY
Series Editor: Judith Orasanu
U.S. Army Research Institute

Metacognition and Reading Comprehension, Ruth Garner
Becoming Literate in English as a Second Language, Susan Goldman and Henry Trueba (eds.)

In preparation

Literacy Development: Comparative Studies in the Acquisition and Practice of Literacy, Stephen Reder and Karen Reid Green

BECOMING LITERATE IN ENGLISH AS A SECOND LANGUAGE

Edited by
Susan R. Goldman
and
Henry T. Trueba
University of California, Santa Barbara

Ablex Publishing Corporation
Norwood, N.J. 07648

Copyright © 1987 by Ablex Publishing Corporation

All rights reserved. No part of this publication may be reproduced in any form, by photostat, microfilm, retrieval system, or by any other means, without the prior permission of the publisher.

Printed in the United States of America

Library of Congress Cataloging-in-Publication Data

Becoming literate in English as a second language.

   (Cognition and literacy)
   Bibliography: p.
   Includes index.
   1. English language—Study and teaching—Foreign speakers. 2. English language—Study and teaching—United States. I. Goldman, Susan R. II. Trueba, Henry T. III. Series.
PE1128.A2B34   1987   428'.007   87-14311
ISBN 0-89391-426-6

Ablex Publishing Corporation
355 Chestnut Street
Norwood, New Jersey 07648

Contents

Introduction: Contextual Issues in the Study of Second
      Language Literacy   1
Susan R. Goldman

1. Mexican Adult Literacy: New Directions for Immigrants   9
Concha Delgado-Gaitan

2. Factors Affecting Development of Second
      Language Literacy   33
Richard Durán

3. Reading in a Second Language: Studies With Adult and
      Child Learners   57
Barry McLaughlin

4. Patterns of Performance Among Bilingual Children Who
      Score Low in Reading   71
Mary Sue Ammon

5. Comprehension of Content Area Passages: A Study of Spanish/
      English Readers in Third and Fourth Grade   107
Marie de la Luz Reyes

6. Oral Reading Miscues of Hispanic Good and Learning
      Disabled Students: Implications for Second
      Language Reading   127
Ofelia Miramontes

7. The Development of Writing Skills Among Hispanic
      High School Students   155
Benji Wald

8. Metapragmatic Knowledge of School-Age
      Mexican-American Children   187
Louise Cherry Wilkinson and Celia Genishi

9. Teacher Language Use in a Chinese Bilingual Classroom   205
Larry F. Guthrie and Grace Pung Guthrie

10 Organizing Classroom Instruction in Specific Sociocultural
   Contexts: Teaching Mexican Youth to Write
   in English   235
Henry T. Trueba

Author Index   253

Subject Index   258

Introduction

Contextual Issues in the Study of Second Language Literacy

Susan R. Goldman
University of California, Santa Barbara

Over the past decade, there has been an increasing recognition of the limitations of single discipline approaches to just about every domain of human endeavor. There are numerous indications of this trend. It is mirrored in the formation of professional associations and publications designed to foster cross-discipline communication. Increasingly, theories of development and of intellectual functioning reflect an appreciation for the multifaceted nature of human thought and behavior. For example, Sternberg's triarchic theory of intelligence places strong emphasis on adaptation and culture as well as on cognitive processes involved in specific performances (Sternberg, 1984). Theoretical and empirical work on language has a long and rich history of profitable interactions among linguists, psychologists, sociologists, and anthropologists. Such collaborations have contributed importantly to our current understanding of language and communication. Finally and happily, it is no longer possible to discuss schooling and classroom practice without being informed by research emanating from multiple disciplines (see, for example, Bloome & Green, 1984; also Cazden, 1986).

This volume brings together two domains of inquiry which are perhaps sterling, exemplars of the necessity and utility of cross-disciplinary perspectives, literacy and English as a second language. Scribner (1984) described literacy as a "many meaning-ed" entity, and, to those trying to grasp it, English oftentimes must appear as a many meaning-ed language and one not terribly consistent in how meaning is made. An important and advantageous consequence of cross-disciplinary perspectives on literacy and English as a second language is that unidimensional definitions of literacy are dispelled rather quickly. Scribner has "defined" literacy by way of three metaphors, all of which have validity and a special cogency when considered in the context of linguistic minority individuals.

Scribner's three metaphors are *literacy as adaptation*, *literacy as power*, and *literacy as a state of grace*. Each metaphor captures a unique perspective on literacy, and, taken together, they reflect the mosaic of the concept. *Literacy as adaptation* encapsulates the survival or pragmatic value of literacy. Such functional literacy is broadly conceived as "the level of proficiency necessary for effective performance in a range of settings and customary activities" (Scribner, 1984, p. 9). Critical issues that arise within this metaphor do not concern definitions of literacy per se; rather, functional competencies and cultural and linguistic variation in language proficiencies necessary for successful functioning are the foci. As well as the group specification of necessary and desired literacy competencies, there is the individual's self-perceived need and definition of the competencies demanded of him or her. This metaphor has driven the research efforts of a large number of individuals attempting to characterize the functional literacy skills for successful schooling (e.g., Wong Fillmore, Ammon, Ammon, Delucchi, Jensen, McLaughlin, & Strong, 1983). Typically, psychologists and sociolinguists have been heavily involved in this view. It has also contributed to a resurgence in interest in Vygotsky's developmental theory.

Scribner's second metaphor is *literacy as power*, a concept emphasizing the relationship between literacy and group or community advancement. According to this view, literacy is a necessary tool for sociopolitical and economic advancement. To be illiterate is to be in a state of victimization. As our society becomes increasingly "technologized," those who possess the literacy skills affording participation will be able to create an impact on their own and the lives of other members of their respective groups. However, Scribner (1984) points out that literacy per se may not be a single and sufficient causal agent in participation. Some have suggested that attainment of functional literacy levels beyond certain rudimentary skills is in fact detrimental and leads to conditions of overqualification for the employment possibilities available to individuals in certain minority groups (see, for discussion, Delgado-Gaitan, this volume; Ogbu, 1983).

The third and final metaphor is *literacy as a state of grace*, a metaphor by which Scribner depicts the tendency in many societies to give favored status to the literate person, or to imbue this individual with special virtue and powers. This metaphor captures the elitist status accruing automatically to the possessor of reading and writing skills. This individual has access to the accumulated knowledge of humankind and enjoys a favored intellectual status among the populace, the majority of whom do not possess such skills. Thus, the mark of an educated man is the ability to read, interpret written communication, and write back in response to such a communication. This last metaphor then assumes a certain specialness about the possessor of reading and writing skills, as if universal possession of such skills was an unattainable, or perhaps undesirable, state of affairs.

Scribner's three metaphors reflect the input of perspectives on literacy from a number of different disciplines. Each metaphor communicates a part of the whole common sense understanding of the literacy concept, and indicates why becoming literate appears to be so important. Each metaphor can be felt in the way our educational system is organized and in the generally accepted goal that it is the job of the schools to teach literacy skills, with the latter usually translated into reading and, increasingly, writing skills. Implicitly and explicitly, and by multiple constituencies, schools and teachers are evaluated on the basis of the degree to which they have fostered the process of becoming literate. In turn, students are evaluated by teachers and the educational system on the basis of how successful they have been in becoming literate. Of particular concern, in the case of those becoming literate in English as a second language, is the assessment of how literate they have become and whether such assessment is based on first and home language as compared to English. An additional concern is whether the degree of literacy achieved by the student is seen as under the control solely of the student, or whether other forces are seen as bearing responsibility for the student's progress. Individual differences in the degree of literacy achieved are not the problem; such differences are to be expected. The problem is the implications and conclusions drawn based on the existence of the individual differences.

Thus far, I have intentionally hesitated to use terms such as "second-language learning and learners" and "second-language acquisition and acquirers." This reluctance is related to the assessment issue and the conclusions drawn on the basis of assessment. The two terms, "learning" and "acquisition," have always struck me as having different nuances that always seemed to be escaping articulated discussion. In the present context, the different nuances in learning and acquisition seem to key two contrasting points of view on the nature of the process of becoming literate and the nature and responsibilities of the individual engaged in becoming literate. Although I am not wedded to the association that I will make between each term and the viewpoint, the contrast in the viewpoints is very real. The term *acquisition* seems to place the burden of responsibility on the individual who is engaged in the task of becoming literate in English as a second language, with minimal responsibility for progress assigned to significant others in the environment.

This viewpoint derives from a type of nativist position on language development. Recall Chomsky's (1965) postulation of a Language Acquisition Device and efforts to specify what such a device would have to come equipped with to accomplish the feats of first language development so rapidly. According to this perspective, success or failure are the individual's responsibility: if you fail, don't look to the environment for an explanation. After all, everyone had the same opportunity. In fact, much of the research on classroom discourse indicates that not everyone does have the same opportunities and language input, even when it might appear so on the surface (see, for example, Eder, 1982; DeStefano, Pepinsky, & Sanders, 1982; see also reviews by Bloome & Green, 1984; Cazden, 1986).

In contrast, second language *learning* carries a connotation of an active and engaged process in which there are conscious and explicit efforts on the part of tutors and tutees, broadly speaking, to come to grips with the English language system. Within this view, the product, namely progress toward becoming literate, is not a property of the learner, nor a property of the tutor, but a product of the interaction. Responsibility is shared and literacy is actively constructed.

The importance of the latter view is in making clear that literacy, whether in first or second languages, is both a cognitively and an interpersonally constructed phenomenon. The language learner is not victimized, tossed wildly about, by sociological factors, nor kept imprisoned by internal, cognitive structures. Rather, the language learner cognizes with a particular internal context and is embedded in sociocultural and linguistic contexts. We would expect that differences within a group of individuals as well as differences between groups of individuals would be accounted for by internal *and* external contexts and their *interaction*. Furthermore, it becomes important for literacy in English *as a second* language to attend to the identification and understanding of aspects of literacy that are general, as compared with those that are language specific.

The perspectives reflected in the contributions to this volume are consistent with the second viewpoint on becoming literate in English as a second language. That is, the process is an interactive one in which literacy is constructed and responsibility for the outcome is shared by the individual and by sociocultural and economic factors, such as those present in school, home, and community contexts. Three major themes are reflected throughout the chapters:

- The home/community setting provides an interpersonal context for literacy learning events and its impact on the individual's cognitive and affective propensities is critical.

- Specific cognitive skills are involved in learning to read and write. Some of these skills are specific to English; some transfer from first to second language. It is necessary to understand more precisely which reading and writing skills are general, and which specific.
- Assessment, diagnosis, and evaluation need to be based upon careful, cross-situational analyses of performance requirements and the relationships between those requirements and general and specific cognitive-linguistic skills. Furthermore, the interpretation of performance patterns is profitably informed by an appreciation for the individual's perspective on the functional value and adaptive significance of the task and performance on it.

Different degrees of emphasis are placed on each of these themes by the various chapters. Specifically, the first two chapters address contexts associated with successful literacy learning in English as a second language. Delgado-Gaitan focuses on the home/community context of literacy and the various factors that determine academic success. She is particularly concerned with the value attached to literacy by significant adult figures and with why literacy is valued in the way(s) that it is. The empirical work describes the varied viewpoints of a group of adults participating in an English-language literacy program. Several aspects of literacy and schooling are discussed by these adults, including their perceptions of literacy, of their role(s) in society, of the value of schooling, and their own goals for themselves and their children. Durán begins with a discussion of various perspectives on the nature of bilingualism and the cognitive and sociocultural factors that influence the degree to which minority language group members become literate in English. He reports data from two large scale surveys that indicate that both interpersonal and intrapersonal factors are important predictors of educational progress. Using ethnomethodological techniques, Durán pursues the meaning of the two factors, emphasizing the importance of the nature and structure of literate behaviors and the contexts in which these behaviors are embedded.

A more specific focus on school contexts and tasks is reflected in the remainder of the chapters. Five chapters are concerned with specific reading and writing tasks and the elucidation of specific and general literacy skills. Reading receives attention in four of the chapters, the first three of which share an information processing orientation to comprehension. McLaughlin's contribution lays out general theoretical assumptions regarding the cognitive skills that are important in learning to read in English and the particular implications the information processing view has for learning to read in English as a second language. Empirical work on the nature of the comprehension difficulties experienced by second language learners is reported. Concern is with whether these difficulties are qualitatively similar to difficulties experienced by native speakers. Ammon's chapter continues this theme, but stresses the importance of beginning both research and diagnostic assessment with a developmental model of reading. She reports on the performance of Hispanic and of Chinese students on reading comprehension items. Her analyses emphasize the elucidation of the strategies and thinking in which students are engaged when they select particular answers. Of particular interest are the variations within the sample of students.

Reyes deals directly with the issue of transfer of learning from text strategies. She reports the comprehension performance of elementary school students learning from reading informational texts in first (Spanish) and second (English) languages. Her findings suggest that strategies for getting new knowledge from printed material qualify as general literacy skills. However, she points to the importance of the context in which reading to learn skills are assessed, emphasizing the importance of an informal and accepting task environment. The final chapter on reading addresses questions of both skill-related and first-language related differences in reading performance. In this chapter, Miramontes describes comprehension strategies that are inferred from the patterns of oral reading miscues reflected in the performances of skilled and of less-skilled readers for whom English is the first vs. the second language. Patterns of miscues when reading in the first language are compared to those when reading in the second language. Wald's chapter on writing completes the section on the cognitive and linguistic characteristics of school based tasks. Specifically, Wald is concerned with transfer of linguistic aspects of written Spanish and English and the identification of language independent writing skills. The writing samples of adolescents differing in amount of experience with the English language are analyzed in terms of features that are similar in Spanish and English and in terms of those that are different. The findings support educational programming that continues literacy skills in the first language *at least* during the time period in which a student is in the process of becoming literate in English as a second language.

The final section chapters emphasize a different aspect of classroom performance and one associated with how language is used to structure and organize the classroom and literacy experiences within it. Wilkinson and Genishi examine the knowledge and awareness of the *request* function of language in first and third grade Mexican-American English speaking children. Wilkinson and Genishi find that English language proficiency is related to the variety of language forms used for making requests. Furthermore, these students seem to place more emphasis on being polite when making requests than do Anglo students. Wilkinson and Genishi suggest that this difference reflects the impact of cultural norms and values. Emphasis switches to the teacher in the last two chapters. Guthrie and Guthrie concentrate on the importance of teachers' use of language to communicate the content as well as the appropriate participation structures in the classroom. Comparisons of two teachers, a bilingual Chinese-English and an English-only teacher, working with a group of native speakers of Chinese, reveal both similarities and differences between them. Of particular interest is the way in which the bilingual teacher used Chinese, the students' first language, to achieve specific and often metacognitive goals. The final chapter, by Trueba, explicitly returns to the importance of the interpersonal context in literacy events in dealing with teachers as conveyors and instigators of literacy events. Student writing samples were gathered when working with a dozen teachers on improving writing instruction. Strategies for improving writing instruction were based on home-based literacy events. Of particular interest in this chapter are the teachers' descriptions of what they learned about how the students learn, especially the importance of the relevance of the activity to the student.

There is a fourth theme that permeates the volume and it is one that seems particularly apt at the conclusion of an introduction. Becoming literate in English as a second language is a multifaceted endeavor and a phenomenon that belies simplistic description and linear combinations of independent factors. Rather, the phenomenon is a linguistically and culturally rich experience upon which complex factors bear. Research that rises to the challenge of this complexity is difficult and labor intensive. This volume represents a rich sample of such research.

References

Bloome, D., & Green, J. (1984). Directions in the sociolinguistic study of reading. In P. D. Pearson (Ed.), *Handbook of reading research* (pp. 395–421). New York: Longman.

Cazden, C. B. (1986). Classroom discourse. In M. C. Wittrock (Ed.), *Handbook of research on teaching* (3rd ed., pp. 432–463). New York: Macmillan.

Chomsky, N. (1965). *Aspects of the theory of syntax.* Cambridge, MA: M.I.T. Press.

DeStefano, J. S., Pepinsky, H. B., & Sanders, T. S. (1982). Discourse rules for literacy learning in a classroom. In L. C. Wilkinson (Ed.), *Communicating in the classroom* (pp. 101–129). New York: Academic.

Eder, D. (1982). Differences in communicative styles across ability groups. In L. C. Wilkinson (Ed.), *Communicating in the Classroom* (pp. 245–264). New York: Academic.

Ogbu, J. U. (1983). Literacy and schooling in subordinate cultures. In D. Resnick

(Ed.), *Literacy in historical perspective* (pp. 129–153). Washington, DC: Library of Congress.

Scribner, S. (1984). Literacy in three metaphors. *American Journal of Education, 93*(1), 6–21.

Sternberg, R. J. (1984). Toward a triarchic theory of human intelligence. *Behavioral and Brain Sciences, 7,* 269–315.

Wong Fillmore, L., Ammon, P., Ammon, M. S., Delucchi, K., Jensen, J., McLaughlin, B., & Strong, M. (1983, May). *Learning English through bilingual instruction: Second year report.* (Contract #400-80–0030). Washington, DC: National Institute of Education.

1

Mexican Adult Literacy: New Directions for Immigrants

Concha Delgado-Gaitan

Department of Education
University of California at Santa Barbara

This ethnographic study is a part of a larger study on the social meaning of literacy among Mexican immigrant families in La Perla, California. The research is based on the concept that adult illiteracy is a consequence, not a cause, of underemployment: peoples' position in the economy largely dictates their opportunities to become literate, which in turn opens up avenues to better employment for them. This notion is opposite of the traditional explanation that Mexicans are underemployed because they are illiterate. The Cultural Ecological theory proposed by Ogbu (1981; 1983) and his predecessors is an appropriate framework for this study, allowing the examination of the concept of literacy within the social and economic environment of the given population. Furthermore, it is important for us to analyze how Mexican immigrant people living in low socioeconomic conditions can gain literacy skills, become aware of their status in society, and, in Freire's (1973) terms, become conscious enough to participate in their liberation. Following a brief discussion of relevant studies, I will present the function and meaning of literacy in La Perla and draw pragmatic implications for purposeful literacy programs at a community level. The final section of the paper reveals the nature of literacy as experienced by the families in the study, and their determination to ensure the success of their children in school.

Literacy Revisited

Significant contributions have been made by U.S. linguists, anthropologists, and psychologists who focused on the sociocultural context of literacy (Hymes, 1964; Au, 1980; Au & Jordan, 1980; Clark, 1983; Cole & Griffin, 1980b, 1983; Duran, 1983; Gumperz & Cook-Gumperz, 1981; Heath, 1980, 1982, 1983; Olson, 1980; Trueba, Moll, Diaz, & Diaz, 1984; Woods-Elliott & Hymes, 1980). The studies have generally focused on shifts in the larger societal contexts for literacy. Some studies, however, examined specific effects on particular communities and on the daily life of its members. Researchers have concluded that the nature of oral and written communication is contextual, i.e., its meaning, is determined by the context of the communication: who communicates with whom, about what, in what situation, in what specific form, for what purpose, in front of whom, and before and/or after what chain of events. Interaction with text as a communication process indeed merits additional investigation. A number of studies (Au & Jordan, 1980; Cole & Griffin, 1983; 1980, Heath, 1980a; Scribner & Cole, 1981; Trueba, 1984; Trueba et al., 1984) have made pragmatic recommendations that would enhance the congruence between the home and school learning environment for the specific population being studied.

Although the literature on literacy and the Mexican adult population in the U.S. is scant, inadequate and vague, literacy research of U.S. populations generally supports the view that people's social and economic condition is a consequence of literacy. For example, adult and child literacy within Mexican communities has been studied in the context of the cultural deprivation theory (Zintz, 1969; Coleman, 1966). In these studies, children were viewed as lacking reading and writing skills because of the parents' lack of literacy skills (see Carter & Segura, 1979, for additional discussion). Some researchers have disputed the deficit theory (Cervantes & Bernal, 1976; Neale, Gill, & Tismer, 1970). They claimed that the school failed to teach Mexican students basic literacy skills due to the discontinuity between the home and school values, resulting in conflicts which made culturally different students feel negative toward school. Ogbu (1978) and Carter and Segura (1979) argued that the crucial element in young Mexican students' achievement was not just the relationship between home and school, but also the economic and social status of the broad Mexican population.

Academic achievement of Mexican students is determined by many factors, not the least of which is socioeconomic. Minority people of low socioeconomic status have traditionally occupied the lowest ranks in the labor market. In turn, socioeconomic conditions affect the acquisition of literacy for adults: job ceilings (Ogbu, 1978, 1983) limit opportunities and resources, thus restricting exposure to oral and written text stimuli that could contribute to the academic achievements by adults and by their children. Restricted socioeconomic conditions, however, do not mean that Mexicans cannot learn or are not intelligent. The issue of limitation refers only to economically and socially imposed stratifications. It is this complex relationship between the practice of literacy in the daily life of people and their socioeconomic environment which is the focus of this paper.

I will begin by describing the school performance of Hispanic students. In 1980, Mexican children constituted 74% of the total pupil count in San Antonio, 45% in Los Angeles, 32% in Denver, and 28% in Houston. In California alone, 77% of the Mexican students of limited English proficiency are underachieving (Pifer, 1984). Furthermore, over 45% of the Hispanic (i.e., persons of Latin, Mexican, Puerto Rican, or Latin American, heritage) students in grades 9–12 drop out before completing high school (Cervantes, 1982; Hayes-Bautista, Minicucci, Acosta, Margolis, & Keith, 1984; Schnick, & Chapa, 1983). Employment and adequate literacy programs in the schools are among the issues surrounding the problems of functional illiteracy among Mexican immigrant adults and their children. The meaning of literacy in minority communities has been described by many researchers. Notable among them is Ogbu (1979), who has consistently reminded us that, in a racially and economically stratified society like the U.S., social, occupational, and political roles, as well as cognitive, motivational, and social skills associated with those roles, tend to be stratified.

There is a wide gap between our understanding of this situation and practices that might rectify the conditions that breed illiteracy. Few anthropologists have risked bridging the theory–practice dichotomy because, as Trueba (1984) has argued, experiments cannot be transplanted; they need to be developed within each community's own unique circumstances. In his work, Freire (1973) provided an excellent example of how to design appropriate solutions for illiteracy while avoiding cultural invasion. He adamantly stated that literacy is more than reading and writing—it involves people's capacity to participate effectively and productively in society. People are able to participate effectively only when they have economic power (Freire, 1973, 1983). Ogbu (1983) has referred to people's knowledge of their resources as their knowledge of their effective environments.

Literacy and the Effective Environment

The literacy study presented in this chapter examines the possible application of the cultural ecological theory as proposed most recently by Ogbu (1979, 1983). (For previous formulations of cultural ecological theory, see Geertz, 1962; Goldschmidt, 1971; Netting, 1968.) Ogbu has applied this theory primarily to Black communities. The major constructs of Ogbu's formulation are applied here to the Mexican community in La Perla.

According to Ogbu, cultural ecology is the study of socially transmitted behaviors, in interdependence with environmental features (1979, 1983). For example, in a modern industrialized nation such as the U.S., a given population's effective environment is one in which people know the available resources. Successful adaptation of a person is determined by his or her ability to learn about the resources and the competencies required for achieving within his or her social group.

The school acts as the principal institution for adapting children to a bureaucratized industrial economy. It teaches them the basic skills of reading and writing. It provides the credentials needed for entering the work force, and it prepares them for more specialized training once they obtain a job (Bottein, et al., 1979; Bourdieu, 1977; Jencks, 1978; Ogbu, 1983). To ensure the perpetuation of cultural resources which would otherwise disappear along with the agents who bear them, the school has to resort to the systematic inculcation of these. Such inculcation is made possible by instruments of cultural communication, such as reading and writing (Bottein, et al., 1979; Bourdieu, 1977). Literacy and other academic qualifications, like money, have a fixed value which Bourdieu (1977) calls cultural capital (pp. 180, 187). All literate people with a diploma are relegated to a single labor market which converts cultural capital into money at a determined cost in labor. Ogbu (1983) argued that for Mexican and other subordinate minorities, illiteracy is a consequence of the economic structure as a result of that group's role in society. The traditional argument reversed this statement by faulting minorities for not being literate and consequently creating their own underemployment (Berreman, 1972; Johnson, 1966; Warner et al., 1945).

Ogbu's Stockton study (1978, 1983) showed that most people did not view schools as cultural transmitters or a place to study for its own sake. Rather, Stocktonians believed that more and better schooling would lead to more and better jobs. While that may be true for the White population, it was not the case for Blacks in Stockton, as Ogbu showed. Nor was it true for Mexicans, according to the work of Grebler, More, and Guzman (1970). They concluded that differences in the adult socioeconomic statuses of adult Anglo and Mexican groups were best explained in terms of job ceiling rather than differences in educational attainment.

The lack of representation of Mexicans in the white collar urban work force also has been attributed to job ceiling rather than to lack of education (Schmidt, 1970; Schmidt and Koford, 1975). Schmidt also contended that the job ceiling against Mexican Americans contributed to their low performance in school by training them for low-status positions in the work force. Blair (1971, 1972) suggested that Anglos can expect increasing economic gains from more schooling, but for Mexicans who drop out of school, the employment possibilities usually decrease.

Getting Acquainted with La Perla

La Perla is a working class community located near the Silicon Valley, one of the wealthiest industrial centers in the country. A large Mexican immigrant population resides in La Perla, their residency varying from a few months to 20 years. Some families live in cramped one-room apartments, while others live in more spacious single-family dwellings. This residential community has a number of small industries, such as lumber, tool-and-die, and automotive plants, as well as two major railroad tracks for both commercial and passenger trains. Family businesses (e.g., restaurants, garages, clothing, and grocery stores) around the community reflect an environment of cultural maintenance through the products sold, the services rendered, and the predominant use of Spanish as the language of interaction.

Ethnic composition of the community, in descending order of representation, is Anglo, Mexican, Black, and other minorities. However, the four elementary schools which serve the community are over 70% minority (Mexican, Black, Tongan). Spanish bilingual programs exist for the limited English proficient students. The bilingual programs are transitional: The students' first language is used for instruction, until they learn to speak English at a designated level in the Idea Kit English as a Second Language Curriculum Program (Redwood City School District, 1981). In spite of special programs for Mexican children, the faculty at one particular school expressed their concern about the students' low level of achievement. In analyzing the problem, many of the teachers pointed out that the parents were not helping their children with their school work and cited that as the reason for the students' failure. At the same time, the teachers were compassionate, excusing the parents for not working with their kids since the parents usually had to work long hours to meet economic needs.

The local school district in La Perla requested federal funds to develop an adult literacy project to deal with some of the concerns voiced by teachers in various schools in the district. Parents of many bilingual children in the four elementary schools were invited to attend the classes. More than 80 enrolled, presenting diverse levels of literacy skills in Spanish and English.

The adult literacy project, which consisted of four classes at various levels, was designed to teach English as a second language as well as

Spanish and English reading skills. Additionally, parents were trained in techniques to help their children prepare for literacy in school. Children of the adults in the night literacy classes also attended classes on the same night the parents did. They were divided into homogenous age groups and received instruction in basic reading skills. On three different occasions during the school year, the students attended classes with their parents and participated in a parent–child activity in which the parents assisted their children. The project teacher supervised the whole class. During the course of the school year, adult student attendance fluctuated in all four classes. In the more advanced class, about 10 adults attended regularly. The author had the role of teacher in the project, and thus was able to observe the entire teaching and learning process as literacy acquisition proceeded.

Eight families were selected from the group that attended regularly to become informants for the literacy study. The number of families selected was determined by the projected time and depth required in working with each family. The study emerged as a way of examining the function and meaning of literacy for the family as a unit. My interest was in understanding how Mexican adults who were acquiring formal literacy used literacy in the home, and how they perceived their role in society given their literacy experiences. The eight families selected were in the advanced literacy group, which meant that they read between a 2nd and 6th grade level in English. This group of families was selected because the families could provide a broader view of their experience as they evolved from illiterate to literate.

The eight families were contacted personally in their homes and invited to participate. They agreed to being observed and interviewed at home and observed in their literacy class. Not only were they willing to work with me, they began inviting me to their homes to talk with them about their future plans for employment and to assist them with especially difficult translations that were required of them in their jobs. Interviews were conducted primarily with the adult in the advanced literacy class, although the spouse and children usually came into the room for part of the interview.

Two different interview styles were used. One style was a form of ethnohistory in which the informants were allowed to talk about their past and relate those events they felt were most important in their lives. The events did not necessarily have to deal with text. The subjects spoke freely about their childhoods in Mexico, their arrival in the U.S., and the many struggles they encountered on a day-to-day basis to find employment and organize their families to ensure their success in school. Several such interviews were conducted.

Another type of interview was more formal, and involved structured questions posed to the adults and to the children. Each family participated in two of these interviews, about 2 hours in length each time. Adults as well as the children were asked to provide specific information about their use of text in the home and on the job. The adults talked about their conceptualization and their attainment of literacy and their application of these skills. The children who were old enough to understand the questions provided very insightful information about their reading and writing in both languages and their relationships with their parent(s) who were learning English skills.

Observations in the home were limited to spontaneous verbal or text-oriented interaction between the parent and the children after school. More predictable and sequential observations occurred in the adult literacy classes, where the parents learned to read in Spanish by using the texts the children were using in their classrooms. In addition, it was possible to observe the adults' use of text in English and to note their development from level-one text to level-five in the Idea Kit ESL curriculum. It was also important to observe how the adults used what they were taught in the literacy class to work with their children at home. The field research continued for 9 months. It basically encompassed the school year from fall through spring, since that was the duration of the adult literacy project. Additionally, follow-up interviews and observations are planned with these families on a yearly basis. However, the data collected during the 9-month period are sufficient to formulate a descriptive analysis of literacy in La Perla.

All the data are analyzed according to Ogbu's cultural ecological theory, which states that the successful adaptation to society is determined by a person's ability to learn about resources and acquire competencies for succeeding in society. He also theorized that immigrant families are inclined to succeed because they view the U.S. school system as the most important vehicle for their advancement. The data are presented for five areas of relevance to the cultural ecological theory: searching for socioeconomic opportunities, the value of schooling, literacy forms in the home, formal steps to literacy, and parental support for children. For each area, data are reported in both Spanish and English. The informants used only Spanish during the interviews, as well as in most of the interactions at home and in school. Therefore, to ensure full integrity of the data, they are presented in the subject's native language and in the English translation.

Searching for Socioeconomic Opportunities

A common theme in the historical experience of the families in this study is their sociocultural and economic struggle to immigrate from Mexico to the U.S. The "push" for these families was two-fold: They wanted to improve their economic opportunities and those who had children wanted to provide them with a better chance to learn in school. Most of the families came from small towns in Mexico; others came from isolated rural areas where education was impossible because of location. All of the adults in the study came from very poor families where day-to-day survival was barely possible. Yet every adult claimed to have had at least one parent who valued education, even if he or she was too poor to pursue a complete education in schools. One informant, Mrs. Macias, related her story as follows:

> Yo ví en Jalisco, México, que no podíamos hacer una vida buena. Mi esposo y yo trabajamos arreglando zapatos luego su tío vendió el taller donde trabajabamos y no teníamos trabajo. Así es que nos fuimos a Matamoros, pero se nos acabó el dinero; luego sus amigos le dijeron que debía irse a los Estados Unidos para trabajar en lo que pudiera para hacer dinero. Así es que él se vino y yo me quedé con los niños y fue muy difícil para mí porque pasó mucho tiempo donde yo no sabía de él, si estaba vivo o muerto. Luego despues de algunos meses me escribió que quería que nos viniéramos todos, que había encontrado a una tía de él que vivía aquí en La Perla. Así es que vinimos porque el ya habia encontrado trabajo remendando zapatos en la tienda donde estamos ahora. Pero al principio yo no trabajé y comencé a estudiar Inglés.
>
> I saw that in Jalisco, Mexico, we could not make a good living. My husband and I worked repairing shoes; then his uncle sold the shop where we worked, and we didn't have a job. So we moved to Matamoros, but we ran out of money. Then his friends encouraged him to come to the U.S. to work in whatever he could to make money. So he came, and I stayed with the children, and it was very hard because I didn't know if he was dead or alive. Then, after a few months, he wrote that he wanted us to come too, because he had found an aunt of his who lived in La Perla. So we came, because he had found a job repairing shoes in the store where we both work now. But at first I didn't work; I began studying English.

Mrs. Macias relates the sacrifice that she and her family withstood economically and emotionally in Mexico as they prepared to immigrate. The impetus to leave their homeland and risk more hardships was founded on the desperate hope that the familial ties would produce new directions. Mrs. Macias continued to talk about how pleased she was that they had decided to come to the U.S.

> Pues sí, es difícil aquí porque todo cuesta más, pero siquiera aquí pueden estudiar los niños, porque allá en México toda la educación cuesta mucho. Aquí siquiera pueden ir gratis y les dan mucha oportunidad para desarrollarse.
>
> Well, it's difficult here because everything costs a lot, but at least the children can study here because over there in Mexico all the education

costs a lot. Here, at least they can attend free, and they're given a lot of opportunity to develop.

Mrs. Macias and her family have recognized that economic survival is difficult in the U.S., but their strong intention for the children to benefit from the schooling opportunity in this country sometimes compensated for the underemployment, low wages, and substandard living conditions. Both men and women in the study viewed their employment opportunities as fortunate in comparison with their past in Mexico. They explained that they did not have adequate jobs in the U.S. because they spoke limited English, but they also felt that, once they learned better oral and written literacy skills, their employment opportunities would increase. A young single parent, Mrs. Molina, related how she plans to improve her economic situation:

> Yo trabajo limpiando casas y me canso mucho pero es difícil conseguir otro trabajo. Me gustaría ser secretaria bilingüe pero creo que tendría que aprender el Inglés mejor y para estudiar, es difícil porque no tengo quien me cuide a mi niña, porque todos trabajan; cuesta mucho para conseguir así a alguien que la cuide. Y no sé. Se me hace tan difícil aprender Inglés, así es que mejor yo creo que estudio para ser . . . ¿Cómo se dice de esas que peinan el cabello,—que lo arreglan? Así no tengo que saber tanto Inglés. Ahorita no puedo hacerlo porque no tengo bastante dinero guardado para poder estudiar sin trabajar porque todavía estoy pagando los tres mil dolares que me cobraron en el hospital cuando nació mi hijita. Pero si quiero, nomas que yo creo que va a ser algún tiempo antes que pueda hacerlo porque para limpiar casas, pues no es seguro. También tengo una idea de un papel para mandárselo a varias personas que viven en casas ricas así yo puedo ayudar a mí y a mis primas.
>
> I work cleaning houses, and I get very tired, but it's difficult to get another job. I would like to be a bilingual secretary, but I think that I would have to learn better English and in order to study; it's difficult, because I don't have anyone to take care of my daughter because everyone works and it's too expensive to find someone to take care of her. And I don't know. I think it's difficult to learn English, so maybe it's better to study to be . . . how do you call those that fix people's hair? That way, I don't have to learn so much English. Right now I can't do it, because I don't have enough money saved up so I can study and quit work, because I'm still paying the three thousand dollars that they charged me when I had my daughter. But I do want to, because to clean houses, it's not secure. I also have an idea to make a flyer and send it out to rich people's houses so I can help myself and my cousins.

Mrs. Molina had a strong sense of her obstacle to better employment, learning English. Yet she very much wanted to study as a way of securing a better job. In the face of her demanding financial obligations, she planned to organize her house cleaning skills to make herself and her cousins more employable.

Another woman, Mrs. Rojas, discussed her plans for improving her economic situation a bit differently. She was married, had three children, and also cleaned houses for a living. Her husband was frequently unemployed and adamantly opposed to her learning English literacy. Her emotional and physical independence is expressed through her acceptance of her life as it is and the defiance of her husband's opposition to her schooling. Mrs. Rojas' desire to improve her employment stemmed from the embarrassment of her present job.

> Yo me siento muy avergonzada cuando estoy en las casas donde limpio y llegan personas jóvenes como yo y se visten tan bien y saben como comportarse. A mí me gustaría arreglarme y vestirme bien y trabajar donde puedo conocer gente y ser social. Allí en las casas donde limpio no tengo esa oportunidad. Yo siempre he querido aprender a escribir a máquina y estar así entre el público para verme bien así como las muchachas que vienen a visitar a las casas donde trabajo. Lo voy a hacer tan pronto como termine este curso de Inglés y luego me voy a matricular en el colegio de noche para comenzar los cursos de secretaria.
>
> I'm embarrassed when I'm in the homes where I clean and young women come to visit and they're dressed so nicely and they know how to act. I would like to dress and look good and work in a place where I can meet people and be sociable. In the houses where I clean, I don't have that opportunity. I've always wanted to learn how to type and to be with the public, so I can look good, like the girls that come to visit to those houses where I clean. I'm going to do it as soon as I finish this English course, and then I'll enroll in a secretarial course in the community college.

Mrs. Rojas had used the people around her as models for how she wanted to look and act. Her aspirations were linked to the need for more literacy skills in English, and she had investigated the necessary steps for this to occur. In this case, notice Mrs. Rojas did not mention money as her incentive for a better position; rather, she emphasized her appearance more than the daily survival needs. On various occasions, Mrs. Rojas spoke candidly about her attitude toward money and its role in improving her condition.

> No me preocupo porque no tenemos dinero o porque no tenemos otro apartamento más grande. Me gustaría tener mejores cosas pero nunca me da miedo que no lo tendremos. De alguna manera lo hacemos, porque, mire, yo sola con las casas que limpio he mantenido a mi familia mientras que mi esposo no trabaja y ya pasa de seis meses. El nomás paga la renta y yo tengo que pagar lo demás. Mi familia le compra la ropa a los niños. Pero eso no me molesta, lo que sí me molesta es que él a veces me trata de interrumpir cuando quiero leer porque a él no le gusta leer.

I don't worry about not having money or because we don't have a bigger apartment. I would like to have better things, but I'm never afraid that we won't have it. Somehow we'll do it because, you see, with the houses I clean, I alone have supported my family while my husband has been out of work and that's been over 6 months. Even when he works he doesn't help much. He only pays the rent and I have to pay the rest. My family buys my children all their clothes. But that doesn't matter; what does bother me is when he interferes with my studying and tries to interrupt because he doesn't like reading.

Mrs. Roja's attitude toward literacy seemed partly due to her need to be independent. She saw a different job as a way of being away from her husband's domineering ways, as well as an opportunity to demonstrate her confidence and social manners. Mrs. Rojas, unlike Mrs. Molina, did not find it necessary to quit work in order to study. She was willing to attend school at night, especially because her husband could stay and care for their three children who are 7 years and under.

The common thread among the three examples cited, as well as the rest of the families, appears to be their interest in improving their social and economic conditions through acquiring higher literacy skills. Although all of these families seek educational responses to their circumstances, we must not ignore the marked diversity of perceptions within the group. Each family addresses a different personal need for advancing their skills. Yet we cannot overlook the fact that the underlying commonality this group shares is their immigrant status and their optimism that regardless of the circumstances, life will improve when they develop better literacy skills in English.

The Value of Schooling

School is unquestionably a high priority for these families. They viewed the role of school as one of educating children in English and providing them with other skills that would assist them in obtaining a job. Much of their appreciation for the educational system in the U.S. stemmed from their own lack of opportunity to receive an adequate education in Mexico. The high value on schooling motivated the parents to develop their own literacy, so they could, in turn, assist their children with English. Thus, bilingualism was required. One informant responded in the following way to the question on her views about the importance of schooling.

Allá, fíjese que, yo nomás estudié hasta el cuarto grado porque mi mamá no pudo pagar y tanto que quería ser enfermera. Ahora sí les digo a mis hijos que estudien porque así pueden tener una carrera buena.

> Over there (in Mexico), you see, I only studied up to the fourth grade because my mother couldn't pay and I so much wanted to be a nurse. Now I tell my children to study, because that way they can have a good career.

This parent felt adamantly that she could not allow her children to suffer as she had, especially since children do not have to purchase their own book supplies in the U.S.

Most of the families in the literacy study, like those in the examples cited, had only minimal formal schooling in Mexico. Only one of the parents interviewed actually completed the equivalent of a high school education in Mexico. Consequently, they have had an informal experience of "education," yet they have a clear perception of how "educated" people behave, since "education" connotes the degree of politeness and respect which people display to one another.

Parents have great trust that their children will receive all the academic skills they require for an adequate job. However, they are not always confident that schools teach proper social behavior. They have noticed that their children begin to lose respect for other people once they get into higher grades in school. Parents then are forced to be more strict in order to provide their children with "una buena educación." In these homes, children's behavior toward adults and others is of primary importance, and parents see that their responsibility is not only to train their children to pursue academic interests, but also to inculcate in them good manners toward everyone.

Another skill which parents strongly expected their children to maintain was their oral and literate ability in Spanish. They spoke to their children only in Spanish regarding their personal and school tasks. Most parents expressed the idea that their children's knowledge of Spanish was necessary for them to communicate effectively. Some parents felt defeated when their children preferred to speak English to them at home; one parent insisted on Spanish at home:

> Yo le voy hablar en Español a mis niños aunque no quieran y también voy a seguir insistiendo que ellos hablen in Español porque yo no se muchas cosas en Inglés todavía y a fuerzas les tengo que hacer entender lo que sé yo y si yo les hablo en Inglés entonces no les puedo explicar precisamente lo que pienso. Algún diá me lo van agradecer. Ahora me sale mi niña con que quiere ser rubia y que no le gusta su cabello negro y que no quiere hablar Español. Yo no la voy a dejar que siga con esas cosas locas, por eso les sigo hablando y leyendo en Español y quiero que en la escuela sigan apprendiendo a leer el Español.
>
> I'm going to speak in Spanish to my children even if they don't want to, and I'll continue insisting that they speak in Spanish, because I don't know a lot of things in English yet and I must speak to make them understand me in Spanish, since I can't explain what I think exactly in English.

One day they'll appreciate it. Now my daughter wants to be blonde and refuses to speak Spanish. I won't let her continue with those crazy notions; that's why I'm going to continue speaking and reading in Spanish and I want them to continue learning to read Spanish at school.

Family cohesion was a very strong motive for maintaining oral proficiency in Spanish, as cited above. Furthermore, parents wanted their children to remain in bilingual programs in the schools to develop their literacy skills in Spanish. They were aware of the value of bilingualism and the employment demands for bilingual people, particularly in California. Parents recognized that their children would have an especially important talent by knowing two languages. One parent shared his views about the opportunities which his children could have as a result of being bilingual.

A mí me parece que los niños deben de saber los dos idiomas porque los trabajos que valen algo ahora requieren que hablen el Español no solo el Inglés. Como en el trabajo de mi esposa, ella debe de saber el Inglés mejor, también es bueno que sepa el Español porque vienen a veces visitantes de otros paises y ellos solo hablan Español porque la dueña tiene negocios en muchos paises de habla Española.

I think that my children should know both languages, because the jobs that are worth anything at all require that they speak Spanish, not only English. For example, in my wife's job she should know English better than she does, but it's good that she knows Spanish also, because many visitors come from other countries, since the owner has business in other Spanish-speaking countries.

This informant has witnessed the value of bilingual employment, and we note that he indirectly expressed a desire for his children to obtain an adequate position. He also saw bilingualism as a prestigious skill to possess.

The children, too, have learned the urgency of maintaining their first language. The older children in the families who talked more openly about their experience in school emphasized their desire to speak and read in both languages because they could do well in the Spanish courses in school and be able to understand when the relatives spoke to them in Spanish at home. A junior high school student, Julia, spoke about her bilingual literacy skills.

Sí, yo quiero seguir estudiando el Español porque así mi mamá tiene algo para ayudarme en mi tarea. Ella me puede ayudar a leer y escribir en Español. También yo puedo trabajar en otros paises cuando acabe de estudiar aquí. A mí me gusta la música y por eso me ayudaría otro idioma.

Yes, I want to continue studying in Spanish because that way my mother has something that she can help me with. She can help me read and write in Spanish. I can also work in other countries when I finish studying here. I enjoy music, and that's why I think knowing another language would be helpful.

Julia has found a way to utilize Spanish as an academic asset as well as a unifying tool between her and her mother. Her mother has played a major role in developing Julia's attitudes to, and practices in, Spanish. Julia's mother explained in detail her efforts to encourage both her daughter and son to pursue literacy in Spanish. She provided them constant rewards for successful accomplishment in their studies at school.

The systematic rewards which every family gave their children for high grades in school and for completing their homework is also evidence of the value placed on schooling. Parents also rewarded their younger children who were not in school but were beginning to learn to talk and to notice text in their environment. For example, one parent said that she felt so pleased when her 2-year-old daughter recited the alphabet when watching Seasame Street that she hugged her and squeezed her. The child burst into laughter, recognizing that she was appreciated.

Rewards to children for school grades were abundant. Parents were quick to recognize completion of homework, respectful behavior and good grades. Children could expect to receive hugs, kisses, special food treats, small gifts like pencils, or rides to out-of-town places on the weekend. Although these actions seem inconsequential, they carry a great deal of meaning to these families. Both for the parents and for the children, there is a common understanding of high standards set by the parents.

The value families place on school as a place to train for a good job and to obtain literacy in both languages is reinforced by the attention given to the children's successes. The pre-school as well as the school-age children knew that they were expected to learn oral and written literacy in both languages for academic purposes and family unity. Literacy is not only a question of adults teaching their children reading skills, but, more importantly, it is the relationship between the development of literacy and the transmission of cultural values which are highly esteemed in the parents' minds. The high value parents attributed to developing and maintaining Spanish literacy is an indication that there was no separation between culture and literacy.

Literacy Forms at Home

Families used written text at home in a variety of ways that were not academic in nature. That is, parents were not merely reading their children's school texts.

The process of identifying precise text in the home required careful questions and observations. Many of the adults were initially unaware of their actual involvement with text. They did not identify their activities as reading because they did not perceive themselves as readers. Through much probing parents disclosed the variety of items they read either in English or Spanish in their daily activities.

Shown in Table 1 are the types of literacy forms found in each home and the languages involved with the given forms. The data in Table 1 indicate that letters from family members in Mexico and school bulletins were the most commonly read texts in these homes. In home six, the

Table 1. Families

Literacy Forms	1	2	3	4	5	6	7	8	
Letters from family		s	s						Children
	s	s	s	s	s	E/S	s	s	Adult
Bible & other prayer books		s	E/S						
		s	s			s			
Child story books/ Adult story books	e/s	e/s				S			
	e/s	E/S	E/S	e	e/s	e/s	S		
Popular magazines (Women's Day, Readers' Digest)									
		e		e	E				
Direction for using household products (camera and cooking recipes)									
	e		e		e	e			
Newspapers									
		e/s	e/s				E		
School Bulletins									
	E/S	E/S	e/s	E/S	e/s		e/s	E/S	
Children's School Text	e	e	E/S	E/S	E		E	E/S	
	e/s	e/s	e	E/S	e		e	e/s	

Note:
1) The S and E indicate the language in which the items are read.
2) Capital letters indicate the most frequently used form of literacy in that particular household by adults or children.
3) In each row, entries above the dashed line indicate child use; entries below adult use.

single parent had no children in school, her only daughter being 2 years old, so she was not receiving bulletins from school. All the remaining households received the school bulletins in English and Spanish, because at least one of their children was in a bilingual program.

Fewer households indicated use of newspapers, magazines, story books, Bibles, instructions, or cooking recipes. Those families who claimed no experience with this type of text usually felt that they could get whatever information might be provided by these literacy forms through either visual media like television, or phone calls, or just by asking someone. The following is a comment by one adult who did not find it necessary to read newspapers, magazines, or any instruction manual.

> Mire, en mi trabajo me piden que sepa escribir poco para tomar los mensajes que llegan por teléfono. Luego ya cuando llego a la casa me siento tan cansada y luego me pongo a cocinar para la familia. ¿Quién va tener tiempo de leer el periódico? Yo le prendo ahí a las noticias en Inglés y así sepo (sic) lo que esta pasando. Y para hacer cualquier trabajo aquí en la casa, si no sé cómo componer algo, le pido a mi esposo o a los niños que me ayuden de alguna manera. En el asunto de la comida, pues ahí yo les hago lo que sé cocinar, pero nunca uso cosas asi que requieren recetas ni nada de eso. Si por ahí me encuentro con poco tiempo para leer, mejor me pongo a estudiar unos de los libros en Inglés para adelantarme más.
>
> You see, in my job, they ask me write some things like messages from telephone calls that come in. But when I get home, I'm so tired, and then I start cooking dinner for my family; who has time to read the newspaper? I'll turn on the news or the T.V. in English, and that way I know what's happening. And for whatever job I have here at home, if I don't know how to fix it, I ask my husband or the children to help me in some way. Regarding the cooking, well, I just fix whatever I know how to cook, but I never use things that require a recipe.

This woman functioned quite adequately with minimal interaction with text; rather, she used verbal communication with those close to her. The reason given for her way of organizing her daily home routine was that she was able to carry out all her activities without reading. One conclusion is that she sees literacy strictly as a pragmatic vehicle to employment.

Literacy items were carefully selected by adults in the families interviewed. Certain parental attitudes toward reading were pervasive: reading was viewed as a functional instrument to perform a necessary household task or as a means of assisting their children to complete academic tasks. Only one adult in the study expressed a profound interest in reading *Reader's Digest* stories, for her own edification as well as for better employment. Since parents recognized their responsibility for their children's success, they wanted to continue their own development in English literacy. Improved English skills could provide more opportunity for steadier and more skillful jobs. It was this kind of thinking that allowed them to move into more complex uses of literacy through formal instruction.

Formal Steps to Literacy

This aspect of the analysis constitutes a separate paper in and of itself; however, I will present only a brief segment of the analysis, depicting the learning process that these students followed in their literacy class. This segment demonstrates their best efforts at being good students by acquiring the skills which they believed were essential for them to help their children.

The night literacy class which the adults attended stressed only reading, not writing. The English texts generally dealt with popular topics of interest to the parents. For example, the *Barnell Loft Series* (Redwood City School District, 1981), presented factual accounts of people who performed record-breaking acts. Other texts included a newspaper published specifically for English-as-a-second-language (ESL) classes. The parents were usually asked to read the selection silently and answer questions about the text. When parents first began to read English, they were asked only simple factual questions about the content, because, although they could read complex material, they did not have the linguistic competence to understand and/or answer complex questions.

Students were taught to analyze the text, diagram the information contained in different parts of it, and then study the lexicon involved in each step. Gradually, the students developed the linguistic structures for answering more analytical and evaluative questions. For example, in a story about a turtle who returned to its original home after a 4-year absence, students had factual questions such as, "How long did it take the turtle to return home?" More complex comprehension questions were "What part of the story is almost fiction?" and "How would you train the turtle to find its way home?" Most of the parents had no difficulty answering the questions, since they were reading stories at a low level of difficulty. Every week, the parents were given a reading selection at a somewhat higher level and homework was assigned.

Homework was not always completed by the adults. Explanations predominantly referred to their massive amounts of housework and their tiredness. An average of 12 students attended weekly classes, although they were not always the same 12 students. A group of 8 attended regularly. Of the 12 parents in class, between 5 and 7 completed their homework, but they were not always the same students. There was no real system of accountability for homework and attendance. Attendance and completion of homework reflected the students' eagerness to learn. One parent expressed what was a common attitude at class time—her interest in attending despite her tiredness. She yawned and said:

> ¡Ay maestra, estoy tan cansada desde esta mañana! Luego fuí a limpiar casas y me cansé todaviá más.
> Oh, teacher, I'm so tired. Since this morning, I went to clean houses and I got even more tired. (Teacher made a comment about how she was glad that, despite the student's tiredness, she was present because she had been improving.)
> Pues, ¿qué puedo hacer, maestra? Tengo que seguirle, si no, no puedo entrar al colegio para el curso de secretaria.
> Well, what can I do? I have to continue; if not, I can't get into the college secretarial course.

This student is making a statement about the importance of her sacrifice for future advancement. Cleaning house is a physically strenuous job on top of caring for her three children, but she was willing to persist through her tiredness and put forth effort to participate in class.

Most of the students in this class participated actively in both the ESL and reading class. The teacher structured the class so they could interact with one another as well as with her. The curriculum in both the ESL and reading class usually dealt with topics such as a dialogue between two people going to the store or sitting at a table for dinner. The topics were of cultural relevance, so that students could compare and contrast their experiences in their native culture with that of the U.S. Occasionally, topics related to the students' work and family were explored. Specific grammatical structures like adjectives and the present tense were learned through discussions about their experience in the work force. Most of the time, however, this type of curriculum was discouraged by the literacy project, since the goals of the program called for rather traditional content which did not consider the sociopolitical experience of these specific parents.

Within the traditional ESL linguistic format of the classes, students received the basic skills of past, present, and future tenses in regular and irregular verbs and contractions. One of the most noticeable transformations for the students occurred during the lessons on "asking questions." Prior to these specific lessons, the students generally asked questions by making a statement with an interrogative intonation, e.g., You are going to the beach? All the students found it very awkward to formulate questions beginning with standard question words, such as, *did, who, what, where, when, how,* or *will*. Following a couple of questions, they became more comfortable with the use of interrogatives. At one point, the teacher went to the blackboard and showed the class the difference between asking a question by making the statement with an interrogative intonation, and correctly posing a question. The class listened so attentively that one could hear a pin drop at the end of the example, and, almost in unison, the parents smiled and said, "¡Ah!" One student commented, "Oh, teacher, I been saying it wrong all this years! Now I can ask a lot of questions. When are you going to give us a prize?"

This student's humor illustrates her elation with a newly discovered way of communication. She was immediately able to use the grammatical structure to convey her point correctly. The parents' joy also demonstrated an important awakening of a critical part of language, the skill of asking questions. Without this skill, people are limited in their ability to exploit their environment and acquire the necessary resources.

Parental Support

The literacy project also trained the parents to work with their children at home. As part of this training, parents were asked to bring elementary school age children to class three times during the year, on designated dates. During these classes, the entire class was given a lesson which the children performed with their parents' assistance, while the teacher supervised the process. For example, one activity required the students to look at an advertisement, make a list of adjectives, and then write their own advertisement to sell the product. This activity was adapted for the various levels of children's abilities ranging from 1st to 6th grade. The task was intended to be challenging for even the older students, but they turned out to be much more advanced than expected. The session was successful nonetheless, except that the older students completed the task much faster than the others. The students enjoyed the activity so much that they insisted on doing a second advertisement.

The parents coached the students on the task, since they had performed it earlier. Parents explained the activity to their children in Spanish, although it was an English task. The only instruction given to parents on how to assist their children was that they were not to give the child the answer. Rather, they were to help the child figure out the correct answer. They were told to use the dictionary as a resource for spelling, and to be patient and allow the children to think of their own adjectives and ideas. The activity lasted about 40 minutes, at the end of which the children shared their projects. When asked how they felt about the process, they were all too inhibited to talk in the presence of their parents other than to say it was "fun."

When the children returned to their own classes, a few parents opened up about their uneasiness during the task. The four parents who expressed their discomfort with the process explained that their children knew so much more English than they knew. They felt inadequate to help their children with their homework. One parent said that he supported them by saying: "I don't know much about my girl's work, but I has to sit with her and tell her that I's care if she does her homework and she has to tell it to me the homework and what she knows."

This parent recognized that supporting his children academically went beyond his ability to assist them with the skills. He believed that, even though his own English skills were limited, he could still be interested in what his daughter was doing. Further, he could make the young girl accountable for her own work. This was a common attitude among the families interviewed. That is, even though the adults did not understand some of their children's English assignments, they designed other systematic ways of supporting them to succeed academically.

Some parents assisted their children in school work by sitting with them to do homework and working out the problem, showing them examples for solving their problems, encouraging them to do their homework before playing, reading to them, taking the children to the community library, and providing them with a space at the kitchen table to do their homework. Thus, parental support in these families meant, not only academic assistance, but emotional and physical comfort.

Summary and Conclusions

This chapter has presented a rather brief glance at a few important issues facing the Mexican immigrant families in La Perla, California: (a) These families were grateful to be in the U.S. where conditions were relatively better than those in Mexico. They were aware of sociopolitical and economic limitations, but hoped that their situations would improve once they learned English. (b) Written text played an important role in these households. A great deal of written material came from family correspondence, school bulletins, and student homework, but there was less involvement with popular literature. (c) Motivation to learn English stemmed from many sources, from personal embarrassment at not knowing English to a desperate need to obtain steady employment. The adults in this study saw their position in society as oppressed but not necessarily hopeless, since they attributed most of their low socioeconomic condition to their inadequate English literacy skills. (d) Schooling was held in high regard by these families. Every adult in the study regarded schools an important route to better education for their children and then to greater employment opportunities. Although parents did not speak English well, they assisted their children intellectually, in the way that they encouraged the children to study and explained the consequences of education. Parents also supported their children by providing emotional and physical comfort. Since adults viewed the school as the most available avenue to success, they were not critical of the school curricular programs; rather they were grateful for the opportunity to attend free public school.

Ogbu (1983) reminds us that the value which this population places on schooling for themselves and their children is a means of pursuing the rewards which they see Anglo mainstream people acquiring as a result of advanced training. Their approach to literacy involved taking English classes which stressed linguistic competence, because they believed that English language skills alone would be sufficient to help them obtain better employment. The specific English literacy and parent training program in La Perla valued highly the family unit. Family members provided support to one another. Parents not only learned to assist their children, but the children were often in the position of teaching their parents English. Because the children's English competency was often more advanced than that of the parents, they accommodated by having the parents tutor the children in Spanish. There was a great deal of emphasis on the mechanical and linguistic structures of the language. This exclusive focus on linguistic competence did not begin to address the communicative competence and political consciousness required for immigrants to understand their role and status in society.

Freire (1973) stated that, in order for people to overcome their oppressed socioeconomic conditions, they must become active participants in the process that moves them through that level. He further delineated the process of literacy consciousness as one where people must become aware of their day-to-day conditioning. A purposeful program would provide not only linguistic competence for Mexican adults, but also a strong foundation for their role in society.

References

Au, K. (1980). Participation structures in a reading lesson with Hawaiian children: Analysis of a culturally appropriate instructional event. *Anthropology and Education Quarterly, 11*(2), 91–115.
Au, K., & Jordan, C. (1980). *Hawaiian talk-story. Sibling work groups, and learning to read: The culturally-congruent shaping of an educational program.* An unpublished paper, Kamehameha Early Education Program.
Berreman, G. D. (1972). Race, caste, and other invidious distinctions in social stratification. *Race, 24* (4).

Blair, P. M. (1971). *Rates of return to schooling of majority and minority groups in Santa Clara county, California*. Ph.D. dissertation, Stanford University, Stanford, CA.

Blair, P. M. (1972). *Job discrimination and investment analysis: A case study of Mexican Americans in Santa Clara County, California*. New York: Praeger.

Bottein, J., Elmandjra, M. and Maritza, M. (1979). *No limits to learning: Bridging the human gap*. New York: Pergammon.

Bourdieu, P. (1977). *Outline of theory and practice*. Cambridge, MA: Cambridge University Press.

Carter, T., & Segura, R. (1979). *Mexican Americans in school: A decade of change*. New York: College Entrance Examination Board.

Cervantes, R. (1982). *Hispanic underachievers: The neglected minority*. Paper presented at the Hispanic English Dominant Student Conference, San Diego University Lau Center Anaheim.

Cervantes, R., & Bernal, H. H., (1976). *Psychological growth and academic achievement in Mexican American students*. San Antonio, TX: Development Associates.

Clark, R. (1983). *Family life and school achievement*. Chicago, IL: University of Chicago Press.

Cole, M., & Griffin, R. (1980). Amplifiers reconsidered. In D. Olson (Ed.), *The social foundations of language and thought* (pp. 343–365). New York: W. W. Norton.

Cole, M., & Griffin, P. (1983). A socio-historical approach to re-mediation. *The Quarterly Newsletter of the Laboratory of Comparative Human Cognition*, 5(4), 69–74.

Coleman, J. S. (1966). *Equality of educational opportunity*. Washington DC: Office of Education, U.S. Department of Health, Education and Welfare.

Duran, R. P. (1983). Cognitive theory and Chicano children's oral reading behavior. *The Quarterly Newsletter of the Laboratory of Comparative Human Cognition*, 5(4), 74–79.

Freire, P. (1973). *Education for critical consciousness*. New York: Seabury Press.

Geertz, C. (1962). *Agricultural involution: The process of ecological change in Indonesia*. Berkeley, CA: University of California Press.

Goldschmidt, W. (1971). Introduction: The theory of cultural adaptation. In R. B. Edgerton (Ed.), *The individual in cultural adaptation: A study of four East African peoples* (pp. 1–22). Berkeley, CA: University of California Press.

Grebler, L., More, J. W., & Guzman R. (Eds.). (1970). *The Mexican People, the nation's second largest minority*. New York: Free Press.

Gumperz, J., & Cook-Gumperz, J. (1981). Ethnic differences in communicative style. In C. Ferguson & S. B. Heath (Eds.), *Language in the USA* (pp. 430–445). Cambridge, MA: Cambridge University Press.

Hayes-Bautista, D., Schnick, W., & Chapa, J. (1983). *The Hispanic portfolio: A prospectus for investment*. Sacramento, CA: Hispanic Affairs Council.

Heath, S. (1980a). *What no bedtime story means: Narrative skills at home and school*. Paper prepared for the Terman conference, Stanford University.

Heath, S. (1980b). The functions and uses of literacy. *Journal of Communication*, Winter, 123–133.

Heath, S. (1982). Protean shapes in literacy events: Evershifting oral and literate traditions. In D. Tannen (Ed.), *Spoken and written language* (pp. 91–116). Norwood, NJ: Ablex.

Heath, S. (1983). *Ways with words*. Cambridge, MA: Cambridge University Press.

Hymes, D. (1964). The ethnography of communication. *American Anthropologist*, 66 (3), part 2, 6–56.

Jencks, C. (1978). *Inequality*. New York: Basic Books.

Johnson, K. R. (1966). *Teaching the culturally disadvantaged pupils*. Palo Alto, CA: Science Research Associates Inc.

Minicucci, C., Acosta, L., Margolis, S., & Keith, R. (1984). *Making high schools work for linguistic minorities*. Sacramento, California: A Research Partnership Report Prepared by Assembly Office of Research Reports on High Schools.

Neale, D. C., Gill, N., & Tismer, W. (1970). Relationship between attitudes toward school subjects and school achievement. *Journal of Educational Research*, 63(5), 232–237.

Netting, R. (1968). *Hill farmers of Nigeria*. Seattle, WA: University of Washington Press.

Ogbu, J. U. (1978). *Minority education and caste: The American system in cross-cultural perspective*. New York: Academic.

Ogbu, J. U. (1979). Social stratification and the socialization of competence. *Anthropology and Educators Quarterly*, 10(2), 1–20.

Ogbu, J. U, (1981). Origins of Human Competence: A cultural-ecological perspective. *Child Development*, 52 413–429.

Ogbu, J. U. (1983). Literacy and schooling in subordinate cultures: The case of Black Americans. In D. Resnick (Ed.), *Literacy in historical perspective* (pp. 129–153). Washington, DC: Library of Congress.

Olson, D. R. (1980). Some social aspects of meaning in oral and written language. In D. Olson (Ed.), *The social foundations of language and thought* (pp. 90–108). New York: W. W. Norton.

Pfifer, A. (1984). The Challenge of Higher Education. Keynote address at President Arciniega's Investiture, May 24, 1986, California State College at Bakersfield, CA.

Redwood City School District (1981). *Procedures Manual for Bilingual Education*.

Schmidt, F. H. (1970). *Spanish surnamed American employment in the Southwest: A study prepared for Colorado Civil Rights Commission under auspices of Equal Employment Opportunity Commission*. Washington, DC: U.S. Government Printing Office.

Schmidt, F. H., & Koford, K. (1975). The economic condition of the Mexican-American. In G. Tyler (Ed.), *Mexican Americans Tomorrow* (pp. 81–106). Albuquerque, NM: University of New Mexico Press.

Scribner, S., & Cole, M. (1981). *The psychology of literacy*. Cambridge, MA: Harvard University Press.

Trueba, H. (1984). *Xilot: Teachers, revolution, and literacy*. Paper prepared for the American Anthropological Association Meetings, Denver, Colorado, November 14–18.

Trueba, H., Moll L., & Diaz, S. (1984). Improving the functional writing of bilin-

gual secondary school students. ERIC clearinghouse on languages and Linguistics, ED 240, 862. Report submitted to the National Institute of Education.
Warner, L. W. (1945). *Who shall be educated?* New York: Harper.
Woods, E. C., & Hymes, D. (1980). *Issues in literacy: Different lenses.* A commissioned paper for functional literacy project Northwest Regional Educational Laboratory, Portland, Oregon.
Zintz, Miles V. (1969). *Education across cultures.* Dubuque, IA: Wm. C. Brown Co.

2

Factors Affecting Development of Second Language Literacy

Richard P. Durán

Graduate School of Education
University of California at Santa Barbara

Introduction

This chapter discusses some core issues and research findings of importance to understanding acquisition of English literacy among persons for whom English is a second language. The chapter begins with an overview of bilingualism as a social and psychological phenomenon based on previous research and theory. Attention is shifted in the bulk of the chapter to a discussion of results from two survey studies investigating the educational achievement and academic skills preparation of students from language minority backgrounds.

The next section of the chapter discusses some of the contributions made by ethnographic research to the understanding of literacy development among linguistic and cultural minorities which complement findings from survey studies. Attention is given in a final brief section to novel cognitive approaches to research which might further complement the findings of ethnographic research and survey research on literacy acquisition among second language learners.

Social and Psychological Aspects of Bilingualism

Bilingualism is both a social and psychological phenomenon (Wald, 1974). In its social sense, it represents the distribution of two language systems within a society and its activities. Ferguson (1959) and others have argued that there is a tendency for diglossia to be prevalent in societies whose members speak two or more languages. That is, in such societies individuals tend to rely on, and prefer, use of one language over another in different social domains of experience. This tendency toward differential distribution of languages across public and more personal realms of social experience is not coincidental. In part, it stems from social boundaries distinguishing groups and their perceptions of the world from each other, and it thus also stems from political and power relations among groups.

Separation of languages also is likely to serve a cognitive function. Expectations and norms favoring use of one language over another act to reduce cognitive uncertainty and effort to plan and enact communication in everyday life with strangers or with members of the same ethnolinguistic community. Further, since there is also much effort and experience required to acquire extended competence in a second language, monolingual speakers tend not acquire an additional language system unless it is rewarding in some fashion.

Preference for one language over another in different domains of everyday life is also influenced by social factors, these latter factors in turn reflecting historically-based power and political relationships among groups whose first languages differ. Because of these historical factors, there is an inherent link between preferences for languages, acceptance of use of languages, and attitudes and behaviors.

Sociolinguists such as Hymes (1983) and Gumperz (1982) have found that language choice and alternation of languages among bilinguals reflect everyday social identities of individuals at the same time that they reflect more macro-level group relations. Ultimately, factors surrounding language choice affect the distribution of social privileges, rights, and social power among different ethnolinguistic groups within the same society and nation. Heinz Kloss, in his seminal work *The American Bilingual Tradition* (1977), discusses these issues from a U.S. historical perspective.

A related aspect of language choice among bilinguals affecting literacy development in a second language concerns language shift and language loyalty over time. Sociolinguistic research among Hispanic bilinguals in the U.S. has found, e.g., that the children of families who rely on Spanish show less of a tendency to use Spanish themselves (Laosa, 1978; Macias, 1979). Hernandez-Chavez (1978) argues that a critical determinant of Hispanic bilinguals' ability to maintain proficiency in Spanish is the existence of Spanish as a primary form of communication in everyday community life. He argues that bilingual education programs, even those described as Spanish maintenance programs, should not be expected to instill maintenance of Spanish in and of themselves.

Lambert (1977) has introduced the notions of "additive" versus "subtractive" bilingualism, in interpreting contexts associated with successful and less successful integration of bilingual groups into a society. These notions have both a social and psychological referent. Additive bilingualism occurs when an individual's acquisition and use of a second language system is viewed as a personal asset and also as a social asset within a nation or community in question.

Additive bilingualism is also associated with ability to transfer skills and information across languages and also with possible enhancement of cognitive skills. Research by Goldman (Goldman, Reyes, & Varnhagen, 1984), and by Durán (1981, 1985a), for example, has found that bilingual subjects perform similarly in matched discourse recall and problem solving tasks in each of their two languages. Dornic (1980) presents an extensive review of experimental studies of bilingualism investigating differences and similarities in bilinguals' performance of information processing tasks in a familiar versus less familiar language.

Other research studies, involving a number of populations around the world, have found evidence suggesting that proficient knowledge of two language systems enhances cognitive flexibility and metalinguistic skills (Lambert, 1977; Cummins, 1978; Hakuta & Diaz, 1985; DeAvila & Duncan, 1981). Cummins (1981) has suggested that cognitive benefits of bilingualism can emerge only after individuals acquire sufficient proficiency in any one language to permit cognitively demanding language use. Once such a threshold level of proficiency is attained, bilinguals are allegedly capable of transferring learned information with facility across languages.

These views suggest the possibility that learning to be literate in a second language is likely to be affected in a dramatic fashion by literate capability in a first language. If an individual has literate skills appropriate for schooling in a first language, then acquisition of literate skills for schooling in a second language may be facilitated. The exact reasons and mechanisms for such facilitation have yet to be suggested in detail, and they are in need of research.

In contrast to the positive social and psychological benefits discussed above, bilingualism may also be primarily of a subtractive nature in some nations and communities. Subtractive bilingualism is present when acquisition and use of a second language occurs in a manner that socially disempowers and limits possibilities for the development of cognitive and other personal capabilities of the individual. For example, in the U.S. many young Hispanic children whose first language is Spanish acquire marginal facility in English as required for schooling. Further, such children often lack an opportunity for continued development of Spanish skills appropriate for schooling. This lack of opportunity is associated with negative public attitudes towards use of a non-English language. With some notable exceptions, within the nation as a whole, Spanish lacks prestige as a practical medium for the conduct of essential public communication. Folk beliefs and attitudes have developed in the populace at large positing that knowing Spanish is both an impediment to learning English and an impediment to social integration of Hispanics within the U.S. mainstream. These folk perceptions are reinforced by everyday evidence of Hispanics' status within U.S. society. The limited education attainment levels of many Spanish speaking Hispanics, their limited literacy range in Spanish marking advanced educational attainment, and their concentration in the unskilled sectors of the U.S. labor force isolates group members from networks of communication and power essential to management and decision making in public life. In turn, these perceptions may lead to stereotypes that Hispanics are culturally deprived, lack intelligence, and lack social and personality characteristics needed for successful participation in the American way of life (Carter & Segura, 1979).

The psychological reality of negative stereotypes and their connections to language behavior have been demonstrated in experimental research studies on attitudes towards Hispanic speakers of accented English. This research has utilized matched-guise experimental designs and has found that Hispanic speakers whose English carries a Spanish accent are likely to be judged to have less desirable intellectual, personality, and social traits than Hispanic speakers of nonaccented English (Ryan & Carranza, 1977; Ramirez, 1981).

Understanding the occurrence of subtractive bilingualism within the contexts of the U.S. is complicated. Consistent with the earlier discussion on language choice and language loyalty, ethnolinguistic groups within the U.S. show different patterns of bilingualism closely related to their integration into privileged segments of society. Understanding these patterns of social and educational stratification associated with bilingualism requires going beyond language itself. An examination of inter-ethnic group relations is required. Relevant to this concern, Ogbu and Matute-Bianchi (1985) reviewed a wide collection of comparative international education research in search of patterns of intergroup relationships which fostered or limited minority group member's access to formal education. Ogbu and Matute-Bianchi concluded that in the U.S. context, recent Asian immigrants, and U.S. Asians generally, outperform Blacks and Hispanics in schools because the latter two groups are treated as socially stigmatized castes providing an unskilled labor pool for the American economy. In contrast, members of the former groups are more likely to be perceived as persons who might contribute important technological and scientific skills to the American economy. In the Ogbu and Matute-Bianchi analysis, the key to education access among minority group youth lies in the development of personal aspirations fostering pursuit of an education. These aspirations, in turn, are very much influenced by the social attitudes and values that families have towards their position within U.S. society and the expectations that they communicate to children about the value of an education for them. Ogbu and Matute-Bianchi claim that Hispanic and Black families from low socioeconomic and formal education backgrounds are more likely to teach their children that education will not pay off for them as equitably as it does for children from nonminority backgrounds.

Accounts such as those provided by Ogbu and Matute-Bianchi are difficult to verify empirically in any sweeping manner. However, as data described in the next section indicate, there is evidence that language minority children's educational aspirations can be predicted from measures of their language characteristics, family socioeconomic status, and other background and personal characteristics.

Recent Survey Data

This section of the chapter discusses results from a study of Hispanic and White high school seniors participating in the 1980 High School and Beyond longitudinal survey. It also discusses findings from a survey of the self-judged language and literacy skills of Hispanic college freshmen who have taken the Scholastic Aptitude Test (SAT). The data and analyses point out important associations between students' language and other background and personal characteristics, and their aspirations and academic literacy skills. The evidence cited is consistent with other research suggesting that literacy in English is influenced by both cognitive and social factors.

1980 High School and Beyond Data. Fernandez and Nielsen (in press) investigated the prediction of schooling outcomes from personal and background characteristics of Hispanic and White high school seniors participating in the 1980 High School and Beyond survey. The High School and Beyond 1980 survey involved a nationally representative sample of 3,177 Hispanic high school seniors and 14,696 White, non-Hispanic high school seniors. The main purpose of the Fernandez and Nielsen study was to learn about the relative importance of language characteristics of students as a predictors of schooling outcome measures after controlling for the influence of personal and background characteristics on outcome measures. The methodology used was regression analysis.

Four basic groupings of students were examined in separate regression analyses. The groupings were determined by student's Hispanic versus White (non-Hispanic) self-identity and by student's bilingual versus monolingual background. Student's ethnic self identity was based on responses to multiple choice questions regarding racial background and ethnic identity. Self-identified Hispanics were further subcategorized as: (a) Mexican, Mexican-American, Chicano; (b) Cuban, Cubano; (c) Puerto Rican, Puertoriqueño or Boricua; and (d) Other Latin American, Latino, Hispanic, or Spanish Descent. The White group of students excluded students who also identified themselves as of Hispanic origin. Students were categorized as "bilingual" if they indicated familiarity with a non-English language as a result of knowledge of a non-English language or prior exposure at home to speakers of a non-English language. The identification procedure excluded students who had only studied a non-English language as a foreign language. The definition of "bilingual" was broad in that it included students who might not speak or use a non-English language, but who had been exposed to use of a non-English language at home. Thus, the term "bilingual" as operationalized in the study is more appropriately understood as referring to persons from a bilingual background.

The schooling outcome measures examined in the research included measures of school delay, educational aspirations, and achievement test scores. School delay was assessed based on the difference between a student's age and the modal age of high school seniors (17 years) in the survey. Educational aspirations were assessed based on a numerical coding of student's multiple choice response to the question: "As things stand now, how far in school do you think you will get?" Student's achievement test scores included scores on vocabulary, reading comprehension, and mathematics tests especially developed for use in the High School and Beyond survey.

The independent variables used to predict each schooling outcome measure in regression analyses were conceptualized to be of two kinds. The first kind included measures which were hypothesized to affect achievement regardless of the language background of students. These measures included an index of family socioeconomic status, length of residence in the U.S., and student's gender. In addition, among Hispanic students, Hispanic subgroup identity (Cuban, Mexican American, Other Latin American, and Puerto Rican) was treated as a predictor measure of the first kind. In the ensuing regression analyses, membership in each non-Mexican American Hispanic subgroup was contrasted with membership in the grouping Mexican American.

The predictor measures of the second kind were relevant only for those Hispanic or White students who classified themselves as from a bilingual background. These measures assessed student's self-judged proficiency in English, self-judged proficiency in the non-English language, and frequency of exposure to use of the non-English language. The development of the underlying scales for these language measures were based on a factor analysis of language survey items administered students.

Preliminary examination of schooling outcome data across the four major groupings of students revealed that Hispanic and White bilingual background students showed higher mean educational aspirations and achievement test scores, and less mean school delay than monolingual members from the same ethnic/racial background. However, the data indicated that Hispanic students did not perform as well on schooling outcome measures as White students, regardless of language background.

The results of regression analyses indicated that the socioeconomic status of student's family was the most important predictor of schooling outcome measures for each of the four groups considered. Interestingly, followup statistical analyses indicated that family socioeconomic status was a significantly more important contributor to prediction of White monolingual student's educational outcome measures than it was for prediction of White bilingual student's educational outcome measures. In contrast, no similar difference in the importance of socioeconomic status as a predictor of educational outcomes was found between Hispanic monolingual and Hispanic bilingual students. The results also indicated that family socioeconomic status was a more important predictor for White monolingual and bilingual background student's educational outcomes than it was for the educational outcomes of Hispanic monolingual and bilingual background students. Thus, regardless of the language background of students, an increase in the family socioeconomic status of White students was allied with a greater increase in educational outcome measures than was the case for Hispanic students. These differences in the impact of socioeconomic status across Hispanic and White groups were found to be statistically significant.

The most interesting results of the analyses concerned the extent to which language factors contributed to prediction of schooling outcome measures among Hispanic and White students who were from bilingual backgrounds. As might be expected, judgement of higher proficiency in English contributed significantly to the prediction of schooling outcome measures for both Hispanic and White bilingual background students. That is to say, as the student's self-judged proficiency in English increased so did the student's educational aspirations, achievement test scores, and propensity to not be over-aged for a high school senior student.

In addition, self-judgements of proficiency in the non-English language also tended to contribute positively to prediction of three of four educational outcome measures among Hispanic and White bilingual background students after controlling for the predictive contribution to outcomes of other measures—including self-judged proficiency in English. Specifically, as student's self-judged proficiency in the non-English language increased, there was an increase in student's educational aspirations and achievement test scores.

The foregoing results have theoretical significance for the study of literacy and academic skill development among bilingual students. They are consistent with the possibility that increasing proficiency in either language system is associated with increased achievement test scores in English. The results indicated that prediction of student's mathematics, vocabulary and reading comprehension test scores was improved significantly by inclusion of self-ratings of English proficiency and by separate inclusion of self-ratings of proficiency in the non-English language in the regression equations for Hispanic and White bilingual background students.

The results also showed that self-ratings of English proficiency contributed more significantly to prediction of achievement test scores than did self-ratings of proficiency in the non-English language. This is not surprising given that the mathematics, vocabulary, and reading comprehension tests were administered in the English language. Had the tests been administered in the non-English language, one would hypothesize that proficiency ratings in that language would have contributed more to prediction of achievement scores than English proficiency ratings.

It is also worthwhile to note that self-judgements of higher proficiency in English and the non-English language each contributed significantly to the prediction of student's educational aspirations. In other words, higher self-ratings of proficiency in either language led to higher educational aspirations on the part of students.

Self-judged proficiency in English and self-judged proficiency in the non-English language constituted two of the three language measures used to predict bilingual background student's educational outcomes. The third language measure was a composite measure reflecting frequency of non-English language use. It reflected the frequency of non-English language use by a student and also the frequency of non-English language use in a student's home. The results of regression analyses indicated that this third language measure contributed negatively to prediction of educational outcome variables for both Hispanic and White bilingual background students. In the case of mathematics, vocabulary, and reading achievement test scores, bilingual background Hispanic and White students who indicated more frequent exposure to use of the non-English language earned significantly lower scores than bilingual background Hispanic and White students who indicated less exposure to use of the non-English language. In addition, bilingual background Hispanic and White students who indicated greater exposure to use of the non-English language also were significantly more likely to show delay in their schooling—even after controlling for the influence of length of U.S. residence, family socioeconomic status and other predictor measures on schooling delay.

The results on the influence of language factors on bilingual background Hispanic and White students' educational outcomes are somewhat perplexing to interpret. The finding that self-judged proficiency in English and the non-English language both uniquely contribute to enhancement of student's educational outcomes is consistent with theories positing that bilingualism can have a positive impact on student's acquisition of cognitive and academic skills in a second language. But how is it that more frequent use of the non-English language may contribute to lower educational achievement and more schooling delay among bilingual background students after controlling for other predictor measures? This question has yet to be answered answer empirically. Some investigators suggest that the finding (reported earlier by Nielsen and Fernandez, 1982) could in part be explained by incompatibilities between student's social identity and communicative norms and the attitudes of teachers to student's social background and teachers' knowledge of student's communicative norms (Durán, 1983b).

One other result of the Fernandez and Nielsen analyses that is worth mentioning concerns the influences of Hispanic subgroup identity on prediction of educational outcome measures. Among Hispanic bilingual background students, Cuban students manifested significantly higher mathematics, reading, and vocabulary achievement scores than did Mexican American students. In contrast, among monolingual Hispanic students, these differences were not significant for the two groups. The finding is important to note because it reinforces the importance of taking into account both the Hispanic subgroup origin and language background of Hispanic students in analysing factors influencing educational outcomes and literacy development.

Hispanic College Freshmen's Language Characteristics. Durán, Enright, and Rock (1985) conducted a questionnaire survey of the language characteristics of over 700 self-identified Hispanic freshmen entering 4-year colleges in the 1982–83 academic year. The study sought to investigate connections between student's judgements about their language background, judgements of language proficiency in Spanish and English, and student's SAT test scores and academic preparation for college. At the time of the study, the College Board collected only one piece of information about examinees' language characteristics on the Student Descriptive Questionnaire administered to applicants signing up to take the SAT test. This question simply asked: Is English your best language? Responses were simply "Yes" or "No."

Hispanics gaining admissions to 4-year colleges (in the U.S., 50 states and District of Columbia) requiring the SAT test represent a select subsample of all Hispanics in the U.S. This needs to be kept in mind in reviewing results from the survey, since, roughly, 50% percent of high school age Hispanic complete high school, and, of those who do, only about 26% gain an immediate admission to college. Thus, the Hispanic freshmen surveyed represent those few Hispanic with college aspirations and academic credentials supporting 4-year college admission.

About 70% of the respondents to the survey of Hispanic college freshmen indicated that they came from home backgrounds where Spanish was spoken—though about 85% judged English to be their most proficient language. This latter figure was affected by student's Hispanic subgroup identity. About 47% of the respondents were self-identified Mexican Americans, and 97% of these Mexican Americans identified English as their most proficient language. Even so, about 53% of the Mexican American respondents reported use of Spanish in their parent's homes. It was clear however, that self-identified Cuban-Americans, Puerto Ricans, and Other Hispanics were more likely to have been exposed to Spanish than Mexican Americans, and, further, that freshmen from these other Hispanic groups were much more likely to judge that Spanish was their more proficient language than Mexican Americans.

As might be expected, across all Hispanic subgroups the average SAT Verbal scores of those judging English as their most proficient language (SATV = 504) was higher than the SAT Verbal scores of those who indicated stronger proficiency in Spanish (SATV = 458). The average SAT Verbal scores of nonminority freshmen at the institutions surveyed was 521. The strength of association between Hispanics' judgement of their most proficient language and their SAT Verbal scores is conservatively estimated by the point biserial correlation between the two measures in question. The point biserial correlation obtained was $-.19$; the negative sign of this correlation reflects the arbitrary decision to code responses reflecting stronger proficiency in English as zero, while coding higher proficiency in Spanish as one. This correlation value, while not exceedingly large in magnitude, is statistically significant ($p < .001$).

As mentioned earlier, the Hispanic freshmen survey investigated whether it would be possible to find additional language background and proficiency questions which would show more association with SAT Verbal scores than the association of students' dichotomous judgement of their most proficient language with their SAT Verbal scores. Table 1 displays a selected cluster of language survey questions which showed relatively high correlations with SAT Verbal scores, in compari-

Table 1. Self-ratings of Academic English Skills and Their Association with SAT and TSWE Scores[1]

				Correlations with		
				SAT Verbal	SAT Math	TSWE
SDQ 38: Is English your best language? (Yes or No)[2]				−.19	−.09	−.25
23. At the present time how would you rate, overall, your skills in *English* in the following?[3]						
	Poorly	*Satisfactorily*	*Excellently*			
I ...						
a. Understand textbook materials	( )	( )	( )	.38	.23	.32
b. Understand vocabulary terms I read	( )	( )	( )	.45	.23	.38
c. Understand classroom lectures	( )	( )	( )	.36	.24	.29
d. Understand vocabulary terms used in lectures	( )	( )	( )	.39	.24	.34
e. Communicate required information my written assignments	( )	( )	( )	.35	.22	.35
f. Organize my writing to meet instructor's expectations	( )	( )	( )	.32	.17	.31
g. Use appropriate vocabulary terms in my writing	( )	( )	( )	.39	.20	.36
h. Use appropriate grammar in my writing	( )	( )	( )	.38	.24	.43
i. Speak in class	( )	( )	( )	.26	.17	.23
j. Use expected vocabulary in my classroom speaking	( )	( )	( )	.35	.20	.34
k. Use appropriate grammar in my speaking	( )	( )	( )	.35	.22	.37
	1 2	3	4 5			

Notes:

1. The sample size varied between 593 and 681. All correlations are significantly different from zero at the p<.01 level, single tailed significance test.
2. This is the sole language background question occurring on the 1982-1983 Student Descriptive Questionnaire.
3. This is question cluster 23 on the survey of Hispanic college freshmen described in Durán, Enright, and Rock (1985).

son to other survey questions and in comparison to the −.19 correlation between judgments of English as a "best language" and SAT Verbal scores. The survey questions *not* selected for inclusion in Table 1 pertained largely to students' preferences for English and Spanish in different activities, attitudes towards use of one language or another, and previous schooling in Spanish or English. These latter questions were not related as dramatically to SAT scores as the questions included in Table 1.

The table also displays the correlations of responses to the related questions with SAT Verbal scores, SAT Mathematics scores, and Test of Standard Written English (TSWE) scores. The TSWE results have as yet to be fully examined and they are not discussed at any length in this chapter. Nonetheless, some data obtained on this test and its association with SAT Verbal scores is included here for purposes of completeness, given its relevance to the topic of the chapter. Performance on this multiple choice test is intended to reflect student's mastery of grammatical, vocabulary, diction, and other skills believed to be necessary in college writing assignments.

The content of the cluster of survey questions given in Table 1 is important in light of the literacy characteristics they reflect. The questions were designed to gather information on student's perceptions of their ability to use English for academic purposes in all four modalities of speaking, oral understanding, writing and reading. The correlations between responses to survey questions and SAT Verbal scores ranged from .26 to .45; the correlations between survey questions and TSWE scores were similar. These patterns of correlations verify the hypothesis that more can be learned about student's verbal and literacy skills preparation on the basis of specific questions about language skills than simply by considering whether students judge themselves more proficient in Spanish than in English.

A series of stepwise regression analyses indicated that virtually all of the survey questions in Table 1 significantly improved prediction of SAT Verbal scores beyond the level possible by considering only responses to the simple question about whether English was the most proficient language or not. Given the wide variation in proficiency characteristics that existed across groups, it was important to investigate whether questions would be equally useful across groups in contributing to prediction of SAT Verbal scores. Accordingly, analyses were conducted using a Bonferroni hypothesis testing procedure for each of five separate groupings of survey respondents: All Respondents, Cuban Americans, Mexican Americans, Puerto Ricans, and Other Hispanics. Results from these analyses are presented in Table 2. The entries displayed in the body of the table indicate the percentage of increased SAT Verbal score variance accounted for by each question, above and beyond SAT Verbal score

Table 2. Increment in R^2 for Language Background Questions that Contribute Significantly to the Prediction of SAT Verbal Scores

R^2 with SDQ 38 Entered Alone	Group				
	All Hisp. .04	Cuban Amer. .03	Mex. Amer. .02	Puerto Rican .01	Other Hisp. .07
Language Background Question					
23a	.12**	.14**	.14**	.16**	NS
23b	.18**	.19**	.15**	.25**	.12**
23c	.12**	NS	.13**	.12**	.09**
23d	.13**	.13**	.13**	.13**	.16**
23e	.10**	.17**	.09**	.16**	NS
23g	.12**	.15**	.12**	.15**	NS
23h	.11**	.15**	.11	.14**	NS
23i	.05**	NS	.06**	.08**	NS
23j	.10**	NS	.09**	.15**	NS
23k	.10**	NS	.10**	.14**	NS
Sample Size	682	107	325	136	114

*p<.10, Bonferroni criterion.
**p<.05, Bonferroni criterion.

variance already accounted for by responses to a question inquiring whether English was the best language.

Virtually every survey question tabled improved prediction of SAT Verbal scores for the All Hispanic grouping of students and for each subgroup, Cuban American, Mexican American, and Puerto Rican groups by at least 10%; these improvements in prediction were all significant at the $p < .05$ level. Improved prediction was not as noticeable for the Other Hispanics subgroup. No other cluster of language background and proficiency questions in the survey showed as consistent and strong a pattern of utility in improving prediction of SAT Verbal scores of respondents. These results suggest the potential importance of self-knowledge of literacy skills in students' academic preparation. Students in the survey seemed to have an accurate sense of their general knowledge of English, as required in academic settings when SAT Verbal scores were considered as a criterion measure. This knowledge conveyed information about SAT Verbal scores not captured by simply knowing that English was or was not the student's best language.

Ethnographic Research on Literacy Acquisition

The two survey studies described in the previous section identified significant associations between personal and background factors and students' academic literacy as reflected by reading achievement test scores and verbal subtest scores on a college aptitude test. The survey studies displayed certain quantitative methodological strengths, owing to their large sample sizes, instrumentation, and statistical methods. The studies were effective confirming the importance of certain variables, such as parental education background, students' educational aspiration levels, and students' perceptions of their academic literacy skills, for predicting students' achievement test scores and verbal aptitude test scores. The findings of the studies were consistent with global accounts of how a second language background is related to psychological and sociological phenomena, and of how literacy development impacts on educational attainment among students from language minority backgrounds.

Nonetheless, survey studies such as the ones described also have major limitations. They are not designed to render causal accounts of literacy development, and they are not capable of investigating literacy development as a day-to-day process involving many interacting social and psychological variables that shape the lives of individuals residing in specific communities (see Cicourel & Mehan, 1985, for a review of this point). The earlier discussion of bilingualism and its social and psychological characteristics has suggested the fundamental importance of interacting social and psychological influences on second language learners' development of literacy skills. Investigations of these interactions are possible through ethnographic research on literacy practices and literacy development in community settings.

Another advantage of ethnographic approaches to literacy acquisition is that these approaches do not require rigid a priori operationalizing of constructs under investigation, as surveys do. In educational surveys, test scores and responses to questionnaire items are designed to reflect specific constructs. Ethnographic studies, on the other hand, permit a more functionalist account of literacy skills, and they also permit active, improvised exploration of how the exercise of literacy skills is intimately tied to real, tangible units of everyday behavior.

Understanding how literacy skills are martialed in the service of meaningful behaviors is important. Edelsky (1981) has criticized the mistaken but prevalent belief that reading achievement test scores actually represent reading skills directly. She suggests that reading performances are integrated into broader units of activity that may rely on higher-order cognitive functions and which may serve social communicative functions. The relationship which is developed between a text and reader is likely to be multifaceted, shaped by the current purpose for reading. For example, reading a story for the purpose of compiling a book report to be shared with others may involve use of decoding and comprehension strategies which are influenced by the nature of the story, the degree to which story information may be relevant to a book report, and knowledge about the characteristics of a book report audience. Further, reading and writing activities may alternate in complementary ways, the reader going back and forth from writing the book report to (re)reading portions of the text.

Edelsky notes, in contrast, that reading achievement tests sample a very narrow range of skills which are important to real world reading activities. Ethnographic approaches to the study of literacy behavior are more appropriate to investigate literacy skills as they are enacted in real life, because they can develop descriptive accounts of reading and other literacy performances based on how such performances are imbedded within the social and cultural realization of communicative events.

Ethnographers have applied the term "literacy event" to describe the immediate social and communicative context surrounding a person's reading and writing (Anderson & Stokes, 1984). In addition, the term "participation structures," adapted from the work of Philips (1972), has been introduced to refer to the norms for interaction and communication that interlocutors negotiate in literacy events, and in speech events of all kinds more generally. Ethnographic analyses of the conduct of literacy events and their participation structures have proven productive in uncovering factors affecting literacy development among language minority youth.

A number of ethnographic research studies have focused on literacy skills development and participation in literacy events of members of ethnic minority and language minority communities. Other contributions to this volume more adequately review these efforts, and a review of relevant research is also provided by Durán (1985b). Examples of relevant studies includes the research of Au, Crowell, Jordan, Sloat, Speidel, Klein, & Tharp (1986) on the reading behavior of Hawaiian children; Heath (1983), comparing literacy practices in southern black and white working-class communities; the research of Scollon and Scollon (1981) on development of literacy among Athabaskans; the research of Moll, Estrada, Diaz, and Lopez (1980) on effects of tracking on bilingual children's reading development; and the research of Gumperz and colleagues on development of minority children's literacy skills (Gumperz, 1981; Cook-Gumperz & Gumperz, 1981; Collins & Michaels, 1980). All of the foregoing research has highlighted the importance of social expectations on children's and adult's development of literacy skills. Each study found evidence that individuals must not only learn structural features of a language which are important to literate expression, but also expectations about how to participate effectively in situations demanding the use of literacy.

The research of the Kamehameha Early Education Program (KEEP) with low achieving Hawaiian school children is one of the best examples of such research (Au et al., 1986). KEEP has designed reading instruction so that it draws on children's out-of-school cultural repertoire for communication. And evaluations of KEEP indicate that implementations of the program contribute to significant gains on children's reading achievement test scores (Tharp, 1982).

Anthropological research on adult Hawaiian's story telling led to the identification of certain patterns of interaction—participation structures and speech styles—that were characteristic of this type of communicative event. These patterns included active audience participation in story telling in a manner that drew on styles and modes for interaction that were part of participants' extended oral culture and history. Teachers and research investigators at KEEP discovered that conducting part of reading lessons at school in a manner resembling story telling in community settings facilitated children's participation in reading lessons. This "bridging" of classroom and school culture is especially evident at the outset of small group reading lessons, during which children are expected to discuss stories in terms of their previous experiences. During this phase, children actively contribute to discussion of the possible topic and contents of a story which is about to be read. Similar to adults' story telling in the community, children discuss the possible contents of a story in a manner that is improvised and under minimal control by the main story teller, the teacher, in the context of the classroom. In carrying out their discussion, children freely interrupt each other to add information and to comment on each others' ideas. Au (1980) presents a detailed analysis of the ensuing participation structures and the similarities and differences between these norms and narrative behavior in community settings.

KEEP children's discourse behavior during the orienting phase of reading lessons appears to be effective, because it permits children to draw resourcefully on communications skills which are familiar to them. At the same time, the occasion for exercise of these skills is a reading lesson within the context of a classroom—an environment presenting many cultural requirements and constraints on behavior not found in the community. Hence, children are able to experience a continuity between their out-of-school identities and capabilities, and identity and competencies required in classrooms.

It is important to note that Hawaiian children participating in the initial portion of KEEP small group reading lessons devoted to discussion of stories are not corrected for their use of pidgin English. Thus, children are not distracted from concentrating on development of ideas pertinent to the stories they are to read. Acceptance of pidgin as a legitimate variety for discussion of stories further strengthen the links between children's existing language skills and cultural background and their in-school literacy experiences. It is also noteworthy that children are exposed only to standard English in the materials they read or hear read and that teachers use standard English in probing student's understanding of stories after they have been read. Thus, KEEP small group reading lessons permit students to rely on familiar language skills during an introductory portion of lessons, but by the end of a lesson, competent performance on the part of students depends on skills reflecting mastery of standard English. These contexts for language use more clearly resemble an additive bilingualism/bidialectal context than a subtractive one, since children's knowledge of a language variety different from the standard acts as an asset to school performance rather than as a detriment.

Directions for New Research: An Example

The discussion thus far suggests that understanding literacy acquisition among second language learners benefits from a multidisciplinary approach to research, and that there remain relatively unexplored directions for such research. One of those innovative directions concerns individuals' mental representations of knowledge about their own literacy and how such knowledge is integrated with knowledge of social identity in the enactment of literacy events. Cognitive psychology research on representation of knowledge and knowledge acquisition contributes paradigms and points of view allowing investigation of literate discourse behavior as goal driven problem solving—albeit that such approaches need to be modified to include knowledge of individuals' online, dynamic construction of social relations with others while communicating.

A preliminary attempt to combine cognitive and ethnographic approaches towards this end is described by Durán and Guerra (1982) and Durán (1983a). This research investigated ways in which mental models might be used to describe children's knowledge of literacy events, and of how to perform in them. The approach was influenced by the fact that sociolinguistic descriptions of the components of speech events (Hymes, 1974) bore a strong resemblance to memory structures termed "scripts," which were posted by cognitive psychologists to represent knowledge about how people engage in everyday activities (Schank & Abelson, 1977). Freedle and Durán (1979) outline these correspondences in detail.

Durán and Guerra (1982) and Durán (1983a) describe how the organization of a second grade bilingual child's oral reading from a storybook at home revealed her knowledge of an oral story reading script encountered at school, as well as other forms of knowledge about how to interact with an audience at home. The child in question, Lili, demonstrated strategic oral and paralinguistic behaviors which she had learned from adult readers at school, and which she adapted to fit the conduct of her story reading script within the social and cultural ambience of the home setting. The discourse and paralinguistic strategies enacted by Lili were diverse. They reflected a number of different forms of knowledge about linguistic and social interaction and how discourse and accompanying paralinguistic behaviors might be deployed strategically to aid in delivery of a story and management of a story audience. These strategic behaviors included:

- Deliberate fluctuation of intonation, stress, and other prosodic cues to mark text delivered by the omniscient narrator or by fictional characters quoted in the story text
- Strategic use of intonation, stress, and prosody to mark semantic relations occurring in a text such as distinctions between given and new information, boundaries between phrases and sentences, cohesion relations, etc.
- Embellishing a story by stepping out of the role of literal text-reader to comment on a story or story pictures.
- Interrupting of story reading to manage the attentive behavior of the audience, sometimes with an accompanying switch in language to mitigate a speech act.
- Interrupting reading of a story to ask for help in pronouncing words.

The range of behaviors identified above suggest a complex interleaving and deployment of many forms of knowledge in the conduct of oral reading. These forms of knowledge were made more interesting and complex by Lili's facile switching between languages and cultural perspectives, as she alternatively conveyed knowledge of Hispanic and Anglo ways of behaving and interacting. The strategic behaviors which were observed were not applied in a wooden fashion resembling rote enactment of previously learned behaviors. Enactment of discourse strategies appeared improvisational to a large extent. It seemed clear that the strategies were based upon previous learning, but, at the same time, they appeared to be spontaneously composed for the purpose of contending with immediate needs and contingencies that arose unexpectedly in the literacy context at hand. Such a composition of strategies must have required an active monitoring of several layers of social and linguistic cues affecting the immediate interpretation and conduct of communication.

Durán (1984) reported a very different quality to the English oral reading performance of a child, Juan, who was involved in the same research study. Juan was not as proficient in English as Lili, and experienced great difficulty in reading stories. He concentrated on attempting to pronounce individual words in isolation and displayed very limited strategic use of intonation, stress, and prosody to mark units of syntactic and semantic meaning in the story texts. His oral reading was also characterized by repeated miscues. Other researchers, such as Goodman and Goodman (1977), have reported at length on the occurrence of miscues in oral reading. These investigators have hypothesized that various forms of miscues reflect specific information processing strategies which children deploy as they read. The Goodmans have discussed differences in the sorts of miscue errors enacted by children with higher as opposed to lower English proficiency. The miscue errors made by more proficient children, e.g., synonym substitution, minimally affect the meaning of phrases and sentences being read. On the other hand, children with low English proficiency are likely to show severe problems in the decoding of several words within a sentence, substituting words which are clearly inappropriate within the intended semantic context of a sentence. Research on miscue analysis in bilingual children's oral reading thus is consistent with the hypothesis that children are actively engaged in monitoring their own comprehension processes as they read.

The Durán and Guerra research also suggests that monitoring processes and strategic behaviors during oral reading may go beyond comprehension of the literal information in a text. These additional monitoring processes and strategic behaviors can be hypothesized to regulate the overall coordination of discourse behavior in a setting based on expectations about how behavior is to proceed. These additional behaviors are sensitive to the nature of the activity at hand and its construction, accommodating to the social and cultural characteristics of the unfolding, immediate environment.

Cole and colleagues (Cole, 1984) and other investigators in cognitive anthropology (see Rogoff & Lave, 1984, for a recent collection of papers) working in the ethnographic tradition, have given some attention to descriptions of knowledge structures and cognitive strategies which might underlie literate behavior and the sorts of strategic discourse behaviors which have been described. Studies of verbal reasoning in everyday contexts by Luria (1976), and by Cole, Gay, Glick and Sharp (1971) have found that many apparent "errors" in logical reasoning were in fact systematic and strategic responses to problems based on the organization of experiences and problem solving practices characteristic of the rural cultures in question. In reviewing this work, Scribner (1981) has suggested that individuals acquire knowledge about how verbal reasoning problems are stated and that this knowledge is coupled closely to the way in which reasoning tasks are approached and solved. One may generalize this point of view to suggest that individuals develop knowledge through prior experience about how discourse form and structure are likely to be tied to the cognitive and social problem solving demands of literacy events.

From the foregoing point of view, knowledge about the nature and structure of activities within which specific literate behaviors are embedded stands out as a critical factor. The possibility that knowledge about event structures is fundamental to all cognition (and not just to literate behavior) is discussed by Cole (1985). Citing the research of Vygotzky, Luria, and Leontiev, he posits that people perceive many of their experiences in terms of activity types that are culturally instrumental ways of behaving. Thus, one may inquire how individuals in a second language might develop literacy competencies tied to knowledge of the characteristics of literacy events as recurrent meaningful social activities.

These views suggest fertile territory for new research on acquisition of literacy skills among second language learners. They seem especially promising because they suggest the possibility of treating the interaction of social and psychological variables that influence the occurrence of bilingualism and literacy development in a more integrated manner than has been possible in the past. These new approaches to studying second language literacy acquisition promise new knowledge, complementing the contributions to knowledge made by quantitative surveys and noncognitively based ethnographic studies of literacy acquisition.

References

Anderson, A. B., & Stokes, S. J. (1984). Social and institutional influences on the development and practice of literacy. In F. Smith, H. Goelman, & A. Oberg (Eds.), *Awakening to literacy* (pp. 24–37). New York: Heineman.

Au, K. H. (1980). On participation structures in reading lessons. *Anthropology and Education Quarterly, 9*(2), 91–115.

Au, K., Crowell, D., Jordan, C., Sloat, C., Speidel, G., Klein, T., & Tharp, R. (1986). Development and implementation of the KEEP Reading Program. In J. Orasanu (Ed.), *Reading comprehension: From research to practice* (pp. 235–252). Hillsdale, NJ: Erlbaum.

Carter, T. P., & Segura, R. D. (1979). *Mexican Americans in school*. New York: College Entrance Examination Board.

Cicourel, A. & Mehan, H. (1985). Universal development, stratifying practices, and status attainment. *Research in Social Stratification and Mobility, 4*, 3–27.

Cole, M., Gay, J. K., Glick, S., & Sharp, D. W. (1971). *The cultural context of learning and thinking*. New York: Basic Books.

Cole, M. (1984). *LCHC: A Program of Research and Training in Cultural Psychology*, La Jolla: University of California, San Diego, Laboratory of Comparative Human Cognition.

Cole, M. (1985). The zone of proximal development: Where culture and cognition create each other. In J. Wertsch (Ed.), *Culture, communication, and cognition: Vygotskian perspectives* (pp. 146–161). New York: Cambridge University Press.

Collins, J., & Michaels, S. (1980). The importance of conversational discourse strategies in the acquisition of literacy. *Proceedings of the Sixth Annual Meeting of the Berkeley Linguistics Society, 6,* 143–156.

Cook-Gumperz, J., & Gumperz, J. J. (1981). From oral to written culture: The transition to literacy. In M. Farr Whiteman (Ed.), *Writing: The nature, development, and teaching of written communication. Volume 1: Variation in writing: Functional and linguistic-cultural differences* (pp. 89–109). Hillsdale, NJ: Erlbaum.

Cummins, J. (1978). Bilingualism and the development of metalinguistic awareness. *Journal of Cross-Cultural Psychology, 9*(2), 131–149.

Cummins, J. (1981). The role of primary language development in promoting educational success for language minority students. In California State Department of Education (Ed.), *Schooling and language minority students: A theoretical framework* (pp. 3–49). Los Angeles: Evaluation, Dissemination, and Assessment Center, California State University, Los Angeles.

De Avila, E., & Duncan, S. (1981). Bilingualism and the metaset. In R. Durán (Ed.), *Latino language and communicative behavior* (pp. 337–355). Norwood, NJ: Ablex.

Dornic, S. (1980). Information processing and language dominance. *International Review of Applied Psychology 29,* 119–140.

Durán, R. P. (1981). Reading comprehension and the verbal deductive reasoning of bilinguals. In R. Durán (Ed.), *Latino language and communicative behavior* (pp. 311–336). Norwood, NJ: Ablex.

Durán, R. P. (1983a). Cognitive theory and Chicano children's oral reading behavior. *Quarterly Newsletter of the Laboratory of Comparative Human Cognition, 5*(4), 74–79.

Durán, R. P. (1983b). *Hispanics' education and background. Predictors of college achievement.* New York: The College Entrance Examination Board.

Durán, R. P. (1984). *Children's sense of self and literacy development.* Paper presented at the American Anthropologication Annual Meeting, Denver, CO.

Durán, R. P. (1985a). Influence of language skills on bilinguals' problem solving. In S. Chipman, J. Segal, & R. Glaser (Eds.), *Thinking and learning skills, Volume 2: Research and open questions* (pp. 187–207). Hillsdale, NJ: Erlbaum.

Durán, R. P. (1985b). Discourse skills of bilingual children: Precursors of literacy. *International Journal of the Sociology of Language, 53,* 99–114.

Durán, R. P., Enright, M., & Rock, D. (1985). *Language factors and Hispanic freshmen's student profile.* (College Board Report No. 85–3.) New york: College Entrance Examination Board.

Durán, R. P., & Guerra, E. (1982). *Chicano children's literacy: Learning at home.* Paper presented at the American Anthropological Association Annual Meeting, Washington, DC.

Edelsky, C. (1981). A critical look at several versions of popular theory. In H. Trueba & B. Blair (Eds.), *Advances in second language literacy.* San Diego, CA, California State University.

Ferguson, C. (1959). Diglossia. *Word, 15,* 325–340.
Fernandez, R., & Nielsen, F. (In press). Bilingualism and Hispanic scholastic achievement: Some baseline results. *Social Science Research.*
Freedle, R., & Durán, R. P. (1979). Sociolinguistic approaches to dialogue with suggested applications to cognitive science. In R. O. Freedle (Ed.), *New directions in discourse processing* (pp. 197–206). Norwood, NJ: Ablex.
Goldman, S. R., Reyes, M., & Varnhagen, C. K. (1984). Understanding fables in first and second language. *Journal of the National Association for Bilingual Education, 3*(2), 35–66.
Goodman, K., & Goodman, Y. M. (1977). Learning about psycholinguistic processes by analyzing oral reading. *Harvard Educational Review, 47*(3), 317–333.
Gumperz, J. J. (Ed.), (1982). *Discourse strategies.* New York: Cambridge University Press.
Gumperz, J. (1981). Conversational inference and classroom learning. In J. L. Green & C. Wallat (Eds.), *Ethnography and language in educational settings,* (pp. 3–23). Norwood, NJ: Ablex.
Hakuta, K., & Diaz, R. (1985). The relationship between the degree of bilingualism and cognitive ability: A critical discussion and some longitudinal data. In K. E. Nelson (Ed.), *Children's language. Volume 5.* (pp. 319–344) Hillsdale, NJ: Erlbaum.
Heath, S. B. (1983), *Ways with words: Ethnography of communications in communities and classrooms.* New York: Cambridge University Press.
Hernandez-Chavez, E. (1978). Language maintenance, bilingual education, and philosophies of bilingualism in the United States. In J. Alatis (Ed.), *International dimensions of bilingual education.* Washington, DC: Georgetown University Press.
Hymes, D. (1974). *Foundations in sociolinguistics: An ethnographic approach.* Philadelphia, PA: University of Pennsylvania Press.
Hymes, D. (1983). Report from an underdeveloped country: Towards linguistic competence in the United States. In B. Bain (Ed.), *The sociogenesis of language and human conduct* (pp. 189–224). New York: Plenum.
Kloss, H. (1977). *The American bilingual tradition.* Rowley, MA: Newbury House.
Lambert, W. (1977). The effects of bilingualism on the individual: Cognitive and Sociocultural Consequences. In P. A. Hornby (Ed.), *Bilingualism: Psychological, social and educational implication.* (pp. 15–28). New York: Academic.
Laosa, L. (1978). Bilingualism in three United States' Hispanic groups: Contextual use of language by children and adults in their families. *Journal of Educational Psychology, 67*(5), 617–627.
Luria, A. R. (1976). *Cognitive development: Its cultural and social foundations.* Cambridge, MA: Harvard University Press.
Macias, R. (1979). *Mexicano/Chicano sociolinguistic behavior and language policy in the United States.* Unpublished doctoral dissertation, Georgetown University, Washington, DC.
Moll, L., Estrada E., Elette E., Diaz E., & Lopez, L. M. (1980). The construction of learning environment in two languages. *The Quarterly Newsletter of the Laboratory of Comparative Human Cognition, 2*(3), 53–58.

Nielsen, F., & Fernandez, R. (1982). Achievement of Hispanic students in American high schools: Background characteristics and achievement. (Contractor's Report to the National Center for Educational Statistics.) Washington, DC.

Ogbu, J., & Matute-Bianchi, M. (1985). Understanding sociocultural factors: Knowledge, identity and school adjustments. In *Beyond language: Social and cultural factors in schooling language minority students.* California State University, Los Angeles, Evaluation, Dissemination and Assessment Center, 73–142.

Phillips, S. (1972). Participant structures and communicative competence: Warm Springs children in community and classroom. In C. Cazden, D. Hymes, & V. John (Eds.), *Functions of language in the classroom.* New York: Teachers College Press, 370–394.

Ramirez, A. (1981). Language attitudes and the speech of Spanish-English bilingual pupils. In R. P. Durán (Ed.), *Latino language and communicative behavior* (pp. 217–232). Norwood, NJ: Ablex.

Rogoff, B., & Lave, J. (1984). *Everyday cognition: Its development in social context.* Cambridge, MA: Harvard University Press.

Ryan, E. B. & Carranza, M. A. (1977). Ingroup and outgroup reactions to Mexican American language varieties. In H. Giles (Ed.), *Language ethnicity and intergroup relations* (pp. 59–82). New York: Academic.

Schank, R., & Abelson, R. (1977). *Scripts, plans, goals, and understanding.* Hillsdale, NJ: Erlbaum.

Scollon, R., & Scollon, S. B. K. (1981). *Narrative, literacy and face in interethnic communication.* Norwood, NJ: Ablex.

Scribner, S. (1981). Modes of thinking and ways of speaking: Culture and logic reconsidered. In R. Freedle (Ed.), *New directions in discourse processing* (pp. 223–243). Norwood, NJ: Ablex.

Tharp, R. G. (1982). The effective instruction of comprehension: Results and descriptions of the Kamehameha Early Education Program. *Reading Research Quarterly, 17*(4), 503–527.

Wald, B. (1974). Bilingualism. *Annual Review of Anthropology, 3,* 301–321.

3

Reading in a Second Language: Studies with Adult and Child Learners

Barry McLaughlin
University of California, Santa Cruz

Contrary to conventional wisdom, second-language learning is not easy and automatic for children (McLaughlin, 1984). For a child to acquire a second language requires a great deal of trial-and-error, creative hypothesis-testing, and awkward experimentation. Especially in the classroom context, second-language learning is a difficult and frustrating enterprise for many children (McLaughlin, 1985). This is a topic of great practical concern in the United States, where it is estimated that 4.5 million children of school age come from families where the home language is other than English.

One area of critical importance is *learning to read* in a second language. For many minority-language children, reading is the beginning of school failure. There have been a number of attempts to explain the difficulties that bilingual children have in learning to read English in the classroom. These range from explanations based on differences in cultural "world view" between minority-language children and children from the dominant culture to those that relate to processing linguistic information in a second language. Unfortunately, there has been little experimental research on the reading difficulties of minority-language bilingual children to test this latter set of hypotheses.

In this chapter, I will sketch a theoretical framework to guide experimental research on reading in a second language. I will describe some research on adult second-language readers and some recent work we have been carrying out with child second-language readers. The claim is made that reading is a complex, multi-stage, interactive process that can only be understood by a theory of learning that allows for discontinuous restructuring whereby procedures involving old components and strategies are replaced by procedures involving new components and strategies.

Theoretical Perspective

Second-Language Learning As Information-Processing

Second-language learning can be viewed as the acquisition of a complex cognitive skill that involves information processing (McLaughlin, Rossman, & McLeod, 1983). Central to this perspective is the notion that human beings have limited information-processing ability. To deal with tasks that would otherwise tax our information-handling capacity we develop organizing strategies. By grouping information into related units, rather than trying to deal with isolated bits, we achieve more effective processing. Thus, complex skills are thought to be acquired by mastering a set of related subtasks and their components. To attain a higher-order goal, subtasks need to be integrated by a "plan" whereby the selection of subactivities is regulated according to overriding goals. This process need not be a strictly hierarchical one with one subtask mastered before beginning on a second. Instead, it is more likely that attention is given to various subtasks on a time-sharing basis, with the learner attending now to one subtask and now to another.

A major tenet of the information-processing approach is that learners master complex cognitive skills by concentrating processing energy on to-be-mastered subtasks, which, once mastered, require relatively little amounts of processing capacity, thereby freeing up the system to work on the mastery of other subtasks. For example, a beginning second-language learner may need to exert considerable cognitive effort simply to realize a correct, or at least an adequate, phonetic expression of individual words in the target language. At the same time, the beginning learner needs to employ appropriate syntactic rules and needs to develop the lexical system. Once one of these subtasks is mastered—once an adequate pronunciation is achieved, for instance—the learner has more processing energy free to devote to other subtasks.

Contemporary cognitive psychologists typically see the mastery of complex cognitive tasks to require the integration of two types of operations—one type of operation that requires relatively large amounts of processing capacity and time, and another type of operation that occurs quickly and takes little processing energy. Shiffrin and Schneider (Schneider & Shiffrin, 1977; Shiffrin & Schneider, 1977) referred to these two types of operations as "controlled" and "automatic" processing, respectively. Controlled processes are tightly capacity-limited, but have the advantage of being relatively easy to set up, alter, and apply to novel situations. Automatic processes, on the other hand, do not require much by way of a capacity investment. They occur quickly and are difficult to suppress or alter. Automatic processes are thus thought to utilize a relatively permanent set of associative connections in long-term store, and are established through an appreciable amount of training. Writing one's name is an example of a skill that involves automatic processing, whereas writing one's name with the opposite hand would, for most of us, require controlled processing.

Learning is thought to involve the transfer of information to the long-term store and is regulated by controlled processes. That is, complex skills are learned and routinized (i.e., become automatic) only after the earlier use of controlled processes. It is controlled processes that regulate the flow of information from working to long-term memory. Learning involves time, but once automaticity is achieved at one level in the development of a complex cognitive skill, controlled processes are free to be allocated to higher levels of processing. Thus, controlled processing can be said to lay down the "stepping stones" for automatic processing as the learner moves to more and more difficult levels (Shiffrin & Schneider, 1977).

Reading as Information Processing

Of all the skills that the child must acquire in school, reading is the most complex and difficult. The child who accurately and efficiently translates a string of printed letters into meaningful communication may appear to be accomplishing that task with little mental effort. In fact, however, the child is engaging in complex interactive processes that are dependent on multiple subskills and an enormous amount of coded information. The fluent reader must have automated language skills, intact visual and auditory memory, the ability to associate and integrate intra- and intermodal stimuli, and the ability to abstract and generalize patterned or rule-generated information (Vellutino & Scanlon, 1982).

In particular, to become an accomplished reader, the child must have mastered three important tasks:

1. The child must master the rules governing symbol–sound correspondence in English.
2. The child must be able to use those rules in learning words and must progressively refine and automate word-decoding operations.
3. The child must acquire and perfect a complex set of processing skills that allows for rapid processing of incoming material and the extraction of meaning.

These three tasks are developmentally linked to each other, and mastery proceeds in parallel time frames. Progress in one task may facilitate progress in the others. For example, a supporting context may speed up word-decoding operations, especially for less-skilled readers (Perfetti, Goldman, & Hogaboam, 1979). Similarly, automated word-decoding operations are thought to be important because they allow space in working memory for retaining evolving discourse meanings (LaBerge & Samuels, 1974; Perfetti & Lesgold, 1977). Poor readers may be hampered at stage 3 by their inability to achieve automatic word-decoding or even by nonautomatic symbol–sound matching.

Furthermore, children who are learning to read in a second language may have more problems than monolingual children have because of their lack of familiarity with the semantic and syntactic constraints of the target language. Research with good and poor readers has indicated that, if children are not able spontaneously to identify and exploit syntactic relations and are not flexible in their use of semantic context as a guide to prediction, their reading comprehension and speed decline (Carr, 1981).

From an information-processing point of view, when skill is low and controlled processes are involved in performing any of the tasks just mentioned, there is competition for limited processing resources. For the skilled reader, on the other hand, component processes are highly automatic and integrated. Furthermore, expertise in one processing component may alter the character of processing for some other component, so that the mechanisms for process interaction may differ for expert and nonexpert readers.

Reading Processes in a Second Language

Second-Language Reading in Adult Learners

One of the assumptions of the theoretical point of view sketched above is that learning occurs slowly, as skills are built up via controlled processes and gradually, through practice, become automatic. In reading, the assumption is that learners acquire symbol–sound correspondences, then, once decoding skills have been mastered, direct controlled attention to deriving meaning from text. Practice makes perfect, in this view. But, as we shall see, some findings from research with adult second-language learners made us question the notion that learning is a slow process of the accretion of skills through practice.

One would expect to find a continual progression in reading skill in second-language readers as they develop facility with the language. The more the reader has automatized mechanical decoding skills, the more attention is freed up to grasp the overall meaning of a phrase or sentence. Good readers use predictive skills based on their knowledge of the syntax and semantics of the language to gain the gist of the text. In contrast, one could expect that poorer readers (and those less proficient in the language) have not yet automatized the basic skills, and therefore utilize less efficient strategies to gain meaning.

There is some evidence that less accomplished second-language readers focus on different things than more proficient second-language readers do. A number of studies indicate that beginning ESL students pay more attention to the details, or form, or graphic characteristics of the text, than do native speakers. For example, in a study conducted by Hatch, Polin, and Part (1970), foreign students studying English and native speakers were asked to cross out every letter "e" on a page of text. The nonnative speakers were more accurate at this task, while native speakers missed "e's" in function words and unstressed syllables. This suggests that beginning second-language learners give equal attention to every word while reading, whereas native speakers can read by focusing only on "important" or "essential" aspects of the text.

Johnston (1972) found that ESL students often do not attend to graphic cues that signal meaning, such as capitalization and punctuation. Thus ESL readers tend to focus on phonologically related graphic aspects of comprehension and vocabulary recognition. After listening to a passage, students were asked to indicate which words they had heard. Low-proficiency learners registered vocabulary items in memory in terms of similarity in sound to other words, while high-proficiency learners registered words in terms of associated meanings. Thus, for example, if the word "pin" had been in the passage, lower-level students would mark "pan," while upper-level students would mark "needle."

In a study of reading in a second language, Cziko (1980) found that seventh graders who were less proficient in a second language seemed to rely on graphic cues while reading, in contrast to more advanced students who relied more on contextual information. For example, if the printed text said, "She shook the piggy bank and out came some *money*," the beginning students might make an error by saying, "She shook the piggy bank and out came some *many*," while the advanced students would be more likely to make an error by saying something like, "She shook the piggy bank and out came some *dimes*."

These studies suggest that beginning and advanced second-language readers use different strategies for reading. From an information-processing point of view, one could say that beginning second-language readers deal with phonological information on a controlled process basis, approaching each word anew, until they become secure and adept at word decoding. At that point, sound–symbol matching can operate under automatic processing, and controlled processing can be freed up and devoted to other aspects of the reading task, such as syntax and semantics. Thus the different strategies used by good and poor readers indicate the extent to which certain reading subskills have become automated or still operate only under controlled processing. This view of the reading process turned out, however, to be inadequate to account for the data from a recent study we conducted with beginning and advanced ESL students and native speakers (McLeod & McLaughlin, 1986).

In this study we wished to examined the extent to which learners at different levels of proficiency in English have achieved automaticity in their reading skills. We expected that as learners became more proficient in a second language, they would be more skilled at decoding graphic cues from text. The errors that more proficient learners make should be more meaningful, because they have automated the mechanical aspects of reading and have freed up controlled processing for drawing meaning from context. Because we wanted to relate reading ability to the ability to use context, we included a 10-item cloze test in addition to the reading task.

We found that the beginning ESL readers made the greatest number of errors, and that only 20% of their errors were meaningful. Their performance on the cloze test also indicated that they did not have enough command of the syntax and lexicon of the language to allow them to make accurate predictions in reading. The advanced ESL students were significantly better at making such predictions on the cloze test and made significantly fewer errors in reading than did the beginning students. However, advanced ESL students also made predominately nonmeaningful errors—only 29% were meaningful, in contrast to 79% for native speakers. Table 1 summarizes our findings.

Thus our advanced ESL readers were not utilizing semantic and syntactic cues as well as they could have. They were not approaching the task as "a psycholinguistic guessing game," (Goodman, 1969; Smith, 1978) in which graphic cues were used to make predictions about what the printed text means—even though the evidence suggests that they were quite capable of making such predictions. Their increasing syntactic and semantic competence enabled them to make nearly twice as many accurate predictions as the beginners on the cloze test. Yet they had not applied this competence to their reading behavior.

Our advanced learners, we argued, had not yet reached the point in their reading performance where restructuring occurs. That is, they were using old strategies aimed at decoding in a situation where their competencies would have allowed them to apply new strategies directed at meaning. Their performance on the cloze test indicated that they had

Table 1. Group Differences on Dependent Variables

Group	Cloze Test[a]		Proportion Meaningful Errors	
	Mean	S.D.	Mean	S.D.
Beginning ESL	3.5	2.2	.20	.14
Advanced ESL	6.8	2.4	.29	.17
Native Speakers	9.7	.6	.79	.17

[a]The Cloze Test consisted of 10 items and scores could range from 0 to 10.

the skills needed to "go for meaning." We assumed they read this way in their first language. But they had not yet made the shift in strategies in their second language. In this language, they did not make strategic use of the semantic and syntactic knowledge at their disposal.

These results made us aware of the need to look systematically at discontinuities in the second-language learning process. Our findings made us wonder about the adequacy of the controlled-automatic processing distinction in accounting for our findings. I argued earlier in this chapter that skilled readers are superior to less skilled readers because they have well-automated decoding skills, which allow capacity to be freed for comprehension processes. Presumably, one should see a steady improvement in the reading process as automaticity in decoding develops and processing capacity is freed for comprehension. But this is not what we found. Instead, our data suggested that various aspects of second-language performance have an emergent quality. Learning at such times involves the modification of organizational structures and the adoption of new strategies and procedures. This is a point that will be discussed more in the final section of this chapter.

Second-Language Reading in Child Learners

The argument was made earlier in this chapter that a complex skill such as reading involves many highly practiced and automatic activities. Among other things, skilled comprehension requires flexibility in the use of semantic context and the ability to identify and exploit syntactic relations. We suspected that children who are learning to read in a second language may have more problems than monolingual children, because of their lack of familiarity with the semantic and syntactic constraints of the target language.

Our research (McLaughlin & Baker, 1985) followed the methodology used by Guthrie (1973) with good and poor readers. Guthrie reported that, when required to fill in text with words that were either (a) syntactically appropriate but lexically inappropriate, (b) syntactically inappropriate but lexically appropriate, or (c) both syntactically and lexically appropriate, good readers made fewer errors than poor readers. He also found an effect of passage difficulty, such that, when passages became more difficult, the performance of the poor readers deteriorated to a greater extent than that of good readers. There was no interaction effect for group x form class, indicating that, proportionally, there was no difference in ability to respond correctly to words from different form classes (nouns, verbs, modifiers, and function words). Guthrie concluded from this that there were no differences in the pattern of errors for good and poor readers, and he saw the results as evidence that the two groups are not qualitatively different in syntactic processing during silent reading.

Whereas Guthrie's research was limited to monolingual good and poor readers, we were interested in both monolingual and bilingual good and poor readers. We wanted to see how monolingual and bilingual subjects differed and how poor and good readers differed. But, most important, we were interested in how poor bilingual readers differed from poor monolingual readers. Thus, in statistical terms, we were concerned with both main effects and interactions.

The bilingual students in our study were Hispanic children in a California school. Most of these children had been in bilingual programs throughout their school career, and many had learned to read and write in Spanish before learning to read and write in English. The experiment was conducted with children in the upper grades, as pilot research has indicated that it is at 5th and 6th grade levels that marked differences between children in reading ability appear. Furthermore, at about the fifth grade children read quite smoothly in units larger than individual words, but are not yet fully mature and skilled readers (Gibson & Levin, 1975). Monolingual groups were chosen from the same grades in the same school.

Good and poor readers were identified on the basis of teacher judgments and CTBS scores. Children who were a grade or more above grade level on the reading subtest of the CTBS and were regarded by teachers as good readers were placed in the "good reader" group. Children a grade or more below grade level on the CTBS and regarded by teachers as poor readers constituted the "poor reader" group. All subjects were also administered the Gates-MacGinitie vocabulary test.

There were four groups of nine subjects each in this study: a monolingual good reader group (MG), a monolingual poor reader group (MP), a bilingual good reader group (BG), and a bilingual poor reader group (BP). Children in the good reader groups were on the average a grade and a half above grade level on the CTBS, whereas children in the poor reader groups were on the average two grades below grade level. The good readers were significantly better than the poor readers on the Gates-McGinitie vocabulary test. There were no significant differences, however, between the MG and the BG groups in CTBS grade-level discrepancy scores or in vocabulary. Similarly, there were no differences between the MP and the BP groups in CTBS grade-level discrepancy scores or in vocabulary.

The children in the study were administered five passages of increasing difficulty containing blanks for which there were three choices: the correct response, a syntactically correct response that was lexically inappropriate, and a lexically appropriate response that was syntactically inappropriate. For example, a sentence might read: "The farmer sold his (cow, mother, harvested) to the young man." The passages were selected from basal-text readers ranging in difficulty from a high second grade to a low fifth grade level. The length of the passages varied from 149 to 209 words (mean 173.6 words).

Children were asked to circle the correct word on their sheet, and told to work without hurrying, as carefully as they could. Each passage contained six blanks that called for a noun, six that called for a verb, six that called for a modifier, and six that called for a function word. There were never fewer than three words separating the blanks where words had to be circled. No words were selected if they could not be found in the Houghton-Mifflin Basal-Word list for grades two to five.

Analysis of total correct responses made by the children in their choice of the appropriate words indicated that good readers performed significantly better than poor readers. Our data also indicated that as reading materials became more difficult, the performance of the poor readers deteriorated, but the performance of the good readers remained relatively constant. When we examined the question of whether different form classes were selected with different degrees of accuracy by the various groups, we found no differences between good and poor readers for different form classes. Good readers were better in correctly identifying words in all form classes.

What was especially of interest in our results was the finding that poor monolingual and bilingual readers made different types of mistakes. For the poor monolingual readers, lexical and syntactic errors occurred with equal frequency. Poor bilingual readers, however, made significantly more syntactic errors than lexical errors. These results suggest that the problems of poor bilingual readers may be somewhat different from the problems of poor monolingual readers. It may be that the bilingual children, because of their relative lack of experience with the language, may make syntactic mistakes that native speakers can avoid. The native speaker presumably has well developed and automatic syntactic knowledge, and so is less likely to make syntactic errors.

In short, our study of good and poor monolingual and bilingual readers indicated that good readers possessed skills that enabled them to predict accurately what words were to appear in the blanks. These skills were less available to poor readers, whose performance became progressively worse as the difficulty of the textual material increased. Poor monolingual readers made lexical and syntactic errors equally frequently, but poor bilingual readers made significantly more syntactic than lexical errors.

The Acquisition of Reading Skill

Interactive Processes in Reading

I argued earlier in this chapter that no single-factor theory is adequate to explain individual differences in reading ability. Reading proficiency is related to a large number of information-processing skills, including the ability to use semantic context as a guide to prediction and the ability to grasp syntactic relationships. But there is much more to the reading process than this, and I do not wish to imply that the only differences between the groups we studied were those we measured.

For example, one factor influencing reading in a second language is what children have learned about the structure of discourse in the two languages. As Bock and Brewer (1985) have pointed out, discourse comprehension involves the construction by readers of mental models synthesized from the information in the text and their general knowledge. To the degree that a segment of discourse makes contact with the reader's schema-based general knowledge, the information can be used to construct a mental model that is much richer than the information explicit in the text. But the real-word knowledge that is assumed to provide the basis for generic schemata differs from culture to culture. Children who have a different cultural experience from the mainstream culture assumed in school reading material, may make schema-driven inferences not justified by the text.

Moreover, the assumption of homogeneity among groups of readers for whom English is a second language is unwarranted (Brown & Haynes, 1985). For some individuals reading in a second language, the basic skills of the first language are so well automated and are so specific to the first language that the fundamental skills of visual and orthographic processing must be learned from scratch. It is also possible, however, that automated skills in the first language facilitate the development of corresponding second-language skills when the scripts of the two languages are the same or quite similar in their visual and orthographic characteristics.

Even within language groups with similar scripts, not enough is known about the way in which transfer occurs from first-language reading to second-language reading. One would expect facilitation at the stage when children were "going for meaning," but there may be negative transfer during the early stages of reading in a second language, as the child is learning to master the rules governing symbol–sound correspondence and using these rules to automate word-decoding operations.

Learning to be a skilled reader involves mastering a complex of interdependent bodies of knowledge and operations. Visual analysis depends on phonological analysis, and visual and phonological analysis in the child's second language depend on visual and phonological analysis in the child's first language. Semantic analysis is basic to comprehension, which also depends upon an understanding of coherence cues and discourse schemata. Syntactic analysis is basic to the ability to anticipate what is coming in the text so that meaning can be mapped onto world knowledge.

Thus, there is a great deal more to be known before one can draw conclusions about the reading problems of children for whom English a second language. Our study with child readers suggests that bilingual children with reading difficulties have problems that are, in some respects, different from the problems experienced by nonbilingual children with reading difficulties. But considerable research is needed on various components of the reading process before conclusions can be drawn that have consequences for the intervention techniques used by teachers.

Restructuring

Our research with adult subjects made us question the adequacy of the argument that skilled readers are superior to less skilled readers because they have well-automated decoding skills, which allows capacity to be freed for comprehension processes (Stanovich, 1980). One should find a steady improvement in the reading process as automaticity in decoding develops and processing capacity is freed for comprehension. Our data with adult second-language learners, however, did not support that continuous learning process. Our advanced subjects were more capable of using semantic and syntactic information to make accurate predictions about what was coming in textual material than were beginning learners. Nonetheless, the advanced subjects were not using this ability in their reading, because they made as many meaningless errors as did beginners. Something more seemed to be necessary than increased skill in using semantic and syntactic information.

We believe that something else to be what contemporary cognitive psychologists call "restructuring," or a modification of organizational structure. Rumelhart and Norman (1978) argued that restructuring is a process that occurs "when new structures are devised for interpreting new information and imposing a new organization on that already stored" (p. 39). They contrasted this type of learning with (a) accretion, in which new facts, data, or information are added to a person's knowledge base, and (b) tuning, in which there is a change in the categories used for interpreting new information. In tuning, categories, or schemata, are modified; in restructuring, new structures are added that allow for new interpretation of facts (see Table 2).

Thus, Rumelhart and Norman argued that learning is not a unitary process, but that there are different kinds of learning, one of which is restructuring. Although their analysis was directed principally at learning as the acquisition of semantic knowledge in memory, it can be applied equally well to learning complex cognitive skills, such as the acquisition of a second language. If one assumes that there are various types of learning, one can argue that some learning occurs continuously and over long periods of time, by accretion. For example, vocabulary learning extends over a lifetime for many individuals. On the other hand, it seems likely that some learning occurs in a discontinuous fashion, by restructuring.

Although the data from our adult reading study did not provide us with definitive information about how restructuring occurs, they have made us aware of the need to look systematically at discontinuities in

Table 2. Three Modes of Learning[a]

	Characteristics	Mechanism	Structural Change	Examples
Accretion	Daily accumulation of information	Exposure	No	Learning lists, new facts
Tuning	Changes in the categories used for interpreting new data	Need to improve accuracy, improve specificity, improve generalizability	Yes	Becoming a better typist, overcoming overgeneralizations
Restructuring	New structures are devised for interpreting new information and imposing a new organization on that already stored	New information does not fit existing schemata	Yes	"Insightful" learning and problem-solving, discovery learning, creativity

[a]Based on Rumelhart and Norman, 1978.

the second-language learning process. The next step in research is to describe these discontinuities more precisely and to determine what conditions lead to restructuring. Are there, for example, certain conditions that lead learners to be more (or less) ready to restructure?

Our study with child readers suggests a whole line of research, aimed at comparing differences in ability between good and poor readers who are reading in first or second languages. The ultimate goal of such research is the development of intervention strategies to assist children who are having difficulty learning how to read with skill in a second language. Restructuring is an important issue in child learners as well. It will be interesting to see if, as the child develops reading skills in a second language, periods of restructuring can be identified, in which components of the task are integrated and reorganized in new ways.

References

Bock, J. K., & Brewer, W. F. (1985). Discourse structure and mental models. In T. H. Carr (Ed.), *The development of reading skills*. New Directions for Child Development, no. 27. San Francisco: Jossey-Bass.

Brown, T. L., & Haynes, M. (1985). Literacy background and reading development in a second language. In T. H. Carr (Ed.), *The development of reading skills*. New Directions for Child Development, no. 27. San Francisco: Jossey-Bass.

Carr, T. (1981). Building theories of reading ability: On the relation between individual differences in cognitive skills and reading. *Cognition, 9*, 73–114.

Cziko, G. A. (1980). Language competence and reading strategies: A comparison of first- and second-language oral reading errors. *Language Learning, 30*, 101–116.

Gibson, E., & Levin, H. (1975). *The psychology of reading*. Cambridge, MA: MIT Press.

Goodman, K. S. (1969). Analysis of oral reading miscues: Applied Psycholinguistics. *Reading Research Quarterly, 5*(1), 11–30.

Guthrie, J. T. (1973). Reading comprehension and syntactic responses in good and poor readers. *Journal of Educational Psychology, 69*, 686–696.

Hatch, E., Polin, P., & Part, S. (1970). *Acoustic scanning or syntactic processing*. Paper presented at meeting of the Western Psychological Association, San Francisco.

Johnston, G. A. (1972). *Some effects of acoustic input on reading comprehension*. Master's thesis, University of California, Los Angeles.

LaBerge, D., & Samuels, S. J. (1974). Towards a theory of automatic information processing in reading. *Cognitive Psychology, 6*, 293–323.

McLaughlin, B. (1984). *Second-language acquisition in childhood. Volume 1: Preschool children*. Hillsdale, NJ: Erlbaum.

McLaughlin, B. (1985). *Second-language acquisition in childhood. Volume 2: School-age children*. Hillsdale, NJ: Erlbaum.

McLaughlin, B., Rossman, T., & McLeod, B. (1983). Second-language learning: An information-processing perspective. *Language Learning, 33,* 135–158.

McLaughlin, B., & Baker, C. (1985). *Are poor readers all the same? A comparison of monolingual and bilingual readers in the upper elementary grades.* Unpublished manuscript, University of California, Santa Cruz.

McLeod, B., & McLaughlin, B. (1986). Restructuring or automatization? Reading in a second language. *Language Learning, 36,* 109–126.

Perfetti, C. A., Goldman, S. R., & Hogaboam, T. W. (1979). Reading skill and the identification of words in discourse context. *Memory & Cognition, 7,* 273–282.

Perfetti, C. A., & Lesgold, A. M. (1977). Discourse comprehension and sources of individual differences. In M. A. Just & P. A. Carpenter (Eds.), *Cognitive processes in comprehension* (pp. 141–183). Hillsdale, NJ: Erlbaum.

Rumelhart, D. E., & Norman, D. A. (1978). Accretion, tuning, and restructuring: Three modes of learning. In J. Cotton & R. Klatzky (Eds.), *Semantic factors in cognition* (pp. 37–53). Hillsdale, NJ: Erlbaum.

Schneider, W., & Shiffrin, R. M. (1977). Controlled and automatic human information processing: I. Detection, search, and attention. *Psychological Review, 84,* 1–66.

Shiffrin, R. M., & Schneider, W. (1977). Controlled and automatic human information processing: II. Perceptual learning, automatic attending, and a general theory. *Psychological Review, 84,* 127–190.

Smith, F. (1978). *Understanding reading.* New York: Holt, Rinehart & Winston.

Stanovich, K. (1980). Toward an interactive-compensatory model of individual differences in the development of reading fluency. *Reading Research Quarterly, 16,* 32–71.

Vellutino, F. R., & Scanlon, D. M. (1982). Verbal processing in poor and normal readers. In C. J. Brainerd & M. Pressley (Eds.), *Verbal processes in children: Progress in cognitive development research* (pp. 189–264). New York: Springer-Verlag.

4

Patterns of Performance among Bilingual Children Who Score Low in Reading

Mary Sue Ammon

University of California, Berkeley

The large number of school-age children in the United States reputed to be handicapped by reading difficulties has long been a major concern. And though the study of reading skills and deficiencies has been a topic commanding the attention of many researchers in education, recently there has been much more cross-disciplinary effort at understanding the reading process. However, there has been little extension of newer models of reading to the questions of individual and cultural/language differences in reading (Beaugrande, 1981) and relatively little study of the nature and impact of different reading strategies, cognitive predispositions, and learning styles on the reading of bilingual students. This theoretical and research gap is an important one to fill, in view of the increasing proportion of limited English speaking students in the school population, and the widespread recognition that some bilingual children learn to speak and read in a second language with much more difficulty than others. Additionally, many suggest that the failure to become proficient in English may be a major factor in the high attrition rates for some of the largest LEP language groups. Hispanics, for example, constitute 74% of the LEP population in California, and have a drop-out rate of more than 35% by grade 12, according to the 1984 PACE report, Conditions of Education in California.

This chapter examines current perspectives on the reading process, especially with regard to the kind of data needed to broaden our understanding of the development of reading skills in both bilingual and monolingual students. It then reports several analyses of data collected from selected Chinese and Hispanic third and fifth graders on a variety of reading tasks.

Cognitive Science Models of Reading

The reading literature has been influenced increasingly by models of reading issuing from the cognitive science perspective. Unlike earlier models of reading that placed primary emphasis on decoding skills (cf. reviews by Danks, 1974; Samuels & Kamil, 1984; Spiro & Myers, 1984; Kleiman, 1982), and unlike explanations of reading disabilities that primarily stressed visual–perceptual deficits or problems mastering the irregular rules governing English sound–symbol correspondences (cf. Morrison, 1981; Vellutino, 1978), these cognitive science models emphasize the multilevel, interactive, strategic, and constructive nature of skilled reading (cf. Introduction in Spiro, Bruce, & Brewer, 1980; Orasanu, 1986). Also, in many of the earlier cognitive models (Gough, 1972; LaBerge & Samuels, 1974), reading was seen as progressing in a uniform, linear manner through discrete stages starting from the "lower level" identification of letters and words and proceeding through larger syntactic and semantic units. In contrast, most current models (e.g., Beaugrande, 1980; Frederiksen, 1982; Just & Carpenter, 1980; Rumelhart, 1977; Samuels, 1977; Stanovich, 1980; Woods, 1980) assert that information contained in "higher" interpretive levels of processing may also influence processing at lower stages. The newer models are also unlike earlier descriptions of the reading process which stressed the dominance of "top-down" procedures (Goodman, 1976; Smith, 1971). In the new "constructivist" models, the degree of influence of one processing level on another, the amount of processing at any one level, and the degree to which processing at various levels operates in serial or parallel all are seen as flexible and dependent on the goals and strategies of the reader and the context and nature of the reading task. In addition, viewing reading as a constructive process suggests that comprehension is not an all-or-none thing, since meaning does not reside in the text but derives from the interaction of the reader's knowledge, procedures, and goals with the particular text and reading context (see, e.g., Beaugrande, 1980; Frederiksen, 1977; Kintsch & van Dijk, 1978; Meyer, 1975; and Schank & Abelson, 1977).

Many of the skills other than word recognition which are implied by the foregoing view of reading might be necessary for language processing in general, especially the processing required in more formal oral language comprehension situations in schools. However, much of the talking and listening that goes on in elementary school classrooms resembles the less formal, interpersonal type of language already familiar to the school-age child, focusing as it often does on regulating behavior and accomplishing classroom procedures rather than on presenting and clarifying informational content (Bloome, 1983; Bloome & Green, 1984;

Heap, 1982; DeStefano, Pepinsky, & Sanders, 1982). Many of the more complex interpretive processes involved in school listening tasks are facilitated in a way that unaided reading tasks are not. For example, prosodic cues in speech facilitate sentence analysis (Bolinger, 1975; Hornby, 1971; Kleiman, Winograd, & Humphrey, 1979); spatial, temporal, and personal reference is simpler and more concrete (DeStefano et al., 1982; Rubin, 1980); and sentence structure is less complex in most listening contexts (DeStefano et al., 1982; Kleiman, 1982).

In addition, some teachers in face-to-face language interactions provide external aids tailored to individual children to help them retrieve relevant prior knowledge, focus their attention on main ideas, and help them monitor their comprehension (Green, 1977; Green & Harker, 1982; Kleiman, 1982; Schallert & Kleiman, 1979). However, teachers vary in the degree to which they provide this type of feedback and support, and there appear to be interactions of this type of instruction with student characteristics. For example, teachers appear to provide more feedback and instruction especially regarding text meaning and interpretation (a) to students in higher level reading groups (Allington, 1983; McDermott, 1976), (b) to students displaying certain types of prosodic behavior in their oral reading (Collins, 1981), and (c) to students displaying a particular topic-centered type of narrative style (Michaels, 1981). Despite such teacher-provided cues, there are many reading tasks that are done unaided by the individual student. Thus, learning to read skillfully presents many unique and difficult demands for the elementary school child, and these demands would seem to be illuminated by cognitive science models of reading.

Despite the increasing agreement about the characteristics of expert reading, cognitive science models have not yet led to fundamental changes in the way reading skills are assessed and remediated in elementary schools. Part of the problem, as Spiro and Myers (1984) suggest, is that even the most detailed current models are not precisely specified and do not integrate all aspects of reading—that is, they are still only "proto-theories" (also cf. Beaugrande, 1981). Resnick (1984) has pointed out another major problem. Though we know more now about what skilled reading involves, we do not possess a theory of reading *acquisition* (i.e., what "learning to read" consists of). Yet, as both Glaser (1973) and Golinkoff (1976) suggest, a developmental perspective may be both pedagogically and theoretically important, since it provides insights about certain subskills which may not be obvious in the automatized, well-integrated performance of skilled readers. So, with just a theory of reading expertise, we can talk about what young readers apparently *fail* to do (e.g., not actively monitoring their comprehension), or we can talk about the number of errors students of various ages make on particular reading tests, but we know very little about how knowledge and processing skills relevant to reading are constructed. Consequently, it is difficult to say what expectations are reasonable, given the age and experience of different populations of readers. Assessment is especially problematic if we allow that qualitative gains in reading may temporarily result in more errors on the usual tests of reading ability, which are not geared to assess partial strategies or procedures that are qualitatively better but not completely adequate.

In the absence of a modern developmental theory of reading, it is difficult to generate a modern theory of reading disabilities, and engage in diagnostic assessment of children, whether they be native English speakers or bilingual students. Ideally, with such a model, we would be able to determine whether a particular pattern of reading behavior represents a delay in the usual pattern of development, a less common but still normal developmental pattern, or an abnormal dysfunctional pattern.

Developing a Model of Reading Acquisition

Integrating Previous Research Findings

In directing our attention to the goal of describing developmental reading patterns, one strategy might be to use existing data concerning readers at various ages, and then to design new research to fill in missing areas suggested by the cognitive science "expert reader" perspective. For example, in describing developmental differences in learner activities and skills, we might try to integrate findings from previous studies in the reading literature that have attempted to contrast good and poor readers at different ages. However, utilizing these findings poses problems for both theoretical and measurement reasons.

Much past research comparing good and poor readers was focused on the analysis of miscues in oral reading, and in many cases the primary emphasis was on the number of reading errors, rather than on the nature and quality of text comprehension (Barron, 1981; Golinkoff, 1976; Kleiman, 1982; Vellutino, 1979). Even studies categorizing oral reading miscues more qualitatively tended not to distinguish between errors likely to interfere with comprehension and those likely to have little or no effect on the reader's interpretation (Allington, 1984). Another type of earlier research comparing good and poor readers employed tasks requiring students to read non-text-like materials and to produce responses unlike those typical in normal reading situations (Samuels & Kamil, 1984). Assessment tasks such as those ignore the possibility that the strategies students develop to cope with "atypical" situations may not represent their usual approach to reading. And, since good and poor readers tend to differ on many dimensions (e.g., IQ), information about poor readers' deficiencies in such tasks may not relate directly to their dominant problems in reading. Past studies classifying students as good and poor readers are also hard to integrate, since they often assessed different student populations and classified readers as good or poor by their total scores on tests composed of widely varying types of items and subtests (Golinkoff, 1976; Kleiman, 1982).

In addition to the above substantive problems, the findings of many studies examining differential skill deficits in poor readers, or the effects of various types of training on good and poor readers (sometimes matched on another measure like IQ), have been clouded by measurement problems. Chapman and Chapman (1973), Hall and Humphreys (1982), and Kleiman (1982) all point out that faulty inferences can be drawn when tests with dissimilar reliabilities, score distributions, and item difficulty characteristics are used. And spurious significant interactions of ability level with specific training or with task characteristics may result from statistical regression or from calculations ignoring the scale of measurement.

New Directions for Research on Reading Acquisition and Reading Disability

Analyses of Individual Reading Performances. Many previous studies comparing good and poor readers have examined the relation between single factors or processing subsystems (decoding ability, phonetic processing, use of context, or vocabulary) and reading failure. However, more recent discussions and the aggregate data on reading disabilities suggest that models of reading failure should involve a number of factors whose effects are weighted differently for various problem readers, or whose effects are interdependent, as they interact and compensate for each other in complex ways (Applebee, 1971; Kleiman, 1982; Spiro & Myers, 1984, Sternberg & Wagner 1982). Both Kleiman (1982) and Sternberg and Wagner (1982) point out that if any of the more complex models of reading disability holds, overall comparisons of ability groups would obscure, not elucidate, the pattern of disability. Kleiman concludes that only detailed studies of individual poor readers, conducted from a cognitive processing point of view, can test the assumption that there is homogeneity within the skills of good and poor readers. Because of the complexity of the reading process and the current status of our knowledge about its acquisition, Campione and Armbruster (1984) also recommend that detailed individualized assessment of strategy execution by young readers in training studies needs to be done in order to avoid attributing improvement in reading to the wrong factor.

Task Analyses and Use of Varied Reading Measures. Since a constructive view of reading emphasizes the way activities of the reader are responsive to, and interact with, different reading tasks and contexts, both reader and task characteristics need to be considered in describing the development of reading skills. Sternberg and Wagner (1982) point out that the types of reading deficits that have been observed in particular studies depend, in part, on the indices used to classify the reading disabled (e.g., comprehension test scores, reading speed, oral reading facility, teacher evaluations). Consequently, Spiro and Myers (1984) and Johnston (1983, 1984a) suggest that we need to spend more time examining the demands of various reading tasks and to turn more to multiple measures of comprehension, including more qualitative, less all-or-none, characterizations of reader responses. Campione and Armbruster (1984) also note that, since particular criterion measures and task difficulty have been shown to influence training study outcomes, there needs to be some variety in the types of tasks used for assessment of gains after instruction.

Post Hoc Analyses of Response Patterns. Airasian and Madaus (1983) show that post hoc analyses of test items or subtests often reveal unique achievement differences among groups—differences that are hidden by total test scores. And Harnisch and Linn (1981) have found large ethnic group differences in response patterns to mathematics tests, suggesting that reading response patterns might also identify bilingual students for whom special caution is needed in interpreting total test scores. A related assessment strategy is to construct tasks in which particular responses or response patterns are diagnostic (e.g., Baker & Herman, 1983; Brown & Burton, 1978; Glaser, 1981; Harnisch, 1983; Tatsuoko & Tatsuoko, 1982). Brown and Burton (1978) have, for example, developed a computerized assessment technique that poses arithmetic problems to students and uses the pattern of both wrong and right answers to determine underlying misconceptions or incomplete knowledge of the subtraction algorithm. This work is important because it shows how an assessment approach based on detecting "semantically meaningful deviations" from an expert's knowledge base (Brown & Burton, 1978, p. 185) can be developed. It also clearly demonstrates how assessment is complicated if one assumes, not only that different "bugs" (malprocedures) can have the same surface manifestation, but that multiple bugs can interact with or compensate each other, often giving the appearance of random or inconsistent behavior on the surface. So far, most diagnostic assessments of this type have been attempted in delimited content areas, such as addition and subtraction. Diagnostic assessment in a multicomponent task like reading may be much more difficult to achieve.

An Investigation of Differences in the Reading Behavior of Bilingual Students

The present chapter reports on preliminary effort to apply a cognitive science model of reading to the assessment and diagnosis of the reading skills of bilingual students. An attempt has been made to examine the demands of a typical reading comprehension test and the way individual bilingual students respond to the task and to other types of reading. Toward that end, our approach has been to specify characteristics of reading comprehension test items that appear to interact with reader characteristics, to examine response profiles of individual readers rather than only overall group characteristics, and to look at a variety of types of information collected on each student to arrive at patterns of performance among bilingual students who would generally be regarded as poor readers for their grade levels.

Two connected types of analyses will be reported. The first is a qualitative analysis of items from a standardized reading comprehension test—items that presented particular difficulties for our sample of low English proficiency students. The second is a set of case analyses of individual problem readers, utilizing information gathered not only from the standardized reading comprehension test but from a variety of language-related tasks, from cognitive style tasks, and from a home interview.

The data discussed in this chapter were collected as part of a larger project (Wong Fillmore & Ammon, 1980) commissioned by the National Institute of Education. The overall purpose of the project was to determine through research the most effective practices for helping limited English proficiency students acquire the oral and written English language skills needed for participation in school. Our purpose was to study the effects of certain instructional practices, not to evaluate the effectiveness of the classes themselves or the programs they represented. Research in second language learning is showing that there are enormous individual differences to be found among children in how fast and well they learn a new language, and that the sources of this variation can be found both in the way learners approach and deal with the complex task of learning a new language, and in the way learner characteristics interact with the language learning situation.

The instructional practices and student characteristics that we set out to examine in the larger study are ones that research on individual differences in second language acquisition has identified as major sources of variation among children in how fast and how well they manage the learning of the school language (Wong Fillmore, 1982, 1983). One such characteristic is the language background of the child. The way we approached studying first language and cultural background was to select for study two groups that we believed would approach language learning somewhat differently, because of differences in patterns of language use and in social and learning behavior. Thus we studied the learning of English by Cantonese-speaking Chinese children and by Spanish-speaking Hispanic children. Previous research (Wong Fillmore, 1983) suggests that these two groups differ with respect to how much they turn to adults versus other children as models for language learning. Another variable that interacts with instructional practices is the student's age at the time of introduction to English. Since a longitudinal study was not possible, we focused our study on third and fifth grade children who had about 2 or 3 years of English. A total of 13 third grade classes was involved in the study (six Chinese and seven Hispanic), but the fifth grade data were drawn from only two classrooms within each ethnic group, as very few self-contained bilingual classrooms were available for study at grade five. Consequently, the data from the fifth grade subjects were used primarily to carry out case-study comparisons. Thus, two learner characteristics defined the groups of students involved in this study: language background (Cantonese or Spanish), and age (third or fifth grade).

Data were also collected to enable us to examine the ways language learning is affected by individual differences in situational, social, or learning styles. Differences among children in the degree to which they were outgoing with both native and nonnative English speaking peers were assessed via a series of observations conducted in the classrooms. Learning style differences were assessed with measures focusing on the following characteristics: (a) ideational fluency, (b) ability to use linguistic contextual information, and (c) propensity to take risks. Home interviews with the families of our subjects were used to examine questions about the effect on the child's continuing L2 development of parents' educational level, the amount of exposure to English in the home and neighborhood, and family attitudes toward schooling and the use of English.

Demographic Characteristics of the Sample

Four school districts in the San Francisco Bay Area participated in the study. Two are large urban districts; the other two are small rural or semi-rural districts. The Cantonese study sites were drawn exclusively from the two urban districts, since the Chinese in the area are concentrated in the two communities covered by these districts. The Hispanic sites were drawn from one of the two urban districts, and from the two rural ones. The rural sites were included in order to make the Hispanic classes more representative of the schools serving Spanish-speaking students in California. The four districts differ considerably in their size and in the ethnic diversity of the student populations they serve. The two urban districts are very large and serve students from a great variety of ethnic and linguistic backgrounds. The two smaller rural districts have much less linguistic and cultural diversity among the student population. The 17 classes located in 8 elementary schools in these districts were selected from the many we considered because they better fit our selection criteria and because the teachers and administrators were willing to participate in the research. The group of target subjects in each class consisted on the average of nine children whose first language was either Cantonese or Spanish, who had had 2 to 3 years' exposure to English in school previously, and who had usually been in the same type of classroom (bilingual or all-English) before. All the target subjects had been identified as limited or non-English-speaking children when they first entered their schools. By the end of the study year, a complete set of data had been collected on 157 students in these 17 classrooms.

Purposes and Types of Language Assessment

It seems obvious that speaking, listening, reading, and writing are all important language activities in school, but language assessments in the past generally have not done justice to the full range of school-related language skills. Consequently, our plan for evaluating reading, like that for assessing speaking, listening, and writing, was multifaceted. We wished our assessment to have face validity in terms of covering basic situations in which reading is evaluated in schools both formally and informally (such as oral reading with teacher corrections and probes, or silent reading with written comprehension questions). But we also wanted to use more diagnostic and varied measures of reading skills to help us discover particular reasons for problems in reading, or the presence of varying degrees of different reading skills in the children being studied.

Description of the Reading Tasks

In order to test reading comprehension at a level of difficulty appropriate for each subject, and to provide a standardized measure of proficiency like that obtained by schools in their testing programs, a screening test was administered to target subjects during the first weeks of the school year. This test consisted of two subtests—Auditory Vocabulary and Word Reading—from the Red Level Stanford Diagnostic Reading Test (Karlsen, Madden, & Gardner, 1976). These two subtests, both of which were presented in English, were then followed by a translation of the Auditory Vocabulary items into the children's first language (i.e., Spanish or Cantonese).

The Red Level SDRT vocabulary subtest was selected because it is designed to relate to the difficulty of words and concepts in reading material used in the early elementary grades. It is also designed to provide an accurate assessment of low achieving pupils in third grade. Additionally, this subtest contains both common types of auditory vocabulary test formats—one requiring choice among pictures and one requiring choice among written word alternatives. The picture choice format requires picture interpretation, but no word reading. The word choice format presents either an additional memory or decoding factor to the concept identification task. Since exact translations of words do not necessarily mean that the items are the same difficulty in the first language as in English, and since answers provided during the English testing might influence choices on the L1 vocabulary test, we viewed this subtest only as a rough screening measure to detect children with widely discrepant scores on the two versions of the test.

The Red Level SDRT word reading task was selected because it seemed to be the most direct measure of word decoding ability available. In addition, the published data from the SDRT standardization sample revealed that this set of items had the highest correlation of all the subtests with the paragraph reading scores from the same test, and also correlated highly with skills such as understanding of phonics and spelling ability.

In the individually administered pretest of reading comprehension that followed the screening test, each child received four different passages to read. Each paragraph was followed by a set of questions designed to test comprehension. Children read the first paragraph aloud, and this oral reading was timed; miscues were recorded and subsequently classified qualitatively. The second paragraph was read silently. After answering the written questions for these two passages, children were asked the reasons for their selection of each answer. The third paragraph was also read silently. After responding to the written questions, each child was asked to reread the passage and then to retell the story orally. Examiners then probed for memory and understanding of points inadequately covered in the summarization. Finally, the fourth paragraph was presented according to a procedure developed by Fillmore (1982) and Fillmore and Kay (1981, 1983), in which the text is exposed one sentence or phrase at a time and children are asked questions about their evolving understanding or envisionment of the text after reading aloud each succeeding piece.

The content of the four paragraphs (i.e., the passages chosen for each kind of treatment) varied according to the child's reading level as established by the screening test, but there was also some overlap in the materials across reading ability designations. A set of similar reading comprehension tasks was administered in a subsequent session to the Hispanic subjects in Spanish. The posttest reading comprehension tasks and procedures were similar to those of the pretest. However, because of time limitations, students read only three instead of four paragraphs. (See Wong Fillmore, Ammon, Ammon, Delucchi, Jensen, McLaughlin, & Strong, 1983, for more details on the classroom sites and subjects, and for more information about the language assessment instruments.)

Specific Goals of the Present Analyses

Since one of the major goals of the larger project was to study the effects of instructional practices on the learning of English by bilingual children, a comparative approach was taken to the question of effectiveness. Thus we compared different LEP students to see which ones moved farther or faster toward proficiency in English. Dependent variables were selected which differentiated between individuals in the groups of students we studied, rather than ones which revealed common characteristics of their performances. Since the present report is not concerned with describing different levels of language knowledge and skills in relation to teaching practices, this constraint was not necessary. Consequently, questions could be asked about whether the reading skills of a given bilingual group looked similar to or different from those of native English speakers at the same grade level. In the first analysis to be reported, an attempt was made to examine the extent to which traditional reading comprehension test items pose the same or different problems to bilingual students such as those we studied.

An important aspect of the reading tasks that were administered was that they were designed to provide information about the process as well as the products of reading. A "process" orientation, according to Collins and Smith (1982), focuses on students' ability to take remedial action when difficulties are encountered, and on their ability to make interpretations and predictions about the text, such as judgments about the main point and themes, or expectations about the events coming up based on an analysis of the characters and the situations. We collected reading "product" data on speed of decoding, the number of major and minor decoding errors, vocabulary scores in English and L1, the number of correct responses on word reading and reading comprehension tasks, and the extent to which basic content was recalled in story summarizations. But we also recorded the type of incorrect reading comprehension responses, the justifications for these choices, the relation of these responses to story summarizations, and the students' ability to interpret different sources of information in texts, to understand the story, and to change their envisionment when confronted with subsequent information or problematic questions. However, the latter, more qualitative analyses required more time to carry out than was available during the contract period of the larger study. Therefore, a specific goal in doing the second set of analyses was to examine this information related to the reading process in a subsample of our target subjects—the students who appeared to have had major problems in performing on the standardized reading comprehension test. The results of these analyses are discussed in the remainder of this chapter.

Item Difficulty Characteristics

The purpose of this analysis was to obtain descriptive information on the type of standardized reading comprehension test items that seem to present particular difficulties to bilingual students. Since the primary emphasis in this study was on the entire reading comprehension process, not simply on word reading, data were examined only from students who had enough decoding ability to enable them to read paragraphs on their own and try to make sense of them. Out of 157 total subjects in our study, 100 fulfilled the criterion of placing at least in the 4th stanine for beginning third graders on the word reading subtest of the Red Level SDRT. There were fewer Hispanic than Chinese children in this subsample (36 vs. 64), because a number of schools involved in our study did not introduce English reading in their Spanish-English bilingual classrooms until the end of the second grade or the beginning of the third grade.

For this analysis, responses were examined from comprehension questions for selected stories appearing on the Green Level SDRT reading comprehension subtest, which is appropriate for use in grades 3 and 4, and with low-achieving pupils in grade 5. The difficulty rating of each of the test items for this sample of students was calculated and compared to the item p-value (the percentage of correct responses by the normative population) provided by the test publisher (Karlsen, Madden, & Gardner, 1976). Items which appeared to be relatively more difficult for our four groups of subjects (Chinese and Hispanic 3rd and 5th graders) were then identified. A "reversal" score was also calculated for each item, indicating the number of students who found it to be more difficult than they should have, given their level of functioning on the test and the item's difficulty ranking based on the published norms. Thus, the score was calculated by plotting each subject's pattern of correct and incorrect responses to items ranked according to their difficulty, and then identifying the items that subjects missed that were easier (according to the norms) than the most difficult item they answered correctly. For 21 of the 32 items, our bilingual readers performed much like the students in the normative sample. But, for 11 items, our sample of subjects showed some indications of unusual comprehension difficulties. Table 1 presents the quantitative data pertaining to the p-values and reversal scores of these 11 items.

As can be seen, five out of the 32 items (Items 1–5 in Table 1) were found to be considerably more difficult for our sample of 100 bilingual students than they were for the normative sample. In almost all cases, all four subsamples (despite the small numbers of subjects in all but the Chinese third grade group) performed significantly below the normative sample on these five items.[1] Items 6–11 in Table 1 displayed more variability in terms of the way the four grade by ethnicity groups responded to them, with some subsamples finding them more difficult than the normative population did, but with other subsamples performing about the same or better on them than the comparison group did. However, these latter six items, as well as the first five, produced a high number of reversals in individual student response profiles. That is, on all of these 11 items, a large number of our bilingual students, 18 to 43% of the sample as a whole, and at least 20% of one or more subsamples, missed these items while getting "harder" ones correct. Moreover, there are some considerations which suggest that, if anything, these calculations may actually underestimate the difficulty of these items for bilingual children who have recently learned English.[2]

Having found 11 reading comprehension items that seemed especially difficult for a great many of our bilingual students, the next ques-

---

[1] The p-values for items 2 and 3 using data from a larger sample of our subjects (bilingual students placing at least in the third stanine of the SDRT word reading subtest) were computed to assess the stability of these findings. These data from 60 Chinese third graders, 47 Hispanic third graders, 19 Chinese fifth graders, and 21 Hispanic fifth graders indicate significantly greater difficulty for all groups of subjects on these two items, compared with the norms, and thus confirm the trends seen in the smaller subsamples.

[2] Two comments need to be made concerning the estimates of the magnitude of difficulties our bilingual subjects had with the test items, both of which suggest that the obtained differences from the norms might underestimate true contrasts between beginning bilingual and monolingual readers. First of all, the demographic information provided about the school districts participating in the standardization of the SDRT tests suggests that there may have been about 4%–5% Hispanic and Asian children in the normative sample, some of whom may have been bilingual. This factor might have attenuated differences between responses produced by the normative sample and those produced by our students due to cultural or language differences. Second, students tested in the standardization research were not screened for decoding ability as our subjects were. If students with serious decoding problems had been left in the group we were examining for this study, overall percentages of correct responses to most of the reading comprehension items would have been much lower than those being reported.

Table 1. Data on "Difficult" Reading Comprehension Items

| | Proportion Correct Responses | | | | | | Published p Value | | Percentage Reversals | | | |
| | Third Grade | | Fifth Grade | | | | | | 3rd Gr. | | 5th Gr. | |
Item	Chin. (n = 47)	Hisp. (n = 20)	Chin. (n = 17)	Hisp. (n = 16)	Ave. (n = 100)		3rd	5th	Chin.	Hisp.	Chin.	Hisp.	Average
#1	.11*	.10*	.35§	.31§	.18*		.30	.50	—	—	—	—	—
#2	.53	.50§	.65*	.69§	.57*		.62	.82	47	56	35	30	43
#3	.26*	.25*	.41§	.25*	.28*		.50	.58	32	25	35	55	36
#4	.49*	.60	.77	.75	.60*		.65	.82	47	38	24	30	38
#5	.55*	.55§	.82	.69§	.62*		.68	.83	45	44	18	35	38
#6	.45*	.80#	.82	.69§	.63		.58	.81	53	13	18	35	37
#7	.55	.45	.71	.50*	.55		.52	.69	17	19	24	35	22
#8	.51	.60	.88	.75	.63		.54	.79	30	25	12	25	25
#9	.79#	.85#	.65*	.94#	.80#		.62	.82	21	19	35	5	20
#10	.75	.80	.88	.81	.79		.70	.86	23	19	12	20	20
#11	.68#	.55	.82	.75	.69		.55	.79	15	19	18	25	18

*p < .05 (significantly *lower* than norms)
§ p-value difference greater than .10 (test publisher's criterion for significant deviations)
# p < .05 (significantly *higher* than norms)

tion that arose was *why* these items seemed to pose such problems. Harnisch (1983), who has described a similar classification of items according to their difficulty and the predictability of student responses to them (Sato's, 1975, Student-Problem analysis), suggests that items which do not discriminate very well between high and low test performers may contain particularly ambiguous phrases or attractive distractors. He also suggests that differences in background experience, motivation, and instructional history might be additional factors leading to unusual response patterns. All of these possible causes of difficulty linked to the nature of the task and the nature of the student might be applicable to the problems of bilingual children in reading comprehension tests such as the SDRT.

To pursue the question of what factors might have increased the difficulty of some of the reading test items for our bilingual students, the same eleven items were examined and described more qualitatively. The only descriptor used by the test publisher to classify the various items on this test was a distinction between "literal" and "inference" questions (Karlsen et al., 1976). The usual definition of literal comprehension is that all the information which is requested is contained in the text. However, all text requires some inferencing, since it never provides enough detail that the reader does not need to rely on some stored knowledge to fill in gaps (Samuels & Kamil, 1984). Also, though a distinction between literal and inferential meaning is often cited in the reading literature to distinguish among different reading abilities, such a gross division hardly reflects the complexity of the knowledge and procedural interactions required for skilled reading according to the cognitive science position. It is also noteworthy that about half of the items found to be unusually difficult for our bilingual students fell into each of these categories, according to the test publisher's description.

A closer, more detailed examination of these harder questions and the common error responses, however, revealed a few common characteristics. First, the difficult items frequently contained distractor responses that would be attractive to children who used either a strategy of trying to find words in the text that matched words in the answer alternatives, *or* a strategy of exclusively using background information and experiences rather than the text to determine the most likely response. The "matching words" strategy is one that might be expected if children lack or have trouble accessing relevant background knowledge, are relatively field dependent, or are focusing most of their attentional resources on decoding and "bottom-up" processing (cf. Adams, 1980; Collins, Brown, & Larkin, 1980; Golinkoff, 1976; Spiro & Myers, 1984). Moreover, since some bilingual children in the early stages of learning to speak English adopt a strategy of using unanalyzed surface phrases or formulas in order to participate in conversations (Wong Fillmore, 1976, 1979), it may be tempting for children who have relied on that language learning style to adopt a related matching strategy in dealing with reading comprehension tests. Stanovich (1980) has suggested that laborious decoding may also lead children who have some knowledge about the text topic to try to escape from or compensate for these "print-analysis" problems by overrelying on their own background knowledge. Word identification difficulties might be especially likely among bilingual children, because of phonological, lexical, and syntactic differences between English and their first language. However, there also might be differences in the incidence of this compensation related to the degree to which stories are viewed more as cooperative, creative ventures in a particular culture, rather than as problems in discovering an author's meaning. These suggestions would explain how text content could interact with the knowledge, skills, and background experiences of the reader in determining the particular reading strategy used at any one time.

Table 2 contains three examples of difficult test items. The top panel presents an item with answer alternatives that might be attractive to readers using either a "matching words" or a "schema-based associational" strategy. (This item was labeled #3 in Table 1.) In this item, children seeking an answer that matches a phrase in the text would choose the second alternative, "in the front of the classroom." As Table 2 indicates, this was both the most common response (.59) and the most common error choice for this item in our data. In contrast, children using their own schematic knowledge rather than the text to guess the location of a bookcart might choose the first alternative, "in the library." In our data, this alternative was chosen only 6% of the time across the entire sample; however, all of these error choices occurred in the third grade data. That is, fifth graders never chose this response, whereas 12% of the third graders' errors were of this type.

For students to understand that the correct response to the question concerning the location of the bookcart is the fourth alternative, "in the back of the classroom," they need to coordinate interpretations of text information with a variety of experiential knowledge. For example, they must understand that the teacher's request "to roll the book cart to the front of the room" specifies the action and the goal location of the bookcart. In addition, they must infer on the basis of common sense and conversational rules that the teacher would not specify "the front of the room" if the book cart were already in that location, and would not use the expression "the room" if the room being specified were not the classroom, the most likely place for students and a teacher to be. This analysis makes it obvious how important shared rules of conversation can be to reading comprehension. It is interesting that the response al-

Table 2. Examples of Types of Difficulties Characterizing "Difficult" Reading Comprehension Items*

Distractors Attractive to Readers Using "Matching Words" or "Exclusive Schema-Based" Strategies: An Example and Associated Choice Frequencies (n = 100)
Story Excerpt: The teacher asked Bill and Bob to roll the book cart to the front of the room. . . . They pushed the cart as hard as they could, but it didn't move.
Question: Where was the book cart?

	a.	In the library	(n = 6)
	b.	In the front of the classroom	(n = 59)
	c.	In the hallway	(n = 7)
	d.	In the back of the classroom	(n = 28)

Distractors Requiring Unwarranted Supplementations Or Requiring Fine Lexical Discriminations: An Example and Associated Choice Frequencies
Story Excerpt: Barbara lived in a big city. . . . One day Barbara asked her father how chocolate milk was made. "The cows eat chocolate grass," her father said. Barbara laughed and said, "Right!"
Question: Why did Barbara laugh?

	a.	Her father did a trick.	(n = 6)
	b.	She knew that cows give milk.	(n = 30)
	c.	She knew her father was joking.	(n = 57)
	d.	There was no grass in the city.	(n = 7)

Item Requiring Specific Syntactic Knowledge: An Example and Associated Choice Frequencies
Story Excerpt: Pat noticed it at the last possible moment. . . . It was the most beautiful shade of blue she had ever seen. Pat decided that it must have fallen out of one of the nests in the tree above. . . . "Oh, good," she thought. "Maybe if I leave it alone, it will still hatch."
Question: What did Pat find?

a.	a nest	(n = 10)	b.	a bluebird	(n = 9)
c.	an egg	(n = 80)	d.	a branch	(n = 1)

*Items were taken from the Stanford Diagnostic Reading Test, Green Level, 1976 edition.

ternative "in the hallway", which 12% of the fifth graders chose, observes most of these constraints, and is plausible if the cart is pictured as just outside the classroom door in the hallway.

The second example, in the middle panel of Table 2 (item #2 in Table 1), contains a distractor that was an inadequate answer to the question posed, but was sufficiently associated with critical ideas in the passage to make it attractive for children who might not be able to differentiate answers that are adequate on their own from those that could be adequate only with unwarranted amounts of amplification. So if children amplified and reinterpreted the second alternative to this test item as, "She knew that cows give milk—not chocolate milk," this alternative becomes acceptable. This, again, could be viewed as an example of the reader contributing too much to the interpretation of the text—of the *over-application* of a strategy which is usually important for skilled comprehension. This type of error might be characteristic of students who are not yet practiced at the "multiple-choice reading test" genre (cf. Drum, Calfee, & Cook, 1980; Smith, 1982). If a number of our bilingual subjects treated the answer alternatives as continuous with the paragraph, they might have tried to interpret each alternative in a way that would make it fit in with the preceding text. Such a strategy is a positively valued one in most reading situations, but it is a poor strategy for a reading test with this format. As Table 2 indicates, 30% of the children in our sample selected the second alternative.

This item illustrates yet another category of difficulty that centers around language knowledge itself—lexical knowledge and differentiation of related items, syntactic specifications of lexical items, and other syntactic rules and constraints related to expressions within the text, the questions, or the answer alternatives. Baker and Herman (1983) have asserted that the variation in performance created by apparently casual manipulation of linguistic features in tests may be substantial. The use of "trick" and "joke" in the first and third alternatives to the second item in Table 2 provides an illustration of how two lexical items which are close in meaning might provide problems, especially to second language learners. Though a joke can be considered a verbal trick, the expression "did a trick" would not usually be considered a good answer to the question, since to most native English speaking children the phrase usually connotes a physical act, most likely the performance of a magic trick. It is interesting that, though this choice on the second item was not frequent in our data, the Chinese third graders made most of these errors (four, as contrasted with two across the other three subsamples).

The third item in Table 2 (item #9 in Table 1) provides an example of the kind of syntactic specifications related to particular lexical items that children must be aware of to rule out some incorrect alternatives. If students thought that the verb "hatch" in the last sentence of the paragraph in the third example was transitive, or if they were unlikely to interpret "it" as "the thing that is hatched" without a passive syntactic construction, they might be led to pick "bluebird" rather than "an egg" as the answer to the question about what Pat found, since it is a bird that has the potential to hatch eggs. Though there were fewer errors on this item then on the other two items in Table 2, nearly half the errors involved choice of this alternative. The other frequent error on this item was "a nest," which might be considered a "matching" error response. In our data, most of these "nest" error choices (9 out of 10) were made by the Chinese third and fifth graders.

Given that these characteristics appeared frequently in the harder items, the next question was whether or not there was additional evidence that these incomplete or unconstrained inferential strategies, lack of adequate schematic knowledge, and lack of specific types of knowledge linked to English syntax and vocabulary were problems for the bilingual subjects we tested. Thus, the purpose of the second type of analysis performed on our data was to look for patterns of skills and problems in the data of individual children.

Patterns of Performance Among Poor Bilingual Readers

To determine whether there were discernible patterns of difficulties among poor readers in our sample, including problems with reading test items such as those suggested above, students were identified whose scores on the reading comprehension items placed them in the lower third of the sample previously described. Data were examined from 26 children who had missed between 33% and 52% of the comprehension questions. There were, again, slightly more than twice as many Chinese as Hispanic students in the sample, mirroring their relative proportions in the original sample of students who were able to approach the reading of third grade materials.

Because this analysis was of a very exploratory nature, an attempt was made first to establish preliminary groupings of these poor readers in order to facilitate the search for patterns of performance. Consequently, error responses on the reading comprehension questions were examined to determine whether these low comprehenders could be classified by the types of items they found to be difficult. While Sato's S-P analysis classifies low test performers into just two groups, according to the predictability of their errors (Harnisch, 1983), there were *three* possible classifications of students in our study. Some of our low comprehenders might be highly predictable in their responses, predominantly getting all easy and no hard items correct (i.e., having a low number of reversals). Such a pattern of responses might conceivably be associated with simple developmental delay, caused by the added task of learning a second language. There might be a second group of students who missed only universally hard items *and* those items found to be difficult specifically for all or some of our bilingual groups. It would be reasonable to guess that students falling in this category might have, for example, insufficient or incorrect schematic or linguistic knowledge, linked to their lack of experience with the rules of English and with American middle-class culture. Other strategy explanations considered earlier in connection with the items found to be especially difficult for our bilingual samples might also apply to such students. Finally, there might also be students who got both some hard and some easy items correct, i.e., students whose errors were more idiosyncratic and less predictable from the normative data or from the information we had on items that were difficult for our sample of bilingual students.

Eight children were identified whose pattern of errors on the comprehension questions was more or less predictable from the difficulty ratings of the items obtained from the published test norms. These children, with no more than four reversals in their answer patterns, thus appeared more or less like a typical monolingual child scoring in the low-to-average range. All of these students turned out to be Chinese third graders.

Another group of 12 subjects had a high number of reversal errors (eight or more), with their error patterns deviating considerably from what would be predicted from the published p-values for the test items. Within this group, however, there was an interesting and statistically significant difference between the seven Chinese and five Hispanic students. The Chinese children's reversals reflected their errors on items which had been identified as difficult for our bilingual sample, whereas the Hispanic children's errors were more idiosyncratic (i.e., less predictable from either the published p-values, or from the data on item difficulty established for our bilingual students as a whole).

In the remaining group of six subjects—those who had a moderate number of reversals—the four Chinese students and the two Hispanic students were similar to the other Chinese students in making a relatively small number of "idiosyncratic" errors. These error data are summarized in Table 3. Since the data from five additional subjects whose comprehension scores were slightly higher than the 26 discussed here revealed very few idiosyncratic errors by either the Chinese or Hispanic students, it may be that some low scoring Hispanic children have additional sources of problems that have not yet been considered. It is also possible that more guessing was done by many of these low comprehen-

Table 3. Mean Proportion of "Idiosyncratic" Reading Errors by Chinese and Hispanic Low Comprehenders Classified in Terms of Their Item Reversal Pattern

	Chinese Subjects	Hispanic Subjects
High Number of Reversals	.30 (n=7)	.47* (n=5)
Moderate Number of Reversals	.29 (n=4)	.31 (n=2)
Low Number of Reversals	.23 (n=8)	—
Totals	.27 (n=19)	.43 (n=7)

*This proportion of idiosyncratic errors for Hispanic High Reversal students is significantly greater than the proportion for the Chinese High Reversal Students (t = 3.54, p < .01).

ders, and that Hispanic children generally feel freer to adopt this strategy when faced with such reading tasks.

These patterns of responses to comprehension items presented some intriguing questions which could only be addressed by a more detailed, qualitative analysis of the total set of data we had collected on each student. Would the Chinese high reversal group, whose pattern of errors resembled the bilingual sample as a whole, be found to have common information gaps and to deal with them in similar ways? And would their skills and background knowledge be different from the Chinese subjects who performed more like the normative population? Would the Hispanic high reversal group exhibit different configurations of skills and strategies than either of these two Chinese groups, in a way that would explain their more idiosyncratic pattern of errors?

For this qualitative analysis of individual readers, the entire set of reading test data plus the information we had on other language and school abilities, social and learning styles, and family background were explored for the same 26 students. Within the reading comprehension data, reading test protocols were examined for the types of wrong answers selected, and for the ways these answers were justified. Special attention was given to the strategies children used to answer the questions—e.g., whether they tried to find a sentence or word in the text that *matched* either the question or a salient word in the question, or whether they used their *background knowledge and experiences* to justify their choice. Miscue analyses, story retellings, and visualizations and predictions for some of the stories were examined in conjunction with these answers to the comprehension questions, to determine how different children dealt with information gaps of various sorts (e.g., those that were due to unfamiliar content, unusual syntactic constructions, or difficulties in decoding). Profiles of performance on school-administered achievement tests, as well as our own tests of oral and written language abilities, were also consulted.

Trying to coordinate and interpret these multiple and varied types of data was a somewhat overwhelming task. At the outset, it should be stressed that each student was unique in many ways, so that this attempt to group students, of necessity, meant focussing on features that relate to the earlier item analyses, and stressing commonalities that seem salient in our sample while ignoring some potentially important differences among these readers. Other studies, using different samples of students, may provide validating evidence for the patterns to be described, or may suggest other common composites of reading skills and behaviors. This study therefore is seen as providing only some hypotheses which need further exploration. Table 4 summarizes some characteristics of the groups that will be discussed.

Table 4. Subject Groups Showing Different Patterns of Performance On Reading Comprehension Test Items and Other Reading and Achievement Tests

Ethnicity Groups	Predictability of Errors on Reading Test	Comprehension Strategies	Retelling Performance	Achievement Test Pattern
1. Chinese (n=5)	High	Balanced	Good Stories	Reading, Vocabulary and Language Arts =
2. Chinese (n=3)	High	Matching	Memorized Words & Phrases	Low English Vocabulary
3. Chinese (n=3)	Low	Associations Intuitions	Sensible but Sketchy	Low English Vocabulary & Decoding
4. Chinese (n=4)	Low	Text-Based Associations	Weak Story Schema	Reading often < Language Arts, Math
5. Hispanic (n=5)	Low	Idiosyncratic Associations, Intuitions	Good Stories, Details Incorrect	Poor Decoding

Within the group of eight Chinese "low reversal" subjects, whose reading error patterns were highly predictable from the published test norms, there appeared to be two subgroups. One group of five subjects used a variety of strategies to answer the reading questions and justify their choices, not just a single inflexible one. Their English vocabulary and comprehension scores were at roughly equivalent levels at the beginning of the year, though three of the five started off the year at a higher level than the other two. And while they demonstrated some problems maintaining a high level of motivation and attention, or sometimes overused their personal experiences in story interpretation, they showed substantial gains across the year in the school-administered achievement tests, with the three more advanced students showing relatively greater gains. This group's pattern of performance suggests that their reading comprehension problems may be only temporary. In fact, for a few of these students, there was evidence that the problems were already disappearing by the end of the school year.

The other subjects with a highly predictable error pattern were different from the first five in a number of ways. The three students in this group had very low English vocabulary scores in comparison to their L1 vocabulary and their achievement scores in English reading comprehension and language arts (spelling, mechanics, etc.). While their SDRT word reading scores were quite a bit better than their vocabulary scores, all three had serious decoding problems in the reading tasks we administered. They also tended to use a matching strategy in answering the comprehension questions, and they frequently strung together memorized words, phrases, and sentences when they retold stories. This connection between an oral language style of relying on memorized phrases and a matching strategy for answering comprehension questions is one that was suggested as a possibility earlier.

Table 5 contains two story retellings from subjects in this last group. It is possible that knowing the meaning of too few English words might leave these children with little choice but to memorize and match surface phrases. This explanation seems to fit with another similarity found among these students: they all came from homes where their parents and siblings spoke a variety of dialects and languages besides Cantonese, a factor which might have complicated the task of learning the English lexicon. However, it is also possible that a strategy of memorizing and matching phrases with contexts interferes with the development of decoding skills and with English vocabulary development, since stu-

Table 5. Examples of Story Retelling from Chinese Highly Predictable, Low English Vocabulary Group

STORY READ:*

Pat noticed it at the last possible moment. It was good that she had, because she had almost stepped on it. It was the most beautiful shade of blue she had ever seen. Pat decided that it must have fallen out of one of the nests in the tree above. She bent down to look at it and saw that it had not broken. "Oh good," she thought. "Maybe if I leave it alone, it will still hatch."

Subject A:

"*Pat notice the last possible moment that she seen . . . when Pat walk she saw a nest that is fallen down and step on it . . . and bend down and look.*"

[What did she see?]
"*It was not broken.*"
[What will she do?]
"*I will leave it alone. Maybe it will get hitch.*"

Subject B:

"*Pat found something. She found a beautiful shade.*"

[How did she feel?]
"*She feel good.*"
[Why?]
"*Because she found a beautiful shade.*"

*Story was taken from the Stanford Diagnostic Reading Test, Green Level, 1976 edition.

dents adopting this tactic may not try to process the text on higher semantic or syntactic levels. Having such a matching strategy would also lead to errors on all questions except those relating directly to sentences in the text—the easier questions in tests of this sort. That would help explain why these three subjects displayed few item reversals.

It is even more intriguing that, within the group of seven Chinese students whose errors were much less predictable in terms of the published item difficulty norms (i.e., the *high* reversal subjects), there was another subgroup of three low English vocabulary students with many of the same characteristics as the one just described. These children achieved only the 1st, 4th, and 5th percentile on the SDRT vocabulary test; two of the three had L1 vocabulary scores that were 10 and 12 items *higher* than their English vocabulary scores. Moreover, their families had only recently immigrated to the United States, speaking little English but often many languages and dialects other than Cantonese. However, this subgroup's predominant comprehension strategy seemed to be the opposite of the other three low English vocabulary students. Instead of focusing primarily on the surface features of the text, they most justified their comprehension test choices by using their own background knowledge, or by giving associations to response alternatives or to words appearing in the text. For example, on the "bookcart" question (item #1 in Table 2), one of these subjects picked the "in the library" response and then explained, "Because in the library many book . . . library have many book." Another justified picking the second alternative to the "chocolate grass" item (item #2 on Table 2) by saying, "Because cowboy eat milk . . . because Barbara think cowboy drink milk is funny . . . go to the store and drink wine and milk." In some cases, using such a strategy appeared to help students pick the right answer—perhaps for the wrong reason (which might help explain the fact that they got both some easy and some hard items correct). For example, on the item in Table 6, which was another "hard" item for the bilingual sample as a whole, two of these three subjects chose "roots" as the answer (getting the item correct), while the other student chose "seeds." Both of these answers might have been facilitated by subjects' reliance on the knowledge that plants usually grow from roots or seeds. In contrast, all of the eight highly predictable students who frequently based their answers on the text got the answer to this question *wrong*, selecting the fourth alternative, which partially matches a phrase in the text.

On the retelling tasks, the three less predictable, low vocabulary Chinese students tried to reconstruct a sensible story, but frequently dropped out entire events, including ones that were crucial to the story's main point, as illustrated in Table 7. The fact that two groups with the same demographic and vocabulary knowledge characteristics adopted very differ-

Table 6. Example of "Difficult" Item Showing Different Patterns of Response by Students Using Matching Words Versus Schema-Based Strategies

Story Excerpt:*

Even though the banana plant looks like a tree, it has no trunk or limbs. Bananas are grown in. . . . They grow from flowers on the plant and are cut down before they get ripe. The banana plant dies down after just one crop. Since the banana does not have seeds like an apple or pear, new plants are grown from the roots of the old plants.

Question:

New banana plants are grown from an old plant's—
- a. seeds
- b. leaves
- c. roots
- d. flowers

*Item was taken from the Stanford Diagnostic Reading Test, Green Level, 1976 edition.

ent strategies for answering questions on reading comprehension tests suggests that other factors, perhaps related to personality or learning style, may mediate strategy choice for students who have severe English vocabulary limitations. In this regard, it is interesting to note that, when stories were presented one line at a time, the latter group of subjects frequently stayed with and did not revise initial responses and visualizations formed in response to early sentence of texts. The same characteristic of sticking to original guesses based on personal associations and knowledge in the face of disconfirming evidence from subsequent text was also seen in the way these subjects performed one of the learning style tasks in which they were given five sentence contexts for a made-up word and were asked to figure out the meaning of that word.

The remaining Chinese subjects with a more unpredictable pattern of errors also predominantly used schema-based or associational knowledge to answer and justify individual comprehension questions. The fact that these less predictable subgroups tended to respond on the basis of their own background knowledge rather than the text would help explain their deviations from the normative error pattern. However, the second subgroup of four students had another common characteristic which made them unlike the other high reversal Chinese subjects. Many aspects of their behavior indicated problems in the development of metacognitive strategies for dealing with the reading task. For example, they often seemed unable to reflect on the reasons for their answer choices and were either unwilling or unaware that they could reread the text when they experienced problems interpreting or remembering key events in the story. When they did refer to the text, they dealt with sen-

Table 7. Example of Story Retelling from Chinese Less Predictable, Low English Vocabulary Group

Story Read:*

One summer, Ricky went camping with the Boy Scouts. He and his friends went swimming every day. They slept in tents and cooked their own food. But they enjoyed scaring the younger Cub Scouts in the next camp most. At night they would creep through the woods to the Cub Scouts' camp, and make noises like wolves. The young boys would wake up and wonder what was outside their tents. One night, while sneaking through the woods, Ricky fell into a patch of poison ivy. The counselors had to send him home. Ricky had to spend the rest of the summer in the hot city.

Subject C:

"One summer, Ricky and her friends went out swimming . . . When they was in the wood, they scared the youngest cubs . . . also, one night . . . some strange sounds that 'ooooh' while the boys waked up . . . at the early night."

[What happened to Ricky while he was trying to scare the younger boys?]
"He made sounds."
[Where did he have to go?]
"Ricky and her friends go to swimming."
[What happened to Ricky at the end of the story?]
"The youngest boy scare."
[What happened to Ricky because of his poison ivy?]
"He scare they youngest boy."

*Story was taken from the Stanford Diagnostic Reading Test, Green Level, 1976 edition.

tences in isolation, as independent pieces of information. They also seemed to lack a well-developed overall organizing schema for stories, which would have helped them integrate information presented in various sentences of the text. In retelling stories, they said very little, and what they did produce was frequently a sequence of unlinked, uncoordinated sentences with no coherent plot and with ambiguous references. Table 8 contains a story retelling by one of these children which consisted primarily of a sequence of unattributed quotes that were not integrated into a narrative framework.

The five Hispanic students with an idiosyncratic pattern of responses on the test items clearly differed from this latter Chinese group, in that they showed a distinct facility for telling coherent stories, even though their summarization scores often suffered because some story details were not quite correct. Sometimes their retellings gave the impression that they were not as far from understanding the main points of the story as their retelling and comprehension scores might suggest. Table 9 contains the story summarizations from two Hispanic high reversal students. They reveal considerable story-telling ability, but they also show how some details of the story were changed or not grasped. Some

Table 8. Example of Story Retelling from Chinese Less Predictable, Low Story Schema Group

STORY READ:*

"Where's the cat?" dad asked. "We can't leave until we take him next door to stay with the Kaplans." "Tink was on the porch," answered Jess. "On the porch!" dad said, frowning. "Jess, I asked you to keep the porch door locked. That cat pushes against the unlocked door and swings it open. Then he disappears for the day." "I did lock the door, dad," Jess said. Mother shouted, "Don't blame Jess! Our suitcases were piled in the hall, and you carried them to the car. You left the porch door open between trips to the car." "So I did," dad said, "and I'm sorry, Jess." Suddenly they heard a noise from the car. "I think I know where Tink is hiding," Jess said.

Subject D:

" 'Where's the cat? We can't leave until we find the cat. I told you to lock the door.' "
[Who said that?]
"Dad. 'I did lock the door. Don't bang the suitcase.' "
[Who said that?]
"Mother . . . mother shouted. . . ."

[Who did Dad blame for the cat being gone?]
" 'Sorry' "
[When Dad couldn't find the cat, Dad blamed someone. Who did Dad blame?]
"Jess"
[Why?]
"Because Jess didn't lock the door."
[So what happened then?]
"The cat went out."
[And what really happened. How did the cat get out?]
"Jess forgot to lock the door and then the cat pushed the door open."
[What did Dad do when he found out it was his fault that the cat got out?]
"Because Jess forgot to lock the door."
[At the end, how did Jess find out where the cat was hiding?]
"He seen . . . heard him"

*Story was taken from the SRA Achievement Test, Level D, Form 1

of the imprecision in the details of these stories may have resulted from decoding problems that all of these Hispanic students seemed to experience. However, in answering comprehension questions, many of these children preferred using intuition rather than the information in the text, even though they had seemed to understand what they read, as shown by their ability to answer the probe questions after a story retelling. This ability to use both text- and knowledge-based information in comprehension, together with a possible bias toward intuitive amplifications of stories, may explain why this group's error patterns were more idiosyncratic and less predictable than those of the other Hispanic and Chinese low comprehenders.

Table 9. Examples of Story Retelling from Hispanic Less Predictable Group

STORY READ:*

"Where's the cat?" dad asked. "We can't leave until we take him next door to stay with the Kaplans." "Tink was on the porch," answered Jess. "On the porch!" dad said, frowning. "Jess, I asked you to keep the porch door locked. That cat pushes against the unlocked door and swings it open. Then he disappears for the day." "I did lock the door, dad," Jess said. Mother shouted, "Don't blame Jess! Our suitcases were piled in the hall, and you carried them to the car. You left the porch door open between trips to the car." "So I did," dad said, "and I'm sorry, Jess." Suddenly they heard a noise from the car. "I think I know where Tink is hiding," Jess said.

Subject E:

"One day they were leaving to a vacation and they didn't saw the cat and they wanted the cat to stay next door with Kaplans and dad told them to lock the porch door and then Jess didn't lock the door. He leave it unlocked and the cat was pushing and swinging the door and his mother shouted, "Don't blame Jess just because he unlocked the door." And then she said that all the suitcases were piled in the hall, so he took them to the car and he left the porch door unlocked.

[Who?]

"Jess. Then they are going to leave when they heard a noise in the car and Jess said, 'I know where the cat is hiding.' "

Subject F:

"His father said, 'Where's the cat.' Then Jess said, 'I don't know what is it.' Then he didn't looking for it . . . And then they were looking for it . . . then somebody knocked on the door. Then his father told him go and lock the door. And then he said that might be the cat. He will go around the yard, so he could see and maybe that's the cat. Then his father . . . his mother unlock . . . then his mother said, 'Unlock the door.' Then his father told him that Jess was the one that locked the door. And then so his father said to Jeff, 'Sorry.' And Jeff was going to leave. Then his father said, 'Oh Jeff, don't go.' Then Jeff stayed if they found the cat. When they found the cat, they went to take it to the neighbors."

*Story was taken from the SRA Achievement Test, Level D, Form 1

Discussion

Considering the exploratory nature of the work reported in this chapter, it would be premature to offer a set of formal conclusions at this point. However, the process of exploring item analyses and profiles of individual poor readers, in the context of constructivist theory, has raised a number of issues that have implications for future research.

The perspective on the reading process taken in this chapter has stressed the need for more detailed analysis of a variety of reading tasks and performances on these tasks by individual readers. A major problem with adopting this approach to studying the development of reading skills is that broadening the definition of reading comprehension means increasing the complexity of assessment and the difficulty of reliable evaluation. Johnston (1984a) notes that only a few researchers (e.g., Goodman & Burke, 1970) have tried to analyze error patterns to tap the nature and balance of strategies used by readers, and that most analyses of this sort have remained qualitative and intuitive rather than being quantified and rigorously evaluated. The results of the analyses in this study have reinforced the need to pursue a number of related issues if the goal is to develop more sophisticated and reliable evaluation that centers on patterns of reading performance.

One of the least developed areas in cognitive science reading models involves understanding ways to represent the background knowledge that students of various ages bring to bear on reading tasks. Because such knowledge is encyclopedic in scope, processing models of reading and writing are faced with a much greater problem in this regard than those designed to diagnose misunderstandings and malprocedures in, say, arithmetic. In looking at individual profiles of readers, it was obvious that particular strategies were not uniformly applied across the board by some students. For example, students who usually consulted the text in answering comprehension questions would sometimes be considerably affected by personal experience or associations with specific story content. And such background knowledge could either facilitate or interfere with the comprehension of the particular story, depending on the way a student used such information. Johnston (1984b) and Sternberg (1981) have suggested that vocabulary measures designed to tap concepts in specific passages can be used to separate knowledge deficiencies from processing deficiencies. Though such an approach might mean restricting the topics of reading paragraphs, the finding in this study of a connection between vocabulary knowledge and the use of extreme matching or associational strategies suggests that such information might be especially useful in explaining such interrelationships. Thus the auxiliary information could make the determination of dominant strategies cleaner than it currently is, since one could then decide whether the application of a problematic strategy occurred because of a knowledge deficit or despite the student's knowledge about the particular topic. Information of this sort seems to have special merit for evaluating the reading skills and strategies of students with different cultural backgrounds, who may lack information assumed to be generally available to students of a particular grade level.

The fact that, within our sample, there were two subgroups of students who achieved a predictable pattern of responses for different reasons suggests that caution may be needed in drawing inferences *both* about the reading abilities of students who display unpredictable test score patterns and about the knowledge and procedures of students who get easy items correct and miss all harder items. Such caution may be especially important when evaluation utilizes tests that have not been constructed within the framework of a theory of reading comprehension. Thus, to establish truly diagnostic multiple choice comprehension tests, more groundwork is needed in order to select reading paragraphs, distractors, and "correct" responses that will enable more certain evaluation of responses and response patterns. Much of this groundwork will have to be provided by case studies of readers such as those carried out here, since many current cognitive science models not only provide no standard for less than perfect readers, but also assume that texts are sensible and appropriate, an assumption that Fillmore and Kay (1983) found to be unjustified in the case of reading tests. In the present study, distractors on some of the hard items on the SDRT could be characterized as appealing to one particular kind of strategy or knowledge deficit, but it was plain that distractors and correct responses on other items could be selected for more than one reason.

Because students were tested individually in this study and individual answers were probed, more data were available than usual to help identify strategy and knowledge application. However, such individualized testing and qualitative analysis would not be feasible with larger samples. In addition, post hoc justification data, like other introspective reports, cannot be treated as invariably reflecting the truth about actual processing. And, while it seems likely that conscious metacognitive knowledge and strategy application are involved in the development of reading skill (cf. Baker & Brown, 1984) and is no doubt an important area to assess, the bulk of the reading process occurs below the level of conscious awareness (cf. Woods, 1980). Thus, it seems that more effort should be devoted to making response selection more clearly diagnostic of unconscious types of processes and skill deficiencies.

Finally, though rich descriptions of individual readers such as the present ones may help avoid erroneous single-factor explanations of reading disability, the previous discussion of multiple antecedents and consequences of different procedural and knowledge deficiencies makes it clear that there need to be more follow-up studies to examine the short- and long-term prognoses for students displaying various reading skill patterns. In addition, these studies need to be carried out with students at various ages, since deficiencies in some aspects of reading may predict continued reading problems only when they occur at certain ages. For example, evidence of underdeveloped metacognitive procedures may have more serious implications in the later elementary years, since all children seem to have problems in this regard early on. Reading diagnoses that are more sensitive to developmental and individual differences will provide a firmer foundation for the kind of reading instruction that is effective in promoting literacy acquisition in both monolingual and bilingual children.

References

Adams, M. J. (1980). Failures to comprehend and levels of processing in reading. In R. J. Spiro, B. C. Bruce, & W. F. Brewer (Eds.), *Theoretical issues in reading comprehension* (pp. 11–32). Hillsdale, NJ: Erlbaum.
Airasian, P. W., & Madaus, G. F. (1983). Linking testing and instruction: Policy issues. *Journal of Educational Measurement, 20,* 103–118.
Allington, R. L. (1983). The reading instruction provided readers of differing reading abilities. *The Elementary School Journal, 83,* 548–559.
Allington, R. L. (1984). Oral Reading. In P. D. Pearson (Ed.)., *Handbook of reading research* (pp. 829–864). New York: Longman.
Applebee, A. N. (1971). Research in reading retardation: Two critical problems. *Journal of Child Psychology and Psychiatry, 12,* 91–113.
Baker, E. L., & Herman, J. L. (1983). Task structure design: Beyond linkage. *Journal of Educational Measurement, 20,* 149–164.
Baker, L., & Brown, A. L. (1984). Metacognitive skills and reading. In P. D. Pearson (Ed.), *Handbook of reading research* (pp. 353–394). New York: Longman.
Barron, R. W. (1981). Development of visual word recognition: A review. In T. G. Waller & G. E. Mackinnon (Eds.), *Reading research: Advances in theory and practice* (Vol. 3, pp. 119–158). New York: Academic Press.
de Beaugrande, R. (1980). *Text, discourse, and process.* Norwood, NJ: Ablex.
de Beaugrande, R. (1981). Design criteria for process models of reading. *Reading Research Quarterly, 16,* 261–315.
Bloome, D. (1983). *Definitions and functions of reading in two middle school classrooms.* Paper presented at the meeting of the American Educational Research Association, Montreal, Canada.
Bloome, D., & Green, J. (1984). Directions in the sociolinguistic study of reading. In F. D. Pearson (Ed.), *Handbook of reading research* (pp. 395–421). New York: Longman.
Bolinger, D. (1975). *Aspects of language.* New York: Harcourt Brace Jovanovich.
Brown, J. S., & Burton, R. B. (1978). Diagnostic models for procedural bugs in basic mathematics skills. *Cognitive Science, 2,* 155–192.
Campione, J., & Armbruster, B. B. (1984). An analysis of the outcomes and implications of intervention research. In H. Mandl, N. L. Stein, & T. Trabasso (Eds.), *Learning and comprehension of text* (pp. 287–304). Hillsdale, NJ: Erlbaum.
Chapman, L. J., & Chapman, J. P. (1973). Problems in the measurement of cognitive deficit. *Psychological Bulletin, 79,* 380–385.
Collins, A., Brown, J. S., & Larkin, K. M. (1980). Inference in text understanding. In R. J. Spiro, B. C. Bruce, & W. F. Brewer (Eds.), *Theoretical issues in reading comprehension* (pp. 385–410). Hillsdale, NJ: Erlbaum.
Collins, A., & Smith, E. (1982). Teaching the process of reading comprehension. In D. K. Detterman & R. J. Sternberg (Eds.), *How and how much can intelligence be increased?* Norwood, NJ: Ablex.
Collins, J. (1981). Differential treatment in reading instruction. In J. Cook-Gumperz, J. Gumperz, & H. Simons, *School-home ethnography project* (Final

report to the National Institute of Education). Washington, DC: U. S. Department of Education.

Danks, J. H. (1974). Comprehension in listening and reading: Same or different? In *Proceedings of the Interdisciplinary Institute on Reading and Child Development.* Newark, DE: University of Delaware.

DeStefano, J. S., Pepinsky, H. B., & Sanders, T. S. (1982). Discourse rules for literacy learning in a classroom. In L. C. Wilkinson (Ed.), *Communicating in the classroom* (pp. 101–120). New York: Academic Press.

Drum, P. A., Calfee, R. C., & Cook, L. K. (1980). The effects of surface structure variables on performance in reading comprehension tests. *Reading Research Quarterly, 16,* 486–513.

Fillmore, C. J. (1982). Ideal readers and real readers. In D. Tannen (Ed.), *Analyzing discourse: Text and talk.* (Thirty-second round table monograph on language and linguistics, pp. 248–270). Washington, D.C.: Georgetown University Press.

Fillmore, C. J., & Kay, P. (1981). *Text semantic analysis of reading comprehension tests.* Progress report (NIE Project 9-0511).

Fillmore, C. J., & Kay, P. (1983, August). *Text semantic analysis of reading comprehension tests.* (Report No. G-790121). Washington, DC: National Institute of Education.

Frederiksen, C. (1977). Semantic processing units in understanding text. In R. Freedle (Ed.), *Discourse production and comprehension* (pp. 57–88). Norwood, NJ: Ablex.

Frederiksen, J. (1982, January). *A componential theory of reading skills and their interactions.* (Tech. Rep. No. 227). Urbana-Champaign, IL: University of Illinois, Center for the Study of Reading.

Glaser, R. (1973). Educational psychology and education. *American Psychologist, 28,* 557–566.

Glaser, R. (1981). The future of testing: A research agenda for cognitive psychology and psychometrics. *American Psychologist, 36,* 923–936.

Golinkoff, R. M. (1976). A comparison of reading comprehension processes in good and poor comprehenders. *Reading Research Quarterly, 11,* 623–659.

Goodman, K. S. (1976). Reading: A psycholinguistic guessing game. In H. Singer & R. Ruddell (Eds.), *Theoretical models and processes of reading* (2d ed.) (pp. 497–508). Newark, DE: International Reading Association. (Originally published 1967).

Goodman, Y. M., & Burke, C. L. (1970). *Reading miscue inventory manual procedure for diagnosis and evaluation.* New York: Macmillan.

Gough, P. B. (1972). One second of reading. In J. F. Kavanagh & I. G. Mattingly (Eds.), *Language by ear and eye* (pp. 332–358). Cambridge, MA: MIT Press.

Green, J. (1977). *Pedagogical style differences as related to comprehension performances: Grades one through three.* Unpublished doctoral dissertation, University of California, Berkeley.

Green, J. L., & Harker, J. O. (1982). Gaining access to learning: Conversational, social, and cognitive demands of group participation. In L. C. Wilkinson (Ed.), *Communicating in the classroom* (pp. 183–222). New York: Academic Press.

Hall, J. W., & Humphreys, M. S. (1982). Research on specific learning disabili-

ties: deficits and remediation. *Topics in Learning and Learning Disabilities,* 2(2), 68–78.
Harnisch, D. L. (1983). Item response patterns: applications for educational practice. *Journal of Educational Measurement, 20,* 191–206.
Harnisch, D. L., & Linn, R. L. (1981). *Identification of aberrant response patterns.* (Report No. G-80-0003). Washington, DC: National Institute of Education.
Heap, J. (1982). *Word recognition, in theory and in classroom practice.* Paper presented at the Ethnography of Education Research Forum, Philadelphia.
Hornby, P. A. (1971). Surface structure and the topic-comment distinction: A developmental study. *Child Development, 42,* 975–988.
Johnston, P. H. (1983). *A cognitive basis for the assessment of reading comprehension.* Newark, DE: International Reading Association.
Johnston, P. H. (1984a). Assessment in reading. In F. D. Pearson (Ed.), *Handbook of reading research* (pp. 147–182). New York: Longman.
Johnston, P. H. (1984b). Prior knowledge and reading comprehension test bias. *Reading Research Quarterly, 19,* 219–239.
Just, M. A., & Carpenter, P. A. (1980). A theory of reading: From eye fixations to comprehension. *Psychological Review, 87,* 329–354.
Karlsen, B., Madden, R., & Gardner, E. (1976). *Stanford Diagnostic Reading Test.* New York: Harcourt Brace Jovanovich, Inc.
Kintsch, W., & Van Dijk, T. (1978). Toward a model of text comprehension and production. *Psychological Review, 85,* 363–394.
Kleiman, G. M. (1982, June). *Comparing good and poor readers: A critique of the research.* (Tech. Rep. No. 246). Urbana-Champaign, IL: University of Illinois, Center for the Study of Reading.
Kleiman, G. M., Winograd, P. N., & Humphrey, M. M. (1979, May). *Prosody and children's parsing of sentences* (Tech. Rep. No. 123). Urbana-Champaign, IL: University of Illinois, Center for the Study of Reading.
LaBerge, D., & Samuels, S. J. (1974). Toward a theory of automatic information processing in reading. *Cognitive Psychology, 6,* 293–323.
McDermott, R. (1976). *Kids make sense: An ethnographic account of the interactional management of success and failure in one first-grade classroom.* Unpublished doctoral dissertation, Stanford University.
Meyer, B. F. (1975). *The organization of prose and its effects on memory.* Amsterdam, Netherlands: North Holland.
Michaels, S. (1981). "Sharing time": Children's narrative styles and differential access to literacy. *Language in Society, 10,* 423–442.
Morrison, F. J. (1981, April). *Reading disability: A problem in learning and word decoding.* Paper presented at the meeting of the Society for Research in Child Development, Boston.
Orsanu, J. (1986). *Reading comprehension: From research to practice.* Hillsdale, NJ: Erlbaum.
Policy Analysis for California Education (PACE). (1984, April). *Conditions of Education in California* (paper 84-1). Berkeley, CA.
Resnick, L. B. (1984). Comprehension and learning: Implications for a cognitive theory of instruction. In H. Mandl, N. L. Stein, & T. Trabasso (Eds.), *Learning and comprehension of text* (pp. 431–444). Hillsdale, NJ: Erlbaum.
Rubin, A. (1980). A theoretical taxonomy of the differences between oral and

written language. In R. J. Spiro, B. C. Bruce, & W. F. Brewer (Eds.), *Theoretical issues in reading comprehension* (pp. 411–438). Hillsdale, NJ: Erlbaum.

Rumelhart, D. (1977). Toward an interactive model of reading. In S. Dornic (Ed.), *Attention and performance VI* (pp. 573–603). Hillsdale, NJ: Erlbaum.

Samuels, S. J. (1977). Introduction to theoretical models of reading. In W. Otto (Ed.), *Reading problems*. Boston, MA: Addison-Wesley.

Samuels, S. J., & Kamil, M. L. (1984). Models of the reading process. In P. D. Pearson (Ed.), *Handbook of reading research* (pp. 185–224). New York: Longman.

Sato, T. (1975). [*The construction and interpretation of S-P tables.*] Tokyo: Meikji Tosho.

Schallert, D. L., & Kleiman, G. M. (1979, July). *Some reasons why teachers are easier to understand than textbooks* (Reading Education Report No. 9). Urbana-Champaign, IL: University of Illinois, Center for the Study of Reading.

Schank, R., & Abelson, R. (1977). *Scripts, plans, goals, and understanding*. Hillsdale, NJ: Erlbaum.

Smith, F. (1971). *Understanding reading*. New York: Holt, Rinehart, & Winston.

Smith, J. K. (1982). Converging on correct answers: A peculiarity of multiple choice items. *Journal of Educational Measurement, 19*, 211–220.

Spiro, R. J., Bruce, B. C., & Brewer, W. F. (1980). Introduction and Global issues. In *Theoretical issues in reading comprehension* (pp. 1–9). Hillsdale, NJ: Erlbaum.

Spiro, R. J. & Myers, A. (1984). Individual differences and underlying cognitive processes. In P. D. Pearson (Ed.), *Handbook of reading research* (pp. 471–501). New York: Longman.

Stanovich, K. E. (1980). Toward an interactive-compensatory model of individual differences in the development of reading fluency. *Reading Research Quarterly, 16*, 32–71.

Sternberg, R. J. (1981). Testing and cognitive psychology. *American Psychologist, 36*, 1181–1189.

Sternberg, R. J. & Wagner, R. K. (1982). Automatization failure in learning disabilities. *Topics in Learning and Learning Disabilities, 2*(2) (Controversy: Strategy or capacity deficit), 1–11.

Tatsuoko, K. K., & Tatsuoko, M. M. (1982). Detection of aberrant response patterns and their effect on dimensionality. *Journal of Educational Statistics, 7*, 215–231.

Vellutino, F. R. (1978). Toward an understanding of dyslexia: Psychological factors in specific reading disability. In A. L. Benton & D. Pearl (Eds.), *Dyslexia: An appraisal of current knowledge* (pp. 61–111). New York: Oxford University Press.

Vellutino, F. R. (1979). *Dyslexia: Theory and research*. Cambridge, MA: MIT Press.

Wong Fillmore, L. W. (1976). *The second time around: Cognitive and social strategies in second language acquisition*. Ph.D. dissertation, Stanford University, Palo Alto, CA.

Wong Fillmore, L. (1979). Individual differences in second language acquisition. In C. J. Fillmore, D. Kempler, & W. S-Y. Wang (Eds.), *Individual differences in language ability and language behavior* (pp. 203–228). New York: Academic Press.

Wong Fillmore, L. (1982). Instructional language as linguistic input: Second language learning in classrooms. In L. C. Wilkinson (Ed.), *Communicating in the classroom* (pp. 283–296). New York: Academic Press.

Wong Fillmore, L. (1983). The language learner as an individual. In M. Clarke & J. Handscombe (Eds.), *On TESOL '82: Pacific perspectives on language learning and teaching* (pp. 157–173). Washington, D.C.: U. S. Government Printing Office.

Wong Fillmore, L., & Ammon, P. (1980). *Learning English through bilingual instruction* (Contract ; 400-80-0030). Washington, DC: National Institute of Education.

Wong Fillmore, L., Ammon, P., Ammon, M. S., Delucchi, K., Jensen, J., McLaughlin, B., & Strong, M. (1983, May). *Learning English through bilingual instruction: Second year report* (Contract ; 400-80-0030). Washington, DC: National Institute of Education.

Woods, W. A. (1980). Multiple theory formation in speech and reading. In R. J. Spiro, B. C. Bruce, & W. F. Brewer (Eds.), *Theoretical issues in reading comprehension* (pp. 59–86). Hillsdale, NJ: Erlbaum.

5

Comprehension of Content Area Passages: A Study of Spanish/English Readers in Third and Fourth Grade*

María de la Luz Reyes

California State, Bakersfield

Introduction

For all students, success in school is largely measured by the extent to which they become proficient not only in learning *how to read*, but especially in *learning from reading*. During the period when the student is learning how to read, the teacher is the primary agent responsible for presenting new concepts and expanding the student's knowledge base. Once the student has mastered the rudimentary skills in reading, the responsibility for acquiring new knowledge shifts from the teacher to the student. This means that, from that point on, the student must depend on his or her own comprehension of informational material as the principal source of knowledge (Reyes, 1984).

In most elementary schools, this shift in responsibility for learning occurs around third grade and coincides with the introduction of content area materials (e.g., social studies, science, geography, etc.) and with the introduction of expository themes in the language arts curriculum. With each year the child continues in school, content area materials (or informational texts) become increasingly prominent (Baker & Stein, 1979; Spiro & Taylor, 1980). Yet, despite the importance of content area materials, very little is known about the factors which influence chil-

---

*The research reported in this chapter was conducted as part of a larger project supported by a Department of Education, National Institute of Education grant (NIE-G-82-0125) to Susan R. Goldman.

dren's comprehension of this type of text (Spiro & Taylor, 1980). Lack of information in this area can be attributed to two factors:

1. Most comprehension research has utilized narratives, or stories, similar to the types of materials which comprise the bulk of readings used in what Chall (1979) calls "the learning-to-read stage," when the teacher is still serving as the primary agent of learning.
2. Of the few studies using expository materials, most have been conducted with adults. Only a handful have been conducted with students who are at the stage when independent learning is critical.

What those studies do indicate, however, is that children acquire a schema for stories; that is, they learn that stories follow a predictable pattern. For example, there is always a setting and a character ("Once upon a time there was. . . ."); there is a goal and a conflict ("who wanted to. . . ., but . . ."); and a resolution of that conflict ("and they lived happily ever after"). This schema for stories is said to aid comprehension (Mandler & Johnson, 1977; Stein & Glenn, 1979).

Goldman, Reyes, and Varnhagen (1984) found that schemas for stories are helpful even when the story is presented in the student's less proficient or second language. In their study of comprehension of fables (a type of narrative) by students dealing with two languages (Spanish/English), they found that higher order skills involved in comprehending stories appeared to transfer to comprehension of stories in students' second languages. When producing story recalls and answering questions about the texts, many students used their first language, regardless of the input language of the text. However, these recalls reflected levels of *comprehension* of story materials that were equivalent for first and second language inputs. For example, native Spanish speakers accurately recalled material from stories presented in English, but did so in Spanish. The converse was true for those acquiring Spanish as a second language, Goldman et al. (1984) interpreted their findings as having indicated that whatever prior knowledge of story content and structure students had acquired through their first language was accessible, available and utilized during comprehension of second language story materials.

The literature on comprehension of expository texts, however, provides no evidence that children acquire or use schemas analogous to those used for stories when comprehending expository texts. Therefore, comprehension of expository materials is believed to be more difficult than comprehension of narratives (Baker & Stein, 1979), and may be more dependent on expertise in a content domain.

While the literature on learning from text for native English speaking children is limited, the information available about Hispanic students' abilities to learn from text is almost nonexistent. Because Hispanic students, limited or non-English speakers, function in a dual language environment, they bring some unique skills and/or problems to the reading comprehension task. The rapidly growing number of minority language students in the public schools begs an examination of the reading performance of those students. In light of the almost 50% drop-out rate of Spanish-speaking students in junior high and high schools, the need for such studies has an even greater sense of urgency.

The purpose of this study was to examine the comprehension of informational material by limited-English proficient students in third and fourth grades who were enrolled in Spanish/English bilingual education programs. In the context of this paper, "expository text" is defined as reading material whose primary function is to provide new information about a specific topic. To distinguish the term "expository" from other uses of the term, this type of text will be referred to as "informational text." Specifically, the study was designed to address three questions:

1. Whether access to two languages affects the learning of new information by bilinguals when there is no prior knowledge of the topic,
2. Whether there is a relationship between what bilinguals learn from passages presented in Spanish and what they learn from passages presented in English,
3. Whether the writing style of the text influences the amount, or quality, of the information learned form the text.

Spiro and Taylor (1980) have suggested that the form of linguistic expression is a potentially important factor that influences learning from informational text. Forms of linguistic expression are related to the level of vocabulary, the range of sentence constructions (e.g., active or passive), and the degree and type of figurative language that appears in texts. Figurative language, such as metaphors, analogies, and personification, is often used to stress or embellish information which may be conveyed literally and explicitly elsewhere in the text. In elementary school readers and in content-area textbooks (e.g., science, social studies), examples of analogy and personification are frequently found. Often, the style of presenting information in these books is informal and directed at the young reader by the use of the second person pronoun "you". Rubin (1980) refers to this medium-related dimension as "involvement." The text may contain contractions, reflecting more of an informal, oral language approach.

This informal approach to presenting content-area material does not appear to have an empirical base. There are, however, two general possibilities regarding the effects of the use of informal linguistic expression in content-area materials:

1. The texts may be easier to learn from, and easier to understand because there is a better match between oral language and written language in the informal version as compared with the formal texts.
2. The closer match to oral language may make learning from the informal text harder because the discourse function (to inform) is masked by the informal linguistic expression.

This study investigated these two possibilities. In addition, it examined how the formal and informal styles affected comprehension of English for Spanish-speaking readers. A hypothesis was that informal expression would be more beneficial to second language learners than to monolingual English students because the "closeness" to oral language might facilitate comprehension for English as a second language (ESL) students, rather than create any potential "interference" (confusion) due to the informality of the passage.

Learning from text was examined using the topic of vanishing animals. The topic and the four specific animals that the passages described were selected for their unfamiliarity to the participants. The focus was, therefore, on the amount of new information that could be learned from passages presented in English and in Spanish by students at different levels of proficiency in each language.

Subjects. Eighty-eight students from third and fourth grade classes from a public school in Southern California participated in the study. The attendance area includes a low-cost, federally subsidized housing project, community housing tracts, various ranches, and a naval military installation. Approximately 90% of the children's parents are considered unskilled or semi-skilled. The school serves kindergarten through fifth grade, and has an enrollment of approximately 500 students. Of the total enrollment, 78% were classified as limited English proficient (LEP) students, with Spanish identified as their first language (L1) and English as their second language (L2). When the study began, the school had just completed 4 years of Title VII (ESEA) funding, and was supporting the bilingual program with state and local funds.

The third grade participants (n = 40) were divided into three groups:

1. Bilingual Spanish readers (n = 16; mean age 8.8 years). The students selected for inclusion in this group had been in the bilingual program for 3 years and were classified as LEP students. They had begun their formal reading instruction in Spanish, and had continued with

Spanish as the primary medium for reading. Students in this group were either at, or above, grade level in Spanish, based on the reading textbook series they were using, or were at grade level based on scores from the *California Test of Basic Skills en Español* (CTBS, 1978), administered at the end of the 2nd grade. When the study began, only four of these students had received 1 month of formal instruction for transition to English reading. This consisted of approximately 1 hour of after-school introduction to English, phonics, and practice in oral English reading conducted on a volunteer basis by some of the designated Bilingual certificated teachers.

2. Bilingual program, English-transitioned readers (n = 8); mean age 8.5 years). These students had been participants in the bilingual program for 3 years, although not all of them had begun reading in Spanish. Four students were classified as fluent English proficient (FEP) when they enrolled in school and had begun formal reading instruction in English; four students were transitioned to English reading by the end of the first grade. None of these students had received formal Spanish reading instruction in either second or third grades. These students were at, or above, grade level based on the reading section of their achievement test scores and were at grade level in English reading textbook series.

3. Monolingual English readers (n = 16; mean age 8.8 years). All of these students had been classified as FEP upon entrance to school. Both Anglos and Chicanos (Americans of Mexican descent) comprised this group. These students had begun formal reading instruction in English and had received no instruction in Spanish, oral language, or reading. None had ever been enrolled in a bilingual program. All were at grade level in reading according to their reading book series, and/or achievement test scores. This group of third graders received only English language versions of the passages.

There was a total of 48 fourth grade students. They were divided into bilingual readers (n = 32, mean age 10.3 years) and monolingual English readers (n = 16, mean age 10.4). The bilingual students had been enrolled in a bilingual program for a minimum of three years and met the following criteria:

1. Were at grade level on the Spanish CTBS (1978) reading section and/or fourth grade Spanish reading series, with a minimum of second grade reading level in English, or
2. Were at grade level on the English CTBS (1977) in reading, and/or were reading fourth grade English language texts, with a minimum of second grade reading levels in Spanish.

The monolingual English group had been classified as FEP upon entrance to school. Both Anglos and Chicanos comprised this group. The only formal reading instruction for this group had been in English. These students were either at grade level on their reading achievement test scores or were using fourth grade level reading books.

Materials and Design

Materials consisted of two versions (a formal and an informal style) in two languages (Spanish and English) of the same four informational passages on vanishing animals: the aye-aye, the chinchilla, the quetzal, and the vicuña. The passages were modified for comparability across the four topics and were subsequently translated to Spanish. Each passage began with a general statement of the endangered animal and was followed by a more detailed description of that animal. The information in each passage was organized into six short paragraphs in all versions of the passages. Each contained information about the problems of extinction, origin of name, habitat, physical description, and diet. Each passage contained six categories of information and 27–28 facts.

The formal version of the set of passages presented information without any direct reference to the reader. No contractions were used. In contrast, the informal version of the set of passages included the "involvement" dimension (Rubin, 1980) and made many direct references to the young reader, utilized contractions, and included humor and personification, thus reflecting more of an informal oral language style. The informal version was developed by taking the formal version in toto and embedding four types of informal mechanisms:

1. Deliberate attempts to involve the reader by addressing him or her in the second person, *"you"*; e.g., "Can you imagine . . .," and "If you were a . . .".
2. Use of humor/personification of animals; e.g., "Chinchillas don't use coats."
3. Comparison of the reader's attributes or characteristics with the animal's attributes or characteristics; e.g., "You work and play during the day; chinchillas sleep during the day."
4. Use of contractions; e.g., "can't," "you're."

There were five informal mechanisms distributed throughout each of the informal passages. As a result, the informal versions were slightly longer than the formal versions. The two versions, however, contained the same number of informational units or facts. Table 1 shows the formal and informal version of the aye-aye passages. For each topic, a reproduction of the photograph of the vanishing animal was prepared.

Latin-square counterbalancing procedures were used to generate four topic orders and four condition orders (language x version) for the students in the bilingual program. These students read four different texts: Spanish, formal; Spanish, informal; English, formal; and English, informal. The monolingual English groups read two formal English and two informal English.

The design, excluding the factors introduced by counterbalancing procedures, was a mixed design with repeated measures for both the bilingual and the monolingual samples. For the bilingual sample, there was one between-subject factor (grade) and two within-subject factors: language of input (Spanish or English) and version (formal or informal). For the monolingual sample, grade (3rd or 4th) was the between-subjects factor, and version the within factor.

Procedure and Tasks

Subjects were tested individually. They were shown a picture of the animal and were asked whether they had ever seen or knew anything about that animal. If they reported yes, they were asked to tell about it. Not one subject was able to provide any accurate information on any of the four topics. The students were then asked to read the passage and afterwards to tell everything that they could recall. In contrast to requiring an input/output language match which is the common practice in the testing of bilinguals, in this study students were permitted to respond in the language of their choice, regardless of the language of the text, consistent with the methodology followed by Goldman et al. (1984).

Comprehension questions were asked immediately following the conclusion of the recall for the passage. Questions were asked orally and in the language the child used during recall, or in both languages, the goal being to ensure that the child understood the question.

Approximately 2 weeks after completion of the reading task, a listening task was administered to the third grade bilingual program participants (both Spanish readers and English readers). The Spanish readers from the bilingual classroom were asked to listen to the two English passages which they had attempted to read earlier. These were presented via audiotapes. Conversely, the English readers from the same bilingual classroom were asked to listen to the two Spanish passages that they had attempted to read earlier. The rationale for this "add-on"

Table 1. Formal and Informal Aye-Aye Texts

Formal voice:

THE AYE-AYE

There is an animal that some people believe brings bad luck. It is in great danger of being destroyed. That animal is the aye-aye.

The aye-aye is a strange animal about the size of a cat. It belongs to the same family as the monkey. Sometimes the aye-aye makes a noise that sounds like "aye-aye." That is how it was named.

The aye-aye lives in trees on a large island off the coast of Africa. It can be found alone among the trees in the forest.

The aye-aye looks like a raccoon. It has a wide bushy tail and very strong teeth. The aye-aye has strange-looking hands. The middle finger on each hand is much longer and thinner than the other fingers.

The aye-aye is nocturnal. It sleeps during the day, and comes out at night. Then it jumps from branch to branch looking for food. With its teeth, it makes tiny holes in tree trunks. Then it reaches in and pulls out little caterpillars that it eats. To drink, it dips one long finger into water and it pulls the finger sideways through its mouth!

The aye-ayes are almost extinct because almost all the forests where they live have been cut down. Many people also try to kill aye-ayes when they see them because they believe that aye-ayes bring bad luck. So the aye-aye is in bad trouble. There are only about 50 little aye-ayes left in the whole world. The aye-ayes may not be able to survive much longer.

Informal voice:

THE AYE-AYE

Can you imagine how it would be if 8 to 10 year-olds were considered bad luck? You would always be in danger. There's an animal that some people believe brings bad luck. It's in great danger of being destroyed. That animal is the aye-aye.

The aye-aye is a strange animal about the size of a cat. It belongs to the same family as the monkey. Sometimes the aye-aye makes a noise that sounds like "aye-aye." That's how it was named.

You're lucky you don't have to live alone. You live in a house with your family. The aye-aye lives in trees on a large island off the coast of Africa. It can be found alone among the trees in the forest.

The aye-aye looks like a raccoon. It has a wide bushy tail and very strong teeth. The aye-aye has strange-looking hands. The middle finger on each hand is much longer and thinner than the other fingers.

You work or play during the day, and sleep at night. The aye-aye does the opposite. It is nocturnal. It sleeps during the day, and comes out at night. Then it jumps from branch to branch looking for food. With its teeth, it makes tiny holes in tree trunks. Then it reaches in and pulls out little caterpillars that it eats. To drink, it doesn't need a glass like you. The aye-aye dips one long finger into water and pulls the finger sideways through its mouth!

The aye-ayes are almost extinct because nearly all the forests where they live have been cut down. Many people also try to kill aye-ayes when they see them because they believe that aye-ayes bring bad luck. So the aye-aye is in bad trouble. How sad it must be for the aye-aye! There are only about 50 little aye-ayes left in the whole world. The aye-ayes may not be able to survive much longer.

activity was to find out the degree to which these students could understand oral presentation of content-area material after 3 years of ESL instruction. The findings from this task are important because the kind of information contained in these passages is similar to content area material which might be presented in a traditional English-only class. Thus, for those students who did not appear to learn from independent reading of content-area texts in English, their ability to listen and learn from the same text was investigated.

The recall protocols and responses to comprehension questions were scored for the number of presented facts that were mentioned. The total number of facts in the formal and informal versions of each text topic was the same, although not each topic had the same number of facts. The texts on the aye-aye topic contained 27 facts, and the chinchilla, vicuña, and quetzal topics each contained 28 facts. Proportion of facts recalled was the measure used in the analyses. This was determined by comparing the number of facts recalled to the total number of possible facts that could have been given for a text topic, i.e., 27 or 28. Thus, if a student recalled 20 out of 27, his or her score was .74.

Results and Discussion

There are two striking results that emerge from a comparison of the recall performance among these five groups:

1. The proportion of facts recalled by each group in its first language is equivalent for all groups within grade levels.
2. The lower performance in English recall among the third grade bilinguals appears to be temporary, and levels off by the fourth grade for those who continue in the bilingual instructional program.

Free Recall Measure. Analyses of variance were conducted on the proportion of facts recalled from each informational passage. Results of this study on comprehension of content area passages indicated that mode of presentation for content area materials, as defined by formal and informal voice, did not facilitate recall. There were no main effects on either amount or quality of recall due to version (formal or informal) of the passages.

With respect to effects due to input language, among the bilingual third graders there was a significant interaction of language and group, $F(1, 22) = 17.53$, $p < .01$. Means for the interaction are given in Table 2. After reading, the third grade bilingual Spanish readers recalled more facts when the input language was Spanish (Mean = .17) than when the input language was English (Mean = .06). Since the primary task involved reading skills, the outcome was not surprising, given that this group had not yet transferred to English reading. The inverse pattern held for the third grade transition group, who were English readers. They recalled more after English input (Mean = .22) than after Spanish input (Mean = .11).

The data indicate a relationship between having had formal reading instruction in a language and the ability to get new information through reading a text in that instructed language. This relationship is totally consistent with LaBerge and Samuel's (1974) claim that the capacity to process codes (i.e., decode words) is critical to proficient reading. In the case of these two groups, it appears that decoding skills in L2 (i.e., English for the third grade bilingual group, Spanish for the third grade transition group) have not become sufficiently automatized and require relatively constant monitoring. There is, thus, little capacity for the processing of new information. This is then reflected in lower levels of information acquisition in during L2 reading.

The fourth grade bilinguals, whose data are also shown in Table 2, recalled exactly the same amount of information after Spanish input as after English input, Mean = .23. Thus, performance after English input was no longer different from that after Spanish input once students had had two-thirds of a year of English reading instruction. The greatest portion of the instruction focused on breaking the orthographic code and learning to read in English, i.e., on learning decoding.

For the third and fourth grade English monolingual students, grade was significant, $F(1, 30) = 4.25$, $p < .05$, whereas version was not. Fourth graders recalled more (Mean = .28) than third graders (Mean = .21).

A comparison of the fourth grade English monolinguals and fourth grade bilinguals revealed that mean recall for both groups after English

Table 2. Mean Proportion of Facts from Recall Task and Probe Task

Group	Recall Task Input Language		Probe Task Input Language	
	Span.	Eng.	Span.	Eng.
Third gr. Bilingual	.17	.06	.19	.08
Third gr. Transition	.11	.22	.10	.21
Third gr. Monolingual	—	.21	—	.24
Fourth gr. Bilingual	.23	.23	.24	.22
Fourth gr. Monolingual	—	.28	—	.28

reading was equivalent, t (46) = 1.28, $p > .05$. Among the third grade groups, a comparison of performance in each group's primary language also indicated that the recall of third grade bilinguals after Spanish reading (Mean = .17) was equivalent to the recall of the English monolinguals after English input (Mean = .21). These results indicate that performance levels for the languages in which children were receiving instruction were equivalent among the third grade groups. An implication of these results is that reading instruction in L1 does not retard literacy skills in L2, and that those learning the skills in L1 are learning them at a pace similar to the pace of the L1 English learners.

Comprehension Questions. Part two of the reading-to-learn task in this study was recall of facts as measured by probe questions. The rationale for this activity was to ascertain whether failures to recall more of the presented information were due to high language production requirements in the recall task or "lack of acquisition" of the information. A general belief is that probe questions assist the individual in recalling information, because they provide a specific direction for the memory search often required during retrieval.

The data from the recall task and the probe task were submitted to analyses of variance. The results indicated that, contrary to expectation, the mean proportions of facts given in the probe task were no different than those in recall. In fact, the pattern of results from the probe task replicated that of the recall task. The relevant data are given in Table 2.

In general, group performance indicated similar quantities of information were remembered under the two tasks. For example, in the fourth grade bilinguals, the mean proportion of facts recalled was .23, for both Spanish and English input; in the probe task, the mean after Spanish input was .24, and, after English, it was .22. Furthermore, the same conclusion applies to individuals: students who performed well in the recall task also performed well in the probe task. A series of Pearson product moment correlations were conducted, and strong positive correlations between the two tasks in each language were obtained in each group. Figure 1 shows the relationship between the two tasks for the fourth grade bilinguals after English (a) input and after Spanish (b) input. For the other groups, the correlations ranged from $r = .63$ to .93, $p = < .01$. For the most part, students did not provide any additional information beyond what they had given in the free recall, suggesting that, when a student has little or no prior knowledge of a topic, probe questions do not provide any particular advantage over free recall.

Relationship Between L1 and L2. At the subject level, this study was also concerned with the relationship between the individual student's ability to learn in his or her first language and second language. The question of interest was the extent to which performance levels in the

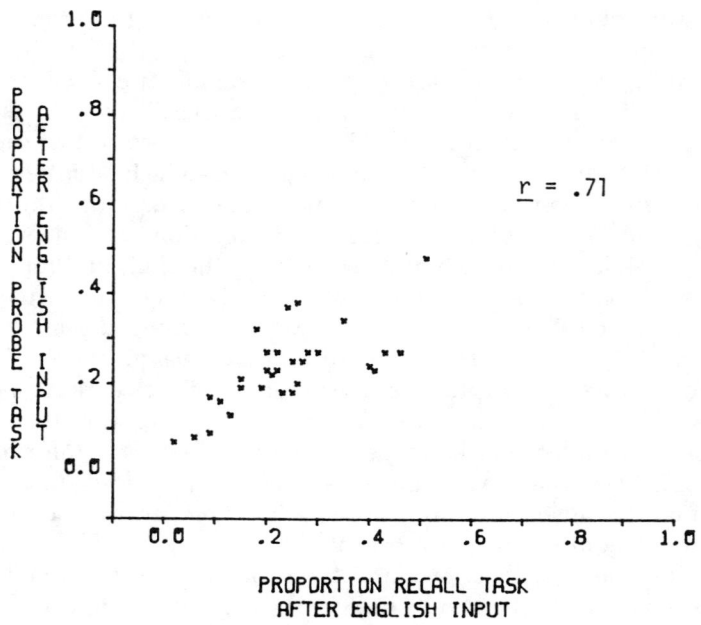

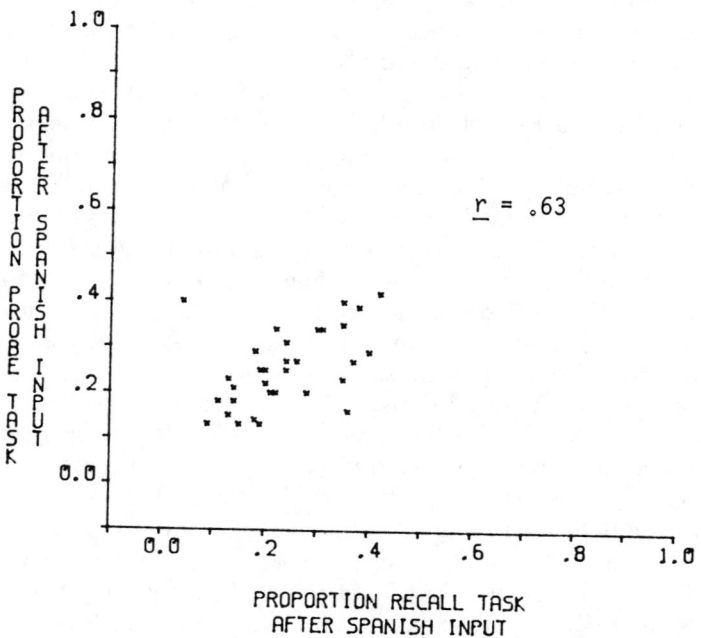

Figure 1. Relationship between recall and probe tasks after English (a) and Spanish (b) input for fourth grade bilinguals.

primary language could predict performance levels in the second language. The relationship is expected to increase in a positive direction as the child improves his or her reading skills. Thus, a positive correlation would indicate that students who performed well in Spanish reading would also perform well in English reading, and that those who would not perform well in Spanish would not perform well in English.

Correlations were computed between recall performance after Spanish input and after English input for the bilingual groups. Figure 2 shows the scatterplot for the fourth grade bilinguals. There is a significant positive correlation, $r = .62$, $df = 30$, $p = < .001$. This suggests that skills involved in the acquisition of new information in Spanish may be transferred to the acquisition of new information in English. For the Spanish-only and English-only third grade readers in the bilingual program, relationships between L1 and L performance were nonsignificant. This was undoubtedly due to extremely low levels of performance in L2 by these groups, neither of whom had had decoding instruction in L2.

Reading Task versus Listening Task. Two separate analyses of variance were conducted comparing the reading and listening task for the third grade bilingual and third grade transition groups. Results of these indicated that task was significant. For the third grade bilingual Spanish readers, performance after listening to English texts (Mean = .16) was significantly higher than after reading English (Mean = .06), F

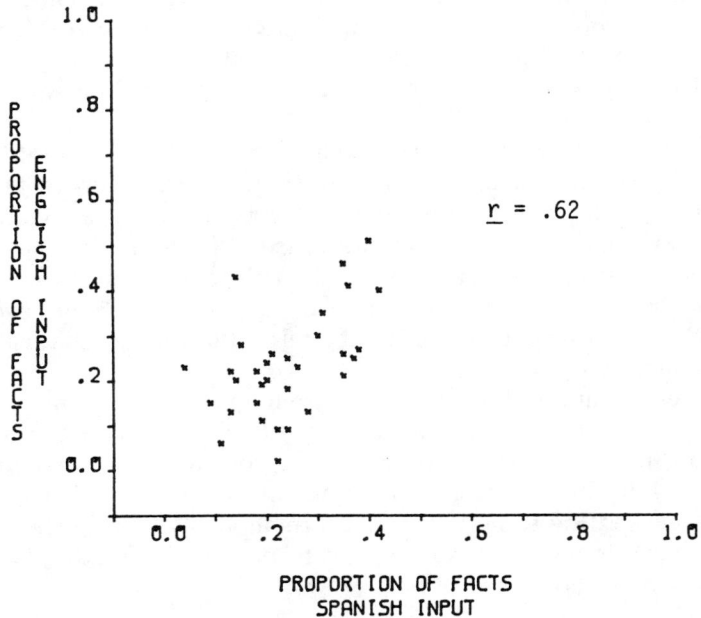

Figure 2. Relationship between proportion of information recalled after Spanish and after English input for the fourth grade bilinguals.

$(1.15) = 15.96$, $p = <.001$. The third grade English readers also performed better after listening to Spanish texts (mean = .18) than after reading them (Mean = .11), $F(1,7) = 10.20$, $p = <.02$.

The data from the listening task is somewhat problematic to interpret because it is a re-presentation of the passages. However, the data demonstrate that, although there are constraints on L2 reading skills, receptive skills are present and enable these students to comprehend content in L2 through a listening mode.

Information Categories. In addition to the quantity of facts recalled, an examination of the quality of recall was conducted. This was done to determine whether the types of information items recalled by students were similar or different. Table 3 shows the breakdown of the aye-aye formal text into the various information categories contained in that text. The results from this analysis indicated that information about (E) diet (Mean = .37), (A) problems of extinction (Mean = .35), and (F) unusual characteristics (Mean = .23) ranked among the top three types of statements recalled by all groups, both bilingual and monolingual. Information relating to physical description (B), habitat (D), and origin of name (C) ranked fourth, fifth, and sixth in order of recall.

The ranking of Category A statements is not surprising, given the organization of the texts. Recall for this category by all groups is consistent with Meyer's (1975, 1979) studies of top-level structure which indicate that students' recall is influenced by passage organization. Since elaboration of the problems of extinction appeared twice in the texts, and the average number of facts for Category A was 5, the results may indicate a facilitative effect of primary/recency factors, and/or redundancy in the recall patterns.

Neither a large number of statements, nor structure, account for the top ranking of information about diet. There was an average of 1.5 of these types of statements across the four texts, as compared to an average of 7 statements for unusual characteristics, for example. The results are not so easily explained, since it is difficult to determine young children's reasons for finding the subject of diet particularly noteworthy. One can only surmise that it might be related to the fact that eating is one of children's central activities.

In general, third and fourth graders, bilingual and monolingual students, appear to have behaved similarly with respect to the types of information items that were best recalled across texts and in both languages. While the fourth graders generally recalled more facts, third graders recalled the same types of information categories. There were no differences in the rank ordering of categories within grades, between grades, or between tasks.

Conclusions and Implications

As stated earlier, there were no significant differences in levels of recall for the formal or informal style of the texts, either between or within grade levels. Two explanations are plausible for this outcome. One is related to the method of developing the informal version (i.e., the informal version included the formal version in toto and embedded five informal mechanisms), the other to the interactional setting provided by the experimenter. Mosenthal & Na (1980) argue that the task organizers, and the interaction between them and the students, may be the most important factor influencing reading comprehension. There are strong indications that, in this study, the experimenter's role as situation organizer may have overridden the formal/informal text manipulations. The experimenter had collected other data at the same school site the previous year, and was acquainted with many of the children who had participated in the study. Being bilingual, familiar with the school, and well acquainted with the children's socio-economic, cultural, and linguistic background, she may have provided a unique social interaction with the students which may have had a greater influence on their recall performance than did the form of linguistic expression of the texts.

Once in the testing room, the bilingual students, in particular, were reluctant to participate, fearing that the situation might call for "un exámen" (a test) in which they would not perform well, or which would require a grade. To allay their insecurities, the experimenter created a highly personalized interaction between herself and the subjects, encouraging them and assuring them that it was okay not to know everything. The experimenter used phrases such as: "No te preocupes, yo te ayudo" ("Don't worry, I'll help you"), "Ándale, dime poquito más. Yo sé que sabes más" (Come on, tell me a bit more. I know you know more"), etc. Outside of the testing situation, and while waiting for the next subjects, the experimenter often chatted with the students during recess, lunch, or after school.

The results of the study, with respect to the influence of the formal/informal version, then, must be interpreted in the context of the interactional setting and the rapport that developed between the experimenter and the students. There were many instances when the bilingual students expressed their lack of confidence with English and the encouragement from the experimenter seemed to make a difference in their efforts. These findings are believed to have significant implications for classroom practice, because they suggest that performance levels of the students with both Spanish and English input might have been much lower with a nonbilingual experimenter, who might have been less sen-

Table 3. Breakdown of Information Categories for Aye-Aye Text

Information Categories

A = problem of extinction
B = physical description
C = origin of name
D = habitat
E = diet
F = unusual characteristics

THE AYE-AYE

A {
1. There is an animal
2. that some people believe brings bad luck.
3. It is in great danger of being destroyed.
4. That animal is the aye-aye.
}

B {
5. The aye-aye is a strange animal
6. about the size of a cat.
7. It belongs to the same family as the monkey.
}

C {
8. Sometimes the aye-aye makes a noise
9. that sounds like "aye-aye."
10. That is how it was named.
}

D {
11. The aye-aye lives in trees
12. on a large island
13. off the coast of Africa.
14. It can be found alone
15. among the trees in the forest.
}

B {
16. The aye-aye looks like a raccoon.
17. It has a wide bushy tail
18. and very strong teeth.
19. The aye-aye has strange-looking hands.
20. The middle finger on each hand is much longer
21. and thinner than the other fingers.
}

22. The aye-aye is nocturnal.
23. It sleeps during the day,
24. and comes out at night.
25. Then it jumps from branch to branch looking for food.
26.
27. With its teeth, it makes tiny holes in tree trunks.
28. Then it reaches in and pulls out little caterpillars that it eats.
29.
30. To drink, it dips one long finger into water
31. and it pulls the finger sideways through its mouth!
32. The aye-ayes are almost extinct
33. because almost all the forests where they live have been cut down.
34.
35. Many people also try to kill aye-ayes when they see them
36.
37. because they believe that aye-ayes bring bad luck.
38. So the aye-aye is in bad trouble.
39. There are only about 50 little aye-ayes left in the whole world.
40. The aye-ayes may not be able to survive much longer.

sitive to the verbal and nonverbal feelings of inadequacy which these second language learners expressed. Sensitivity to students, cultural congruence, and the informal social interaction created by the teacher is believed to be critical in the development of a learning environment which will be conducive to the academic success of bilingual students. Without that positive learning environment, bilingual students may continue to perform at less than satisfactory levels in academic tasks.

Others (see Boggs, 1972; Jordan & Tharp, 1979; Au & Jordan, 1981) have also found that the social context of a lesson is very important to minority language students. In their work with Hawaiian children, Au and Jordan (1981), for example, highlight the importance of this social context by stating that "A teacher who has not already established the proper interpersonal relationships between herself and the children would not be able to teach reading lessons . . . The children simply would not be responsive" (p. 146).

The performance levels of the bilingual groups indicate that, contrary to a general assumption held by many, dealing with two languages in elementary schools does not lead to lower levels of reading performance. On the contrary, beginning reading in the primary language appears to be more effective in the long run partly because it capitalizes on the cognitive and linguistic abilities of the children. In the bilingual classes, the scores for third grade Spanish readers were equivalent to the scores of the third graders who had transitioned to English reading. Additionally, the performance of the third grade English monolinguals who had never received bilingual instruction was also equivalent to the performance of the English reading group who were assigned to a bilingual class. Thus, when performance levels of these groups were compared in the language in which each group was receiving formal reading instruction, there were no significant differences.

The fourth grade bilingual group exhibited equivalent levels of recall after both English and Spanish input. Their performance after English passages was equivalent to that of the fourth grade English monolingual students. By fourth grade, it appears that Spanish and English skills level off for those who remain in the bilingual program, and that there is equal access to learn from text in either language. What this means is that instruction in two languages for bilinguals does not have a negative cognitive effect.

In most cases, the "catching-up" period for these fourth grade bilinguals occurred after less than 1 year of formal instruction in English reading. The period required for the two languages to level off and for bilinguals to reap the benefits of bilingual instruction is, at least in this case, consistent with Cummins' (1981) "threshold hypothesis." That hypothesis maintains that there may be a threshold level of linguistic proficiency which bilinguals must attain in order to derive potential benefits of bilingualism and avoid any negative cognitive effects.

The data from the fourth grade bilinguals offer strong support for the current practice in bilingual programs of introducing literacy skills in the primary language. The performance of this group indicates that, once decoding skills have been sufficiently automatized in Spanish, and when ESL instruction is maintained, transfer from Spanish reading skills to English reading skills occurs within a relatively short time. Acquisition of literacy skills in English is not impaired, and the reading skills already available in Spanish are easily transferred to English. In addition, for language minority students exposure to two languages provides the potential for another positive and desirable by-product: the retention of primary language skills.

References

Au, K. H., & Jordan, C. (1981). Teaching reading to Hawaiian children: Finding a culturally appropriate solution. In H. T. Trueba, G. P. Guthrie, & K. H. Au (Eds.), *Culture and the bilingual classroom studies in classroom ethnography*. Rowley, MA: Newbury House Publishers.

Baker, L., & Stein, N. (1979). The development of prose comprehension skills. In C. Santa & B. Hayes (Eds.), *Children's prose comprehension: Research and practice*. Newark, DE: International Reading Association.

Boggs, S. T. (1972). The meaning of questions and narrative to Hawaiian children. In C. B. Cazden, V. P. John and D. Hymes (Eds.), *Functions of language in the classroom*. New York: Teachers College Press.

California Test of Basic Skills en Español (CTBS). (1978). New York: McGraw-Hill.

Chall, J. S. (1979). The great debate: Ten years later, with a modest proposal for reading stages. In L. B. Resnick & P. A. Weaver (Eds.), *Theory and practice of early reading* (Vol. 2, pp. 29–55). Hillsdale, NJ: Erlbaum.

Cummins, J. (1981). The role of primary language development in promoting educational success for language minority students. In *Schooling and language minority students: A theoretical framework* (pp. 3–49). California State Department of Education. Los Angeles, CA: California State University, Evaluation, Dissemination and Assessment Center.

Goldman, S. R., Reyes, María, & Varnhagen, C. K. (1984). Understanding fables in first and second languages. *Journal of the National Association for Bilingual Education* (NABE), *8* (2), 35–66.

Jordan, C., & Tharp, R. (1979). In A. Marsella, Roland G. Tharp & Thomas P. Ciborowski (Eds.), *Perspectives in cross-cultural psychology*. New York: Academic Press.

LaBerge, D., & Samuel, S. J. (1974). Toward a theory of automatic information processing in reading. *Cognitive Psychology, 6*, 293–323.

Mandler, J. M., & Johnson, N. S. (1977). Remembrance of things parsed: Story structure and recall. *Cognitive Psychology, 9*, 111–151.

Meyer, B. J. F. (1975). Identification of the structure of prose and its implications for the study of reading and memory. *Journal of Reading Behavior, 7*, 7–47.

Meyer, B. J. F. (1979). A selected review of discussion of basic research on prose comprehension. *Prose learning series.* Research Report No. 4. Tempe, AZ: Arizona State University, Department of Psychology.

Mosenthal, P., & Na, T. J. (1980). Quality of text recall as a function of children's classroom competence. *Journal of Experimental Child Psychology, 30*, 1–21.

Reyes, M. (1984). *Comprehension of expository texts: A study of third and fourth grade Spanish/English readers.* Unpublished Ph.D. dissertation, University of California, Santa Barbara.

Rubin, A. (1980). A theoretical taxonomy of the difference between oral and written language. In R. J. Spiro, B. C. Bruce, & W. F. Brewer (Eds.), *Theoretical issue in reading comprehension* (pp. 411–438). Hillsdale, NJ: Erlbaum.

Spiro, R. J., & Taylor, M. (1980). *On investigating children's transition from narrative to expository discourse: The multidimensional nature of psychological text classification.* Technical Report No. 195. Champaign, IL: Center for the Study of Reading.

Stein, N. L., & Glenn, C. G. (1979). An analysis of story comprehension elementary school children. In R. O. Freedle (Ed.), *New directions in discourse processing* (Vol. 2). Norwood, NJ: Ablex.

6

Oral Reading Miscues of Hispanic Good and Learning Disabled Students: Implications for Second Language Reading

Ofelia Miramontes

University of Colorado, Boulder

Introduction

A major thrust in the testing of linguistically and culturally distinct students has been directed toward the identification and development of appropriate, bilingual, nonbiased assessment procedures which will accurately assess student competencies and potential for learning (Baca & Chinn, 1981; Bailey & Harbin, 1980; Duffy, Salvia, Tucker, & Ysseldyke, 1981). A common characteristic of these procedures has been a primary focus on the structural features of language rather than on the semantics and use of language (Holland, 1975; Rees, 1978; Reid & Hresko, 1981). In cases where an effort is made to give language assessment tests in both Spanish and English, instruments usually follow the pattern of those designed in English, focusing on the student's ability to use a "standard" language correctly. These factors serve to highlight student deficits rather than their strength in language use.

Few studies in the area of learning disabilities have focused specifically on Hispanic students (Bernal, 1983). Little is known about these students' characteristics using test instruments which focus on semantic information and reading strategies, and which view these strategies within the context of a first and second language learning interaction. Information is also lacking on the ways in which young primary Spanish readers transfer reading skills to English reading. If the difficulties encountered by second language readers beginning to develop reading skills in English are not understood, they may be perceived as reading disorders or learning disabilities.

Learning Disabilities and Assessment

The area of learning disabilities (LD) deals primarily with language related disorders (PL 94–142), and students are placed in LD classes by a variety of assessment procedures. Language approaches which focus on the structural aspects of language have dominated this field (Rees, 1967; Hallahan & Bryan, 1979). This orientation to the study of language has resulted in a research emphasis on the observable, surface aspects of language.

In recent years, there has been a recognition that the surface structure of language, that is, the appropriate placement of grammatical components within an utterance, merely reflects a more fundamental level of understanding. This perspective of language as communication views the speaker as actively engaged in constructing the meaning of language interaction (Halliday, 1975; Magoon, 1977; Shuy, 1981).

For students who speak a language other than English, this shift in orientation has special implications. Very often, these students are asked to compete academically in an environment where concepts and ideas are encoded in a language they do not understand (Andersson & Boyer, 1978; Carter & Segura, 1979). When a limited English proficient student fails, it may be diagnosed as a learning disability. Yet the home language background and the degree of first language proficiency are often ignored in the assessment process (Cummins, 1984).

Various issues have been raised with respect to assessment and testing of linguistic minority students. One set of issues related to the assessment of all culturally diverse students deals with similarities and differences in acculturation among students, and the validity of testing instruments which reflect a particular culture, values, and life style as the measure of "standard" development of knowledge (Garcia, 1981; Mercer, 1979; Salvia & Ysseldyke, 1981). In addition to cultural assumptions, testing for language disorders assumes a basic level of expected experience and exposure to the English language, during the period of language development. Items are ranked to show this expected average contact. This raises several basic questions about the level of proficiency that children have in the language(s) they speak. The determination of proficiency is confounded by definitions of proficiency (Ulibarri, Spencer, & Rivas, 1981) and by the failure of existing tests to tell anything about the development of children whose language development has been in a language other than English.

The literature suggests that some of the limitations of current special education assessment for Hispanic students include: (a) little attention to early language development (Cummins, 1981; Langdon, 1983); (b) lack of information on home–school language interface (Cummins, 1981; De Avila, Duncan, Ulibarri, & Fleming, 1983; Trueba, 1983); (c) an overemphasis on the structural elements of "standard" English (Holland, 1975; Omark & Watson, 1983); (d) the exclusion of the pragmatic skills of language (Hallahan & Bryan, 1979; Reid & Hresko, 1981); and (e) little information on students' strategies for learning (Cole & Griffin, 1983, Trueba, 1983).

Figures for limited English proficient students in learning disability classes are difficult to gather. The variety and inconsistency in assessment techniques, as well as in criteria, make accurate counts difficult (Dew, 1984; Wright & Santa Cruz, 1983). Reports of Hispanic limited English proficient students in learning disabilities classes have ranged from 6%–7%, representation commensurate with this group's representation in the total school population (United States Comptroller General, 1981), to a 283% overrepresentation in Texas (Ortiz & Yates, 1981).

The study described in this chapter addressed several basic issues concerned with the first and second language reading process. In general, the previously mentioned biases in assessment, plus the absence of any normative data on the acquisition of Spanish reading skills by children not experiencing problems, make it extremely difficult to identify Hispanic learning disabled students. The reading strategies of four groups of students were examined through oral reading miscue analysis: good versus poor readers who had begun reading in English (GE and LDE) and those who had begun reading in Spanish (GS and LDS). For all students, there was some degree of familiarity with the "other" language, and oral reading was tested in both. The testing instrument selected was the Reading Miscue Inventory (RMI). This instrument allowed for a qualitative, as well as a quantitative, analysis of the reading process. A miscue is a misreading of text. This designation indicates that a miscue is a response cued by the context, experience, and language of the readers, and is not necessarily bad (Burke & Goodman, 1972).

Oral reading miscues were first analyzed in order to shed light on reading strategy similarities and differences among the various groups in terms of those that maintain either the structure or meaning of the text versus those that did not. A second set of questions explored differences among the four reader groups in each miscue category (graphic similarities, sound similarities, grammatic relationships, comprehension and grammatical relationships). Comparisons were conducted for both first and second reading languages.

Theoretical Perspective

Much energy has been expended on the issue of "bilingualism" as a causative factor of language problems and interference in language development. Recent research, however, indicates that bilingualism can provide positive cognitive benefits for students and cannot be linked directly with poor school achievement (Lambert, 1983; Troike, 1978). For language minority students language development issues revolve around socio-cultural, political, and educational environmental factors which impact the quality of language development (Tucker, 1980; Gaarder, 1978). Schools often fail to provide these youngsters with normal language development programs (Carter & Segura, 1979; Cummins, 1984; Tucker, 1980).

Most programs for limited English proficient students are compensatory in nature and based on a "philosophy that a non-English language constitutes an educational handicap for a child entering school and should gradually be replaced by English" (Andersson & Boyer, 1978, p. 63). When children come to school unable to speak English they are often perceived to have no language at all (Saville-Troike, 1979). In addition to the attitudinal problems encountered in the education of language minority students, information about the developmental interaction between a first and second language is limited. The fundamental importance of the primary language to the individual is often lost in the complexity of the arguments.

Language and Development

As children enter school, they bring with them a significant amount of cognitive, linguistic, and social skill. By the age of 6, most children have the basic phonological, syntactic, and semantic skills acquired by most native speakers (Saville-Troike, 1979; Padilla & Liebman, 1975). Additionally, children have formed concepts related to the interaction between themselves, their family, and their environment that are encoded in their primary language. These concepts help to shape their view of the world. As children develop they learn to control and modify their environment through familial interactions (Mead, 1977; Vygotsky, 1979). The school takes what children bring and begins to build upon, and expand, this foundation of learning. For all children, the meaning of these concepts and skills is encoded in the language of the home. Limited English proficient children also come to school with a fund of knowledge to contribute to the new learning situation. They are ready to have their conceptual knowledge expanded. Very basically, they can "listen, understand, speak and be understood" (Thonis, 1970) in the primary language. This understanding reflects a knowledge and understanding of thoughts and feelings, ideas, and relationships they have experienced. Therefore, this knowledge will serve as the frame of reference the child uses to understand the information in new settings such as the school.

The development of language plays a vital role in the socialization of the young child. Although research is not conclusive as to the specific relationship between language and thought, the significance of this relationship is clear (Vygotsky, 1979; Ginsburg & Opper, 1979; Mead, 1977; Parsons, 1961). Regardless of the specific place language occupies in the development of the individual personality, it is clear that its role is fundamental in naming, experiencing, and defining peoples' constructs of reality. For an individual developing an understanding of the world, each new experience builds on previous experience. Individuals use their accumulated knowledge to interpret new learning. Learning rests on individuals' abilities to derive meaning from their experiences. What an individual comprehends and does with this understanding is the essence of "learning." In assessing the limited English proficient student, therefore, an understanding of the student's cognitive experiences as well as proficiency in the first language must be an integral part of the assessment process. If these students are to wait for the development of new concepts and skills until they have enough English, they will be effectively blocked from using their available cognitive tools to the level of their full potential.

Assessment

As changes occur in special education assessment, research in this area is being focused on the process used to gain meaning both from communication as well as from print. The broadening perspectives of language assessment are opening new avenues for gathering information on student abilities and needs. These new perspectives shift the focus of assessment from the directly observable aspects of language to the inclusion of social context and an emphasis on how meaning is derived from communication.

In terms of reading, it has shifted the emphasis to the experiential and conceptual base which the reader brings to the printed page, and the process the individual uses to gain meaning from print (Smith, 1978; Spencer, 1979). These include focusing on the experiences and information a reader brings to the task of gaining meaning from print. In 1965, Kenneth Goodman developed a theory and taxonomy for the analysis of oral reading processes. This theory is based on the idea that the reader is an active participant in constructing the meaning of written text. Goodman felt that psycholinguistic reading processes can be revealed by "comparing unexpected responses in oral reading to expected responses" (1969, p. 12). The observed responses reveal both the strengths and weakness of readers.

Deviations from the text are called miscues, "rather than errors in order to avoid the negative connotation of errors (all miscues are not bad) and to avoid the implications that good readers do not make miscues" (Goodman, 1967). Goodman's taxonomy was simplified and developed into the Reading Miscue Inventory (RMI) by C. Burke and Y. Goodman in 1972. The RMI provides an opportunity not only for assessing types of miscues made by readers, but also for observing the reading process in a systematic way. Miscues provide a way of observing and evaluating strategies used by the student to approach the reading task. This type of analysis allows a much broader picture of reading skills than is possible by a reliance only on test scores, the by-products of standardized assessment. It allows a focus on the strengths of the readers. In this way, the strengths brought to English reading by primary language readers of Spanish can be assessed.

Research using the Reading Miscue Inventory has begun to shed some light on the reading processes used by Hispanic students (Hudelson-Lopez, 1975; Barrera, 1978; Eaton, 1979). These studies on Mexican American students have generally been focused on defining Spanish reading as a multifaceted process rather than one which is centered exclusively on any one strategy, particularly phonics. They have also demonstrated that miscues are similar for the readers in both languages, indicating that strategies are being carried over into English reading. None of these studies have included Hispanic learning disabled students.

In summary, factors that can affect the assessment and placement of limited English proficient students in learning disabilities classes include attitudes toward languages other than English, the definition of proficiency, the focus of test instruments, knowledge about first and second language interaction, cultural bias of tests, context and environment of testing, and the preparation and language proficiency of the assessor. In addition, the literature suggests that background information on the child's language development experiences is very important. Other important issues that contribute to inaccurate assessment of Hispanic learning disabled students include a lack of research in the area of first and second language interaction within the reading process (Cummins, 1981; Tempes, 1982). Perceptions and knowledge about the importance of language, about the skills students bring, and about assessment procedures which allow a broad perspective of assessment help shape the expectancies and approaches used in instruction. These expectancies and approaches can result in appropriate instruction geared to the level of student development, or to inappropriate instruction which leads to poor skills development and poor achievement.

The research project described in this chapter investigated the types of text/meaning accurate miscues, by Reading Miscue Inventory category, made by selected Hispanic good readers and readers with learning disabilities. A major focus was to identify similarities and differences which would suggest directions for new approaches to second language reading instruction.

Two major considerations in the design of the study were related to the selection of the test instrument and to the particular types of students to be tested. The instrument needed to allow an assessment of strategies across a variety of behaviors. The protocol for the Reading Miscue Inventory (RMI) allowed, not only the tabulation of miscues across categories, but the observation of the reading process as well.

Student groups were carefully selected to show two primary reading language instructional settings—Spanish and English, and two levels of proficiency within those settings—good readers and readers with learning disabilities. Students were then tested in both languages for all cases possible.[1]

Subjects

Forty upper elementary (fourth, fifth, and sixth grade) students were selected from year-round schools located in a large urban school district in California. The schools were 90% Hispanic and situated within a 12-mile radius. A kindergarten through sixth grade Spanish-English bilingual program was being implemented in each school.

Four groups of 10 students each were selected: (a) good readers whose primary reading language was Spanish (GS); (b) good readers whose primary reading language was English (GE); (c) learning disabled students whose primary reading language was Spanish (LDS); and (d) learning disabled students whose primary reading language was English (LDE).

Students at these grade levels were selected in order to minimize factors of beginning reading instruction particularly for those students designated as good readers. Reading ability at this level should also reflect greater flexibility with the reading process. In addition, the selection of students at these grade levels insured that most students had begun English reading instruction.

School rosters, Comprehensive Test of Basic Skills (CTBS) scores (English/Español), District Reading Program scores, and teacher verification were used to select successful readers. Rosters from the resource specialist program were used to select learning disabled students with reading disabilities.

The characteristics of each group are detailed below:

---

[1] Students were selected for their primary reading language. Therefore, not all students in each group had received second language reading instruction. All students in the (GS) groups had received second language reading instruction in English. Nine of the 10 good readers (GE) had second language reading instruction in Spanish. The number of learning disabled students able to read in their second language was low (LDS, $N = 7$, LDE, $N = 5$).

Group GS. Primary reading instruction for these students had been in Spanish. The GS students represented good readers who had participated in a sequenced bilingual instructional program which included literacy skills in Spanish, and daily oral English-as-a-second-language (ESL) instruction for a minimum of 2 years.

Teachers from the selected grade levels were asked to submit names of "good" readers of Spanish from their classes. Each student selected was screened for a total reading score on the CTBS-Español of no more than 0.05 below grade level ($M = 6.5$). Every student in this group had also begun the transition into English reading in the early part of third grade, and was now receiving English reading instruction (as well as Spanish reading instruction) on a daily basis. These students' mean score on the English CTBS was 4.8. This group was composed of three fourth grade, four fifth grade, and three sixth grade students. Student mean age was 10.5.

Group GE. The GE students represented good readers who had received an all-English basic skills instructional program and had begun reading instruction in English. Each student had been enrolled in this type of program for at least three years at the same school. Teachers from each grade level selected good readers from their classes. Each student was screened for a CTBS-English total score of no more than 0.5 below grade level ($M = 5.7$). Five fourth grade, one fifth grade, and four sixth grade students were selected for this group (mean age = 9.9). Because most of these students were in a school which offered Spanish-as-a-second-language (SSL) instruction for English dominant students, 9 of the 10 had received formal SSL instruction (K-3). Every student in this group had contact with Spanish in the home.

Group LDS. The LDS students had begun reading instruction in Spanish and had been placed in special education specifically for a reading disability, as verified by their Individual Education Plan (IEP).[2] Seven of the 10 students were receiving special education resource room services in English on a pull-out basis. Two of the students were receiving resource room services in Spanish. Only one of the students had taken the CTBS in English, indicating that they had not yet reached sufficient English proficiency (as determined by district policy) to take the test. CTBS-Español scores were available for only four students in this group, Mean = 2.6. This group was composed of four fourth grade, two fifth grade, and four sixth grade students (mean age 10.9).

Group LDE. The LDE students had begun reading instruction in

---

[2] In the schools with strong bilingual programs, few Hispanic students with an all English background were found in special education classes. A possible explanation is that linguistically different students who were experiencing difficulties in all English programs may have been placed in Spanish reading programs as an alternative to special education.

English. All had been referred and placed in a learning disabilities program for reading difficulties. School records indicated a possible Spanish dominance for five of the students, four students were judged to be bilingual, and one was English dominant. For nine of the 10 students, Spanish was listed as the home language. A waiver was on file for five of the 10 students, indicating parent unwillingness to have the student receive instruction in Spanish. Selection of these students as reading disabled was verified by Individual Education Plans (IEP). This group was composed of one fourth grade, three fifth grade, and six sixth grade students (mean age 11.4). CTBS scores were available for 8 of the 10 students ($M = 2.8$).

The Test Instrument

The RMI was developed as a diagnostic instrument. It allows analysis of specific reading skill categories within the context of an entire sentence or paragraph. The RMI provided a vehicle for the assessment of both qualitative and quantitative dimensions of the reading process. Miscues were scored to indicate the function of language, not only within structure, but in terms of the meaning students derived from their reading. In addition, it was possible to observe other aspects of the reading process such as fluency, degree of comfort, coping and avoidance strategies, stress level, and the general quality of the students' interaction with the printed word, although these data are not discussed here.

Preparation of Test Materials

Reading materials unfamiliar to the students and approximately one grade level above their present reading level were selected for the testing. Each story was prepared following the format suggestions in the RMI Manual. One copy of each story was prepared for the students. A second copy was prepared to be used for scoring.

Stories selected for testing ranged from the primer level to a sophisticated literary selection. In order to elicit miscues in the first three categories of the RMI from good Spanish readers, a literary selection which was quite difficult in terms of content and style was chosen.

Testing Sessions

Two 45-minute testing sessions were required for each student. These sessions were scheduled approximately 1 week apart. For the GS and LDS groups, the first session was conducted entirely in Spanish, the second entirely in English. The language order was reversed for the GE and LDE groups. Thus, students always read first in their primary reading language. The procedure outlined in the RMI was strictly followed. Students were asked to read their story and advised that they would not receive any help. They were encouraged to keep reading and if they came to a word they did not know, to skip it and continue reading. They were also advised that they would be asked to retell the story in their own words. Each session was tape recorded.

Miscues were marked in each session with the student and later rechecked from a tape recording of the session. The first page of each recording was not used, although it was marked as the student read. This gave the student an opportunity to adjust to the reading situation. The next 25 miscues from each reading sample were analyzed in terms of the nine basic questions in the categories shown in Table 1. These nine questions were used to derive scores in seven categories, five of which are the focus of the present analysis.

Table 1. Questions and Examples of Miscues for the Nine RMI Questions.

1. DIALECT. Is a dialect variation involved in the miscue?
    Example: Text   Miscue
                    smoke   esmoke
                    Mrs. Miller   Miss Misher

2. INTONATION. Is a shift in intonation involved in the miscue?
    Example: Text   Miscue
                    jumped   jump ped

3. GRAPHIC SIMILARITY. Does the miscue look like what was expected?
    Example: Text   Miscue
    Spanish   alumbrame   alumbrar
                    cavó un hueco   cavo un hueco
    English   geography   gee graphy

4. SOUND SIMILARITY. Does the miscue sound like what was expected?
    Example: Text   Miscue
    Spanish   hondo   honda
    English   Detta   Delta

5. GRAMMATICAL FUNCTION. Is the grammatical function the same as the grammatical function of the word in the text?
    Example:
                                                    sembrando
    Spanish   Anoche un conejo entro al (sembrado) y se comidio todo un surco de tomates.
                                            thirty
    English   Maybe if she's (thirsty) enough she'll take some.

6. CORRECTION. Is the miscue corrected?
    Example:
                                                                    ⓒcasa
    Spanish   Los dos muchachos se acomodaron uno a cada lado de la piedra.
    English   ... then got to his feet and ran for the
                                    ⓒslop
                    tree-covered (slope.)

Table 1. (*Continued*)

7–8. GRAMMATICAL ACCEPTABILITY. Does the miscue occur in a structure which is grammatically acceptable?

8. SEMANTIC ACCEPTABILITY. Does the miscue occur in a structure which is semantically acceptable?
Example:

Spanish   El (consejo) de don Luis no resultó. [conejo]

English   Jackson saw the window spiderweb, break inward with a dull crunch that sent (cubes) of safety glass spraying. [chunks]

9. MEANING CHANGE. Does the miscue result in a change of meaning?
Example:

Spanish   Monica lo llevó a un lado (de la) granja. [del la] Cuanto el Granjo pasó (Junto a Guapo puso) un balde con cepillos [espillos] y una botella de aceite mineral.

English   Gasping, he ducked to avoid the ② (clawing) [①clown] paw that swept in side. ② (Then) the grizzly [①The] [graysly] caught the panel and (yanked,) tearing away [junked] the locked door.

Results

Table 2 presents a summary of mean scores (range 0–25) and standard deviations for each group across each of the five miscue categories. Each miscue was scored with respect to each of the five categories. The data in Table 2 reflect the mean number of miscues that were similar to the original text (a) orthographically, or (b) phonetically, or that retained the (c) grammatical function, (d) meaning, or (e) grammatical relationship of the original text. The first three categories (graphic similarity, sound similarity, and grammatical function) provide an assessment of miscues in terms of the students' literal adherence to the text in their efforts to "read" the word. For purposes of this study, these categories are designated as "decoding" to indicate skills used in the translation of symbols to sounds in the process of gaining comprehension. The last two categories (comprehension and grammatical relationships) provide a semantic factor of analysis and will be designated as "semantic" categories. The

Table 2. Summary of Mean Scores and Standard Deviations for each Group on each of the Five Miscue Categories

		Primary Language						Second Language			
		GE-E N = 10	GS-S N = 10	LDS-S N = 10	LDE-E N = 10	GE-S N = 9		GS-E N = 10	LDS-E N = 7	LDE-S N = 5	
Graphic Similarity											
Yes	$\bar{X}$	14.90	21.90	22.10	17.00	22.67		21.60	21.14	19.80	
	SD	2.56	1.91	2.42	5.08	1.94		2.01	2.73	6.14	
Sound Similarity											
Yes	$\bar{X}$	12.70	21.70	22.00	15.70	22.80		21.20	20.86	20.00	
	SD	3.80	2.41	2.36	6.65	1.79		2.20	2.04	5.70	
Grammatical Function											
Yes	$\bar{X}$	10.50	19.60	18.20	12.40	21.44		19.90	16.14	16.20	
	SD	4.28	2.91	3.39	3.57	2.46		3.31	1.21	6.38	
Comprehension											
No Loss	$\bar{X}$	11.30	13.40	10.30	7.00	11.44		15.50	7.71	10.60	
	SD	2.95	4.97	6.04	2.83	3.75		4.06	2.56	5.90	
Grammatical Relationships	$\bar{X}$	10.70	15.70	10.40	7.30	11.00		15.20	7.57	9.80	
Strength	SD	3.13	3.37	4.85	2.67	4.50		2.14	2.15	5.85	

mean data were analyzed (a) for selected intergroup comparisons across miscue categories and (b) to compare the five miscue categories across the four groups of readers. Separate comparisons were conducted for primary and secondary reading languages.

In the primary reading language, GS readers' miscues preserved the text more often than those of the GE readers. Furthermore, the three "decoding" categories show a greater difference than the two "semantic." The findings for the LDS versus LDE readers was similar. Differences between G and LD groups within each language were not significant. For example about 80% of the GS reader miscues preserved graphic similarity. The percentage was similar for the LDS group. Miscues occurring during reading in the second language showed a different pattern of group differences. Miscues preserved the text equally often across all four groups for the three decoding categories. However, good readers' miscues (GE and GS) were more likely to preserve the semantics than were the miscues of the poorer readers (LDS and LDE). The analyses of the five categories detail these general trends for primary and then for secondary reading languages.

Significant differences between groups were found for every miscue category in the primary reading language analyses. Scheffé tests were used to determine specific group differences within each category.

Graphic Similarity. A "yes" score in the graphic similarity category indicates that the miscue looked like the presented text. ANOVA indicated a significant difference between the groups, $F(3, 36) = 7.14\, p < .01$. Through the Scheffé procedure it was determined that there was a significant difference for Spanish primary readers (GS and LDS) when compared to English primary readers (GE and LDE). Spanish good readers scored higher in the use of miscues which retained graphic similarity to the text. No significant difference was found between good readers and learning disabled readers of the same primary language.

Sound Similarity. A "yes" score in the sound similarity category indicates that the miscue sounded like the word that was in the text. A significant difference was found between Spanish primary language readers (GS and LDS) and English primary language readers (GE and LDE) for this category. Spanish primary readers made miscues which retained a greater degree of similarity to the text than those of the English readers, $F(3, 36) = 12.01, p < .01$. No significant difference was found between good readers and learning disabled readers of the same primary reading group.

Grammatical Function. A "yes" in the grammatical function category indicates that the miscue retained the grammatical function of the presented word. Significant differences existed only between the combined Spanish readers (GS and LDS) and the combined English readers (GE and LDE). No significant difference was found between Spanish good and learning disabled students nor between English good and learning disabled students. In this category, good and learning disabled students of the same language group seemed to do equally well.

Comprehension and Grammatical Relationship. In the comprehension category a significant difference existed between good readers (GS and GE) and learning disabled (LDS and LDE) readers, $F (3, 36) = 3.66$, $p < .05$. Miscues made by good readers retained the meaning of the text more often than those of learning disabled students. No significant difference was found between good and learning disabled readers of the same primary language (GE versus LDE) or (GS versus LDS). A significant difference between the groups was found for the grammatical relationship category $F (3, 36) = 9.32$, $p < .01$. The GS and LDS groups showed a significant difference but no significant difference was found between GE and LDE groups. The miscues of good Spanish readers reflected a significantly greater successful use of this strategy than those of the other three groups. The second language data reflected different patterns across groups than the patterns in the primary reading language.

Graphic and Sound Similarity. All students made miscues in these two categories at about the same rate, and with the same relative text/meaning accuracy. However, for the GE and LDE groups, Spanish reading miscues in the graphic and sound similarities categories were different from the reading miscues made in their primary reading language. In their second reading language, these students made more miscues that adhered to the graphic and sound representation of the text than were evident when they read in English.

The difference between scores for good English readers might indicate some adaptation of strategies by good English readers depending on the nature of the language being read. This may be a viable conclusion particularly since comprehension and grammatical relationship scores were not significantly different from those evident in their primary reading language.

Grammatical Function. A significant difference was found between groups for the grammatical function category, $F (3, 27) = 4.46, p < .01$. A significant difference existed between good readers (GS and GE) and learning disabled readers (LDS and LDE). Good readers were more successful in matching the grammatical function of the words in the text. In contrast, when reading in the primary language, group differences in this category were related to reading language and not to skill.

Comprehension and Grammatical Relationship. In the categories most closely related to semantic criteria (comprehension and grammatical relationships), a significant difference was found between groups for both categories, $F (3, 27) = 5.36, p < .01$ and $F (3, 27) = 6.38, p < .01$, respectively. For both the comprehension and grammatical relationship miscue categories, Scheffé tests revealed that GS readers reading in English more often retained the semantics of the text in their miscues than did LDS readers reading in English. Performances by the GE and LDE groups reading in Spanish were equivalent and similar to the pattern that emerged for these groups when reading in English.

Miscues made during primary language reading indicate that Spanish readers rely on text cues, as reflected in the first three categories of the Reading Miscue Inventory, more literally than their English counterparts. Graphic and sound miscues correspond more closely to the text. Grammatical function miscues retained the function of the word within the sentence more often than miscues made in this category by English readers.

In the categories with a semantic weighting, no significant difference was found between good and learning disabled readers in the same primary reading language. This is accounted for in part by the variability in scores within groups. In the comprehension category, a significant difference existed between the combined group of good readers (GS and GE) and the combined learning disabled group (LDS and LDE). Good readers were better able to retain the grammatical relationship of the sentence if a miscue was made. In the grammatical relationship category, the Spanish primary language good readers (GS) were significantly different from all of the other groups. Miscues made by GS readers were semantically and grammatically acceptable within the text (or were corrected), more often than those of the other three groups.

In contrast, miscues made when reading in the second language tended to retain the orthographic and phonetic properties of the misread word equally often across all four groups. Preservation of grammatical function, relationship, and meaning in the miscues made during second language reading was more likely for good than learning disabled readers. Thus, patterns of miscues made during primary language reading were more similar for students with a common first language; i.e., GE and LDE readers' miscues were more similar than GE's were to GS's, or LDE's were to LDS's. In the second language, similarity was related to skill rather than language group; i.e., GE's and GS's miscues were more similar to one another's than GE's were to LDE's or GS's were to LDS's. These apparent differences among the four groups were explored further through a principal components factor analysis.

Factor Analysis

The factor analysis was used to identify the nature of the constructs underlying differences between these groups. An R-mode factor analysis was carried out on the miscue data for the four reading groups in their primary reading language. The number of factors to be retained in the analysis was determined by retaining only those factors with eigen values greater than 1 (Table 3). Membership of the groups would not change if rotated.

Evaluation of the R-mode factor analysis resulted in the selection of the first two factors as the major causes of variation among the five categories. The first two factors together accounted for 90.7% of the total variance. Although Factor 1 is a group factor showing positive correlations with all five variables (categories), it is most heavily loaded on the first three variables, those representing the first three categories of the Reading Miscue Inventory—graphic similarity, sound similarity, and grammatical function. They correspond to the analysis of the text and can be designated as decoding miscues. Factor 1 therefore can be interpreted as representing text accurate decoding miscue strategies.

Factor 2 was most heavily loaded on the two miscue categories of comprehension and grammatic relations. These categories include an assessment of semantic factors in their analysis. Factor 2 was therefore interpreted as representing a semantic factor. The residual correlation matrix, a measure of the inability of the two retained factors to account for the variability in the original data set, showed residual correlation

Table 3. Calculated Eigenvalues and Contributions to Total Variance for each of the Factors Quantified from the Primary Reading Language Data

Factors	Eigenvalue	% Variance	Cumulative % Variance
1	3.0234	60.46	60.46
2	1.5121	30.24	90.71
3	0.2585	5.17	95.88
4	0.1511	3.02	98.90
5	0.0548	1.09	100.00

Factor Loadings Calculated from the Primary Language Miscue Data

Variable	Factors				
	1	2	3	4	5
1 Graphic Similarity	0.8005	−0.5191	−0.4780	0.3173	−0.5298
2 Sound Similarity	0.8811	−0.4173	−0.1918	−0.2800	0.7161
3 Grammatical Function	0.8962	−0.1485	0.8136	−0.0680	−0.2307
4 Comprehension	0.6232	0.7300	−0.2694	−0.6060	−0.2814
5 Grammatical Relationships	0.6438	0.7166	−0.0148	0.6701	0.2722

values near zero, indicating that the first two factors accounted for most of the variability in the reading miscue data.

A scatter plot of the calculated factor scores for the primary language data is illustrated in Figure 1. The GS, GE, and LDE groups are clearly separated on this plot. This supports the validity of the selection process used to place students in these groups. Spanish and English good readers are clearly separated along Factor 1 indicating that the strategies used by GS readers are more strongly correlated with text accurate decoding skills than those of GE readers.

The LDE and GE groups are clearly differentiated along Factor 2. LDE readers were less successful at retaining the meaning of the text when miscues were made. Furthermore, the LDE group is clearly separated from the GS along Factor 1. GE and LDE readers exhibited a very similar

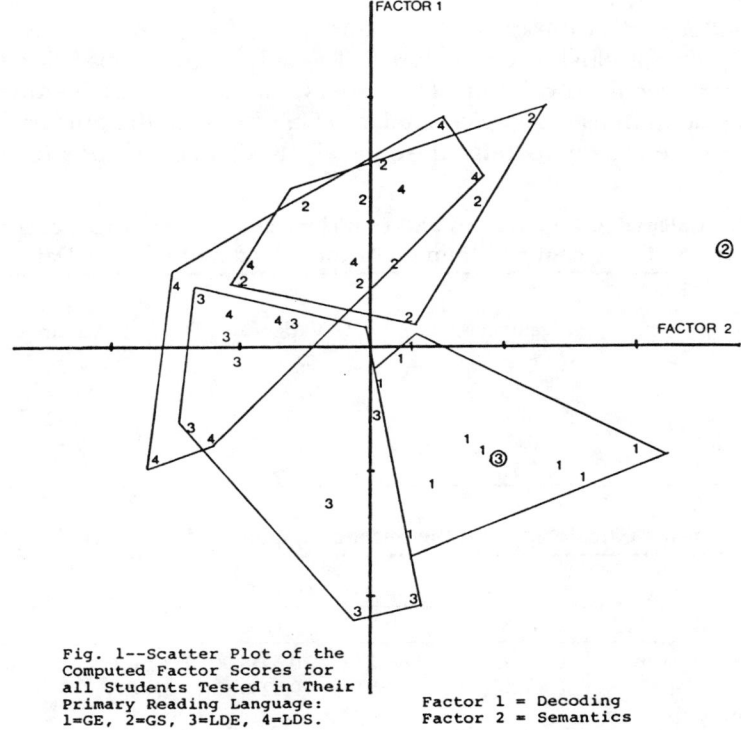

Fig. 1--Scatter Plot of the Computed Factor Scores for all Students Tested in Their Primary Reading Language: 1=GE, 2=GS, 3=LDE, 4=LDS.
Factor 1 = Decoding
Factor 2 = Semantics

Figure 1. Scatter plot of the computed factor scores for all students tested in their primary reading language: 1 = GE, 2 = GS, 3 = LDE, 4 = LDS. Factor 1 = Decoding, and Factor 2 = Semantics.

use of strategies in relation to this factor. Finally, the LDS group is the most diffuse. It overlaps two of the groups—the GS and LDE readers. Half of the LDS students grouped with the GS readers and the other half with the LDE readers. This overlap of groups, along with an evaluation of individual student scores, strongly suggests that possibly 50% of the primary Spanish LD students have been mislabeled as learning disabled by the schools.

A second principle components R-mode factor analysis was done on the secondary reading data and the results are shown in Table 4. The first two calculated factors accounted for 87.26% of the total variance among the five miscue categories.

Loadings are very similar to those in the primary reading language, except that Factor 1 in the second language was most heavily loaded on categories 2 and 3 (sound similarity and grammatic function) rather than on categories 1, 2, and 3.

A scatter plot of the calculated factor scores for the second reading language data is illustrated in Figure 2. The only definite separation was evident between the GS and LDS readers. None of the LDS students who appeared to use strategies similar to GS readers in the primary language (Figure 1) demonstrated the equivalent skill in the second reading

Table 4. Calculated Eigenvalues and Contributions to Total Variance for each of the Factors Quantified from the Second Reading Language Data

Factors	Eigenvalue	% Variance	Cumulative % Variance
1	2.82	56.59	56.59
2	1.53	30.67	87.26
3	0.34	6.95	94.22
4	0.17	3.43	97.66
5	0.11	2.33	100.00

Factor Loadings Calculated from the Second Language Miscue Data

Variable	Factors				
	1	2	3	4	5
1 Graphic Similarity	0.6705	−0.6322	−0.5938	−0.1643	−0.4483
2 Sound Similarity	0.8523	−0.4385	−0.0236	0.4017	0.6753
3 Grammatical Function	0.8779	−0.1190	0.7452	−0.2381	−0.3263
4 Comprehension	0.6891	0.6508	−0.2648	−0.6087	−0.3396
5 Grammatical Relationships	0.6390	0.7099	−0.1465	0.6200	0.3482

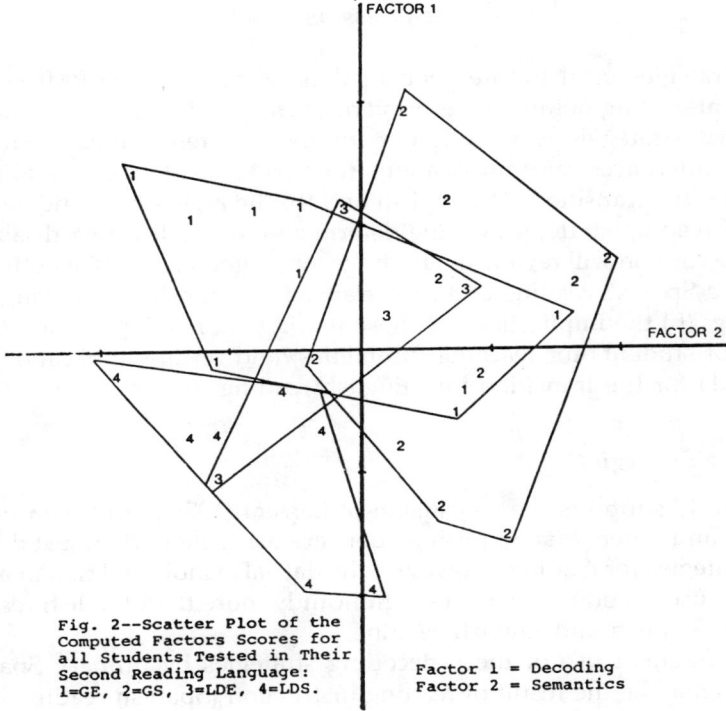

Fig. 2--Scatter Plot of the Computed Factors Scores for all Students Tested in Their Second Reading Language: 1=GE, 2=GS, 3=LDE, 4=LDS.

Factor 1 = Decoding
Factor 2 = Semantics

Figure 2. Scatter plot of the computed factors scores for all students tested in their second reading language: 1 = GE, 2 = GS, 3 = LDE, 4 = LDS. Factor 1 = Decoding, and Factor 2 = Semantics.

language. This may indicate a more limited English proficiency on the part of LDS students as compared to GS students. GE students in their second language demonstrated a much higher correlation with Factor 1 (decoding) than they had in their primary reading language. Of the four LDE readers who were able to read in Spanish, their second language, two of these students showed similar strategy use to that of GS readers. However, the sample size is small and analysis should be repeated with a larger number of students.

In summary, the factor analysis validated the group selection process and showed that in the primary reading language groups could be separated on two factors, decoding and semantic. The results also indicated the possibility that 50% of the LDS group might be mislabeled as learning disabled by the special education assessment conducted to determine a disability.

Discussion

The strategies used by the good readers tested with the RMI lead to some interesting points for discussion. These points revolve around the fact that strategies were different for the selected language groups. These differences raise implications for two areas of educational planning: (a) the transition into English and (b) the assessment and evaluation of reading strategies for the determination of a learning disability. This discussion will review the findings for (a) good readers in both English and Spanish reading and their transfer to English second language reading; (b) the implications of these findings in relation to the assessment of students for learning disabilities; and (c) the implications for curricula for the transition into English reading.

Reading Strategies

This study supports the conclusion of Barrera (1978), Hudelson-Lopez (1975), and others that Spanish readers are using more than just decoding strategies for reading. However, the data also indicated that Spanish readers use decoding strategies significantly more than English readers in both Spanish and English reading.

The frequent use of these decoding strategies by primary Spanish readers may be the result of reading instruction (Spanish reading is often taught using a highly phonetic approach because of the strong sound–symbol correspondence of the language) or an outcome of their effectiveness given the high sound–symbol correspondence of Spanish. These strategies appear to play an important role in the good Spanish readers' skills repertoire. These strategies are not used extensively by good English readers, however. Although it is clear that getting the message is the most important goal of reading, part of the process of obtaining that message may be more closely tied to different strategies depending on the language being read.

The theory that decoding strategies may be a natural part of the Spanish reading process gains support from the results of the miscue analysis of the good English (GE) group. These students exhibited a marked contrast in decoding strategies between English reading and Spanish reading. Although, in English, this group did not make many miscues which were graphically or phonemically similar to the words in the text, they relied twice as much on these miscue categories (decoding) when they read in Spanish, their second language. Two possible explanations can be advanced for the difference between the first and second language reading strategies evidenced by these readers. First, it can be argued that a heavy reliance on decoding strategies in Spanish reflects a more limited proficiency with this language. However, comprehension and retell scores for these readers (GE-S) were relatively high, both in relation to the other groups and in relation to their scores in English reading. A second explanation, given the level of comprehension exhibited in the two reading samples, is that these students were aware that different strategies could be employed for Spanish Reading, and that they were adjusting their strategy use accordingly.

Strategy Transfer

Although data on Spanish readers engaged in English print is limited, Hudelson-Lopez (1975), Barrera (1978), Rodriguez-Brown and Yirchott (1980), and Thonis, (1981) have indicated that many skills from reading in the first language transfer to the second language. The data analyzed in this study also suggest that successful Spanish readers bring a variety of skills to the task of reading English. Among those skills is a well developed use of graphic, phonic, and grammatic clues.

The results indicate that GS readers are using phonetic clues for English reading with a high degree of frequency and with close adherence to the graphic representation and sounds of the text. As indicated above, good English readers do not use these skills extensively. Therefore, a mismatch may exist in the area of decoding between the skills needed in English reading and those that are being brought to this task by the Spanish readers.

Many English transition reading programs use a decoding or phonetic approach. These programs are based on learning a set of consistent sounds of English (such as short vowel sounds), as a basis for English reading. Such an approach serves to reinforce the idea of a reliable, consistent sounding process for English, perhaps creating a false expectation of English reading for a second language reader. These results suggest that students should develop an awareness of the importance of using additional reading strategies for English reading. Students may also require the ability to adapt reading strategies to the nature of the language they are reading, much in the same way that a reader reads in different ways depending on the nature of the text, i.e., recreational, formal, etc.

Possible Misperceptions

The use of decoding strategies may have an impact on how a Spanish reader's proficiency in English reading is perceived. The data have indicated a high use of decoding strategies for Spanish good readers. The high transfer of decoding strategies by good Spanish readers to English reading, may be perceived as a negative factor because of a perception that good readers are not usually bound to the graphic stimulus. It would be erroneous to conclude however, that, because Spanish readers exhibit more use of decoding strategies, they are less proficient in comprehending what is being read. The use of these strategies did not preclude understanding.

Moll and Diaz (1982) have demonstrated that Spanish reading teachers, and teachers who initiate English reading perceive Spanish primary language readers differently. They also found that there was little communication between these teachers with regard to the level of proficiency and sophistication of the transition reader. This lack of interchange of information serves to perpetuate inappropriate and inefficient programs for the transition into English reading. Perceiving the use of decoding strategies as a lack of proficiency may cause students to be given reading materials that are at a level far below their ability to comprehend. This will effectively retard the process of using reading to extend experiences and concepts. If on the other hand, the use of these strategies is perceived as a basic part of a total, successful reading strategy, teachers can direct students in learning how to use decoding skills more appropriately when reading and help students to strengthen other avenues for gaining meaning from print.

A second problem centers on the fact that the Spanish readers' frequent use of decoding strategies focuses attention on the pronunciation of words. Second language readers are also generally in the process of acquiring oral fluency in the second language. This emphasis on the sounds of words may tend to highlight errors made by these nonnative speakers of English. Second language pronunciation and intonation differences may be perceived as a lack of oral and reading proficiency by teachers unfamiliar with the development of English second language learners. As students make the transition into English reading, an understanding of their first language skills can be important in designing programs for a smooth and efficient transition.

Impact on Assessment for Learning Disabilities

The findings discussed above can have a significant impact in the assessment and identification of learning disabilities. The literature indicates that there continues to be a lack of integration of first and second language learning for limited English proficient students (Cummins, 1981; Krashen, 1981; Thonis, 1983). Expectations for these readers are often inappropriate and methods used for instruction are often developmentally inappropriate. Even when testing is done in Spanish there continues to be a lack of information to help integrate these results into an academic learning program for the student.

Some of the factors identified above, such as the transfer of decoding strategies and the lack of information on Spanish reading abilities, could be particularly problematic for the less proficient Spanish reader. Data for LDS students indicated that their miscues were similar to those of good readers, both in categories and in level of adherence to the text, in the primary language. Seven of the 10 LDS students were able to read a story at the fourth grade level or above at the beginning of their present school year.

English assessment of these students, however, indicated important differences in all categories, particularly in the semantic areas. Information collected with the RMI and analyzed by factor analysis suggested that 50% of these students might be misclassified as learning disabled.

The discrepancy between the RMI primary language reading evaluation and the special education classification of these students raises several important questions about the criteria used to determine learning disabilities for limited English proficient students. For example, if the reader demonstrated fluency and understanding in Spanish reading, where does the disability appear? What have the students' previous schooling experiences been, and have these experiences prepared them for the requirements of U.S. schools? Are these adjustments impacting school performance? To what extent is a limited oral English ability impacting the student's ability to read in English? To what extent were Spanish reading skills assessed?

Language Proficiency for Transition

Studies in the area of bilingual education (Wong-Fillmore, 1980; Legarreta-Macaida, 1981) have demonstrated the importance of what Gaarder (1967) has identified as three crucial issues which determine whether a primary language other than English is an asset or a liability. These issues center around (a) how students have interacted with the two languages, (b) to what level of proficiency the first language was developed, and (c) under what conditions students were instructed in the second language.

The students selected for this study represented a variety of school language backgrounds. Significant miscue differences were found to exist between the groups. Of the four groups of readers, the Spanish primary language good readers (GS) demonstrated the highest mean scores in all categories in the primary reading language. They also had the highest mean scores in the second language in all categories except comprehension, where their scores were slightly below those of English good readers. Stories read by the GS group in English however, were at a higher grade level than those of the GE group in Spanish. These GS students had also received the most balanced first and second language instruction for the four groups and their school program included instruction in Spanish across all areas of the curriculum.

Good Spanish readers reflected the best retention of grammatical relationships of the four groups and had the highest level of proficiency in the second language. Lambert (1978) and others have indicated that individuals proficient in two languages are more aware of the interrelationships of language. The results of this study indicate that this higher level of proficiency in both languages is reflected in a greater use of the strategies reflecting grammatic acceptability and semantic acceptability.

English learning disabled students (LDE) on the other hand, had had the most erratic educational experiences. Although parent information indicated that the primary language of communication in the home was Spanish all of these youngsters had begun reading instruction in English. They had received no special instruction in English as a second language. These students showed the lowest overall scores in the semantic categories in the primary reading language. Although no record of Spanish reading instruction was found, three of these students were more successful reading in Spanish than in English.

The group of students who had developed the highest level of bilingual proficiency (GS) also made miscues which reflected the most successful use of miscue strategies, not only in the decoding categories but, more importantly, in the semantic categories. The data suggest that the continuity, sequence, and duration of primary and second language instruction makes a difference in the ability of students to use the processes reflected in the categories tested through oral reading using the Reading Miscue Inventory.

This study addressed several issues regarding reading strategies for linguistically different students. The results suggest the need for in-depth assessments of student skills in the mother tongue, the positive transfer of Spanish primary reading skills to second language reading, the need for a better understanding of the interactions of the first and second language in reading, and the importance of evaluating the features and quality of the child's previous school experiences. Of equal importance was the use of a methodology which provided the opportunity to observe reading strategies from several perspectives. This allowed the possibility of viewing student strengths as well as weaknesses.

Language is at the very core of the interactions between individuals and their world. It is fundamental to the development of the self. In determining instructional language for limited English proficient students, schools hold the key to social and cognitive growth for these students. But, they also hold the power to restrict, control, and limit, closing the door to the full realization of that potential.

References

Andersson, T., & Boyer, M. (1978). *Bilingual schooling in the United States* (2nd ed.). Austin, TX: National Educational Laboratory Publishers, Inc.

Baca, L., & Chinn, P. C. (1981). Coming to grips with cultural diversity. *Exceptional Education Quarterly, 2*(4), 33–45.

Bailey, D. B., Jr., & Harbin, G. L. (1980). Non-discriminatory evaluation. *Exceptional Children, 46*(8), 590–596.

Barrera, R. B. (1978). *Analysis and comparison of the first language and oral reading behavior of native Spanish speaking Mexican-American children*. Unpublished doctoral dissertation, University of Texas, Austin.

Bernal, E. M. (1983). Trends in bilingual special education. *Learning Disabilities Quarterly, 6*(4), 424–431.

Burke, C., & Goodman, Y. (1972). *Reading miscue inventory manual: Procedure for diagnosis and evaluation*. New York: Macmillan.

Carter, T. P., & Segura, R. D. (1979). *Mexican Americans in school: A decade of change*. Princeton, NJ: College Board Publications.

Cole, M., & Griffin, P. (1983). A socio-historical approach to re-mediation. *Quarterly Newsletter of the Laboratory of Comparative Human Cognition, 5*(4), 69–74.

Cummins, J. (1981). The role of primary language in promoting educational success for language minority students. In California State Dept. of Education, *Schooling and language minority students: A theoretical framework* (pp. 3–50). Los Angeles: California State University, Evaluation, Dissemination and Assessment Center.

Cummins, J. (1984). *Bilingualism and special education: Issues in assessment and pedagogy*. San Diego, CA: College-Hill Press.

De Avila, E. A., Duncan, S. E., Ulibarri, D. M., & Fleming, J. S. (1983). Predicting the academic success of minority language students from developmental, cognitive style, linguistic and teacher perception measures. In E. E. Garcia (Ed.), *The Mexican-American child: Language, cognition, and social development* (pp. 59–105). Tempe, AZ: Arizona State University.

Dew, N. (1984). Presentation made at the Council for Exceptional Children, Washington, D.C.

Duffy, J. B., Salvia, J., Tucker, J., & Ysseldyke, J. (1981). Nonbiased assessment: A need for operationalism. *Exceptional Children, 47*(6), 427–433.

Eaton, A. J. (1979). *A psycholinguistic analysis of the oral reading miscues of selected field-dependent and field independent native Spanish-speaking Mexican-American first grade children*. Unpublished doctoral dissertation, University of Texas, Austin.

Gaarder, B. (1978). Statement on literacy in T. Andersson & M. Boyer (Eds.), *Bilingual schooling in the United States* p. 79. Austin, TX: Southwest Educational Development Laboratory.

Garcia, J. (1981). The logic and limits of mental aptitude testing. *American Psychologist, 36*(10), 1172–1180.

Ginsburg, H., & Opper, S. (1979). *Piaget's theory of intellectual development.* Englewood Cliffs, NJ: Prentice-Hall.

Goodman, K. S. (1967). *The psycholinguistic nature of the reading process.* Detroit, MI: Wayne State University Press.

Goodman, K. S. (1969). Analysis of oral reading miscues: Applied psycholinguistics. *Reading Research Quarterly, 5*(1), 11–30.

Hallahan, D. P., & Bryan, T. H. (1979). Learning disabilities. In J. M. Kauffman & D. P. Hallahan (Eds.), *Handbook of special education* (pp. 141–164). Englewood Cliffs, NJ: Prentice-Hall.

Halliday, M. A. K. (1975). *Learning how to mean.* London: Edward Arnold Publishers.

Holland, A. L. (1975). Language therapy for children: Some thoughts on context and content. *Journal of Speech and Hearing Disorders, 40,* 514–523.

Hudelson-Lopez, S. J. (1975). *The use of context by Spanish-speaking Mexican-American children when they read in Spanish.* Unpublished doctoral dissertation, University of Texas, Austin.

Krashen, S. D. (1981). Bilingual education and second language acquisition theory. In California State Department of Education *Schooling and the language minority student: A theoretical framework* (pp. 51–82). Los Angeles: Evaluation, Dissemination and Assessment Center.

Lambert, W. E. (1983). Deciding on languages of instruction: Psychological and social considerations. In T. Usen & S. Opper (Eds.), *Multicultural and multilingual education in immigrant countries.* [Wenner-Gren Symposium Series, 38] (pp. 93–104). Elmsford, NY: Pergamon Press.

Langdon, H. W. (1983). Assessment and intervention strategies for the bilingual language-disordered student. *Exceptional Children, 5*(1), 37–46.

Legarreta-Marcaida, D. (1981). Effective use of the primary language in the classroom. In California State Department of Education *Schooling and language minority students: A theoretical framework* (pp. 83–117). Evaluation, Dissemination and Assessment Center.

Magoon, J. (1977). Constructivist approach in educational research. *Review of Educational Research, 47*(4), 651–693.

Mead, G. H. (1964). *George Herbert Mead On social psychology.* Chicago, IL: University of Chicago Press.

Mercer, J. (1979). *SOMPA technical manual.* New York: Psychological Testing Corp.

Moll L., & Diaz, E. (1982). *Bilingual communications in classroom contexts.* Final report. National Institute of Education.

Omark, D. J. & Watson, D. L. (1983). Psychological testing and bilingual education: The need for reconceptualization. In D. J. Omark & J. G. Erickson (Eds.), *The Bilingual Exceptional Child* (pp. 23–53). San Diego, CA: College-Hill Press, Inc.

Ortiz, A., & Yates, J. R. (1981, April). *Exceptional Hispanics: Implications for special education services and manpower planning.* Austin, TX: University of Texas.

Padilla, A. M., & Liebman, E. (1975). Language acquisition in the bilingual child. *The Bilingual Review, 2* (1,2), 34–35.

Parsons, T. (1961). Social structure and personality development. In B. Kaplan (Ed.), *Studying personality cross-culturally.* New York: Harper and Row.

Rees, N. S. 1978. Pragmatics of human communication: Applications to normal and disordered language development. In R. L. Schiefelbarch (Ed.), *Base of language intervention.* Baltimore, MD: University Park Press.

Reid, D. K. & Hresko, W. P. (1981). *A cognitive approach to learning disabilities.* New York: McGraw-Hill.

Rodriguez-Brown, F. W., & Yirchott, L. S. (1980). *A comparative analysis of reading miscues made by monolingual versus bilingual students.* Paper presented at the Annual Meeting of the American Educational Research Association.

Salvia, J., & Ysseldyke, J. E. (1981). *Assessment in special and remedial education* (2nd ed.). Boston: Houghton Mifflin Co.

Saville-Troike, M. (1979). First and second language acquisition. In H. T. Trueba & C. Barnett-Mizrahi (Eds.), *Bilingual multicultural education and the professional* (pp. 104–120). Boston, MA: Newbury House Publishers, Inc.

Shuy, R. (1981). A holistic view of language. *Research in the Teaching of English, 15*(2), 101–111.

Smith, F. (1978). *Understanding reading.* New York: Holt, Rinehart and Winston.

Spencer, P. L. (1979). *Reading reading.* Claremont, CA: Alpha Iota Chapter of Pi Lambda Theta.

Tempes, F. (1982). A theoretical framework for bilingual instruction: How does it apply to special education pp. 7–24. In A. M. Ochoa & J. Hurtado (Eds.), *Special education and the bilingual child, Proceedings.* San Diego: San Diego State University. National Origin Desegregation Lau Center.

Thonis, E. W. (1981). Reading instruction of language minority students. In California State Department of Education *Schooling and language minority students: A theoretical framework* (pp. 147–183). Los Angeles: Evaluation, Dissemination and Assessment Center.

Thonis, E. W. (1970). *Teaching reading to non-English speakers.* London: Collier-Macmillan International.

Troike, R. C. (1978). *Research evidence for the effectiveness of bilingual education.* Rosslyn, VA: National Clearinghouse for Bilingual Education.

Trueba, H. T. (1983). Adjustment problems of Mexican-American school children: An anthropological study. *Learning Disability Quarterly, 6*(4), 395–415.

Tucker, G. R. (1980). Implications for U.S. bilingual education: Evidence from Canadian research. *Focus, 2,* 1–2.

Ulibarri, D. M., Spencer, M., & Rivas, G. A. (1981). Language proficiency and academic achievement: A study of language proficiency tests and their relationship to school ratings as predictors of academic achievement. *NABE Journal, 5*(3), 47–80.

United States Comptroller General (1981, September 30). Disparities still exist in who gets special education. *Report to the Chairman, Subcommittee on Select*

Education, Committee on Education and Labor, House of Representatives*. Washington, DC: General Accounting Office.

Vygotsky, L. (1979). *Mind in society*. M. Cole, V. J. Steiner, S. Scribner, & E. Soubermann (Eds.), Cambridge: Harvard University Press.

Wong-Fillmore, L. (1980). *Language learning through bilingual instruction*. Berkeley, CA: University of California. (Mimeographed copy).

Wright, P., & Santa Cruz, R. (1983). Ethnic composition of special education programs in California. *Learning Disabilities Quarterly, 6*(4), 387–394.

7

The Development Of Writing Skills Among Hispanic High School Students*

Benji Wald

National Center for Bilingual Research

Introduction

Central to the following paper is the exploration of certain linguistic aspects of the English writing skills exhibited by relatively advanced high school students who are members of the East Los Angeles bilingual community. Of particular interest to the study to be discussed are the similarities and differences between the skills of *early* and *late* learners of both spoken and written English. Subsequent discussion will be more precise on how the concept of early and late learners was operationalized in the study reported below. The general concept distinguishes *early* as having had training in written English from childhood, and *late* as having begun this training in adolescence, not before 12 to 13 years of age.

The theoretical interest pursued below addresses the problem of characterizing linguistic aspects of relatively advanced writing skills—and then ascertaining to what extent these skills distinguish early and late learners. The findings suggest which writing skills are largely independent of the particular language in which they were first learned, and how these skills interact with language-specific knowledge necessary to advanced writing performance in English. Conclusions about the

---

*An earlier version of this paper was presented at a Hispanic SIG session of the 1984 AERA annual meeting in New Orleans on April 23, 1984. I would like to express my appreciation here to the audience for lively and thought provoking discussion during and after the session. The original research from which the present article is extracted was supported by the National Institute of Education through the National Center for Bilingual Research. No endorsement of anything contained herein by either of these institutes is implied by this acknowledgement.

distinguishing features of language-independent and language-dependent writing skills have practical implications for instructional programs aimed at English literacy for learners who are first introduced to English writing, and more generally to English language skills, at a relatively late age (the age of junior high school or later). As discussed below in the section on speech and writing, the strategy of comparing speech and writing for individuals and groups of learners assists in identifying language skills which are specific to or more favored in writing.

In the context of language minority communities, the issue of language-independent literacy skills, as developed below, owes much of its impetus to the research of a variety of scholars. Of particular importance, because of its influence on current thinking about the education of minority language students in the U.S., and its fundamental correctness, is the "interdependence hypothesis" proposed by Cummins (e.g., 1981b), and supported by the findings of Mace-Matluck, Dominguez, Holtzmann, and Hoover (1983), among others. Stated simply, the hypothesis proposes that certain literacy skills, first developed in one language, transfer naturally to other languages, so that initial literacy in one language contributes substantially to the development of literacy in subsequently learned languages. Thus, Mace-Matluck et al.'s 1983 Seattle study of English literacy among students of Cantonese language background reports that, when other factors are controlled for, there is a significant correlation between the literacy level achieved in English and training in Cantonese literacy prior to immigration to Seattle.

A major problem with the hypothesis is that, while studies establish a connection between literacy in a first and second language, they are inexplicit about what the connection is. In brief, they do not identify with any precision those literacy skills which do transfer and those which do not, nor do they specify how the process of transfer occurs. Consequently, they are limited in their ability to inform instructional practice about which skills need more overt attention than others at a given level of general literacy. For the most part, with regard to language minority populations, research has focused on the early stages of literacy, before and in the early grades of elementary school. At the secondary school level there is a noticeable gap in studies of writing skills for language minority students.

Considering what is at stake, given the large size of the major language minority populations, particularly among Hispanics, and the persistent pattern of low academic achievement, particularly among Mexican Americans both in the community studied here and much more generally, the present effort is relatively modest, examining a limited number of features of English writing among a small number of individuals. However, the strategies of observation used and the results obtained suggest directions for more extensive research and for integrating the findings of studies of general language development in first and second languages with the findings of studies of the development of spoken and written language.

The order of the following discussion will be: (a) a sketch of the development of literacy skills, focusing on writing and including indication of controversial areas, (b) the nature of the empirical study of writing skills among early and late learners in the East Los Angeles Mexican American community, (c) the findings of that study, (d) conclusions about the development of writing skills among early and late learners in Hispanic bilingual communities like East Lost Angeles, and (e) implications for educational approaches toward instruction in English literacy skills.

A Sketch of the Development of Literacy Skills

Writing is perhaps the most demanding of the literacy skills, at least to the extent that beyond the most elementary levels, successful writing also implies a certain level of skill in reading. At the most elementary level identified in the literature, that of "graphic sense" (e.g., Ferreiro, 1978), the relationship between reading and writing appears to be highly attenuated. At this level, a child may simply understand that written symbols may be used to represent spoken words or larger phrases. Thus, for example, Vygotsky (1978, pp. 112ff.) proposes that there is an impulse among children toward symbolic representation which transfers from drawing to reading. Vygotsky observes that, in the same way that a child's drawing does not attempt to accurately represent an object, e.g., the human body represented by a head with legs extended downward, initial writing is not intended to precisely represent articulated speech. In view of Read's (1980) further observation that neoliterate children may not be able to read their own writing, it may be inferred that the nature of the relationship between reading and writing, and the usual communicative purpose of writing, may not be clearly understood at the earliest stages. Children's early writing may simply be intended to represent "writing." A child may expect an adult to be able to read the child's own writing, just as adults can read other pieces of writing which the child cannot read. At this most rudimentary stage, two particular language-independent developments have been proposed (e.g., by Ferreiro, 1978). The most primitive is that messages expressible in speech are also representable graphically. The next stage decomposes graphic symbols into independently represented words. These stages may precede school instruction, depending on attention paid to literacy and literate activities in the child's home. They also recapitulate the early history of writing, before the invention of phonological writing systems reflected in syllabaries and alphabets.

Among alphabetic writing systems, formal instruction traditionally begins with alphabeticization and then the spelling of words. As the "phonetic" principle of further analyzing words into constituent sounds progresses, variations in spelling are found among learners (e.g., Edelsky, 1981a). We will later see that spelling variations may persist well into advanced levels of writing. The reasons for these variations may differ, depending on the learner's experience with English spelling. Presumably, at early stages in literacy the variation is the result of individual creativity precipitated by the acquisition of the phonetic principle, accompanied by failure to realize that spelling is conventional, that is, that words have unique spellings regardless of their pronunciation. The conventionalization principle of word representation applies to all languages which have a long history of writing, and apply to all writing systems whether or not alphabetic (e.g., the Chinese logographic system). Thus, the conventionalization principle, by the nature of the universal tendency to standardize written language in the face of diversity of pronunciation in the spoken language, is a language-independent principle of literacy. This principle is acquired early by formally instructed students. This does not mean, of course, that the students immediately acquire the formal conventions for spelling, but simply that they learn that there is a right way to spell a word, and that other ways are wrong, even if the intended word is clear despite the "wrong" spelling, e.g., *I, i,* or *ai* for *eye*. At the same time that students come to realize that the phonetic basis of spelling is mitigated by the conventionalization principle, they are also introduced to numerals and other mathematical symbols which represent words directly without any appeal to their phonological constituents.

In this context, this sketch of the development of writing may move on to more advanced literacy skills. For several decades, the trend in theories of the development of literacy, particularly those dealing with reading comprehension, have moved away from the phonetic principle as a mainstay of reading. Criticising theories and curricula which move from phonological decoding of words to the linear decoding of sentences and larger texts (labelled the "bottom up" theory), "holistic" or integrative theories have emphasized the progressive use of larger features of written context in the development of reading comprehension. Thus, the theories of Goodmans (e.g., 1978) have emphasized that development of reading comprehension relies minimally on phonetic decoding and maximally on integrating a variety of textual clues in the context of any particular word being read comprehendingly.

Early studies in support of integrative theories limited themselves to the analysis of sentences within larger texts. The Goodmans' particular method of miscue analysis among children in mid to late grades of elementary school led them to observe that more advanced readers less often performed reading miscues which were syntactically or semantically incoherent with the following portion of the sentence. Thus,

(1) He *pretended* (miscue for *patted*) him for a minute . . . (Goodman & Goodman, 1978, 4-68)

is an example of a miscue which leads to incoherence with the rest of the sentence, since the verb *pretend* takes an infinitival object, whereas the sentence continues with a direct object. The finding of decreasing miscues of this type among older more experienced readers suggests that a strictly linear strategy of word decoding is not prevalent among more developed readers. Instead, it can be inferred that the reader looks ahead to following parts of (at least) the sentence for cues to the meaning of a particular word.

More recent theories have arisen which go beyond the sentence unit to the role played by larger features of the structure of text in writing and speaking. These theories propose that reading comprehension is further assisted by more general knowledge of the nature of texts (e.g., Schank & Abelson, 1977; Kintsch & van Dijk, 1978; cf. Sanford & Garrod, 1981, esp. Ch. 4). At any point in the reading of a text, expectations are formed about the structure and content of the text beyond what has already been given in the text. This is done on accumulating knowledge about the organization and content of various types of texts (cf. the work of Fillmore & Kay, 1980, on textual prediction).

In general, these further theories involve *anticipatory* strategies, either of the direct type of deviating from a strictly linear pattern in reading for meaning, by scanning forward and then backward while reading, and through expectations about what form and content will be exhibited in further portions of text not yet read. These anticipatory strategies are most probably language-independent skills which are highly developed at more advanced stages in literacy. Later, it will be argued that anticipatory strategies have consequences for how spelling is monitored by early learners, and acquired by late learners. For the moment, however, discussion will turn to theoretical developments in the relation of speech and writing which guided the East Los Angeles writing study.

Speech and Writing

For many reasons, there has been a rapidly growing trend toward comparison of speech and writing. The most elementary consideration is that speech is observed to be universal among human societies, and requires no specific formal instruction to be acquired (except in the case of physiological or neurological impairment), while written language is a specific historical invention which is not universal among societies, and requires formal instruction. In addition, literacy may play different roles and entail different attitudes among different segments of a literate society. This is of particular importance to the study of literacy among language minority groups which have traditionally been relegated in large numbers to lower socioeconomic roles where less education and use of job-related literacy is required. Heath's work (1983) on early literacy experiences among middle class whites and working class whites and blacks in a Southern town exemplifies some of the diversity of practices and attitudes involving literacy within American society. Ethnographers of communication have further pointed out that class and caste-like ethnic differences are often associated with greater and lesser differences between spoken and standardly written languages. These differences extend not only to formal conventions governing vocabulary and syntactic constructions, but also to larger aspects of the organization of information in discourse. The work of Gumperz and associates (e.g., 1982) demonstrates that the manner in which information is organized in discourse is not universal, but varies across language areas. The work of Michaels (1981) suggests that transfer of organizational patterns of information in speech to writing gives an advantage to white middle class speakers, because the spoken conventions for informational organization of the white middle class is closer to the conventions required for writing in public schools.

From a quite different perspective, the work of Cummins (1984) has distinguished the acquisition of speech and literacy skills along the lines of a psychologistic model developed by Olson (1977). This model is based on the characterization of writing as "decontextualized," or, more moderately put, "context reduced," when compared to speech. Illustrative of this approach is the following citation on the "autonomy" of written text:

> Once the possibility develops that text can specify its meanings, it is not simply that the reader must learn to *confine interpretation to the information in the text*. . . The converse responsibility falls upon the writer. His task becomes that of attempting to create autonomous text—to write in such a manner that the sentence meaning is an adequate representation of the intended meaning and therefore relies solely on conventionalized or explicit premises and is not open to personal interpretation. (Olson & Torrance, 1981, p. 249; emphasis in original)

This model identifies two principles governing "autonomy" in writing: conventionalization and explicitness. Typical of theories which acknowledge the importance of social context in only a cursory manner, the notion of "conventionalized premises" is not clearly explicated. As the earlier discussion of ethnographic studies of variation in the structure of discourse across societies has indicated, the particular conventional premises referred to for autonomous text in the above quote may refer to an arbitrary but binding principle in academic writing. Where different societies indicate that there are different ways of organizing a text (or spoken discourse), the conventionalization of information in any particular way is arbitrary.

Much clearer in the citation is the principle of explicitness, traditional in theories of writing. The fundamental insight of the principle of explicitness derives from that aspect of spoken language which is self-evidently absent from written language, a shared physical environment which may supplement linguistic cues to meaning with paralinguistic cues such as gesture, facial expression, and body orientation, as well as the use of props and additional sensory aspects of the situation. Even in the absence of a shared physical environment, e.g., in telephone conversation, intonational contours, tone groupings, and an overlay of expressive phonological devices, as well as inherent sound qualities of the speaker (e.g., often cueing to the sex, age, SES status, etc., of the speaker) contribute to the communication in the situation, and play a role in interpretation of the communication. The absence of this context in writing, according to the theory, puts a greater burden on the use of written language to convey information and signal the context in which the communication is to be understood.

The difference between the amount of information conveyed by speech and writing can be readily appreciated by comparing the most explicit script with a theatrical performance based on it—or, better yet, two theatrical performances based on the same script (and similarly for written music where written cues for sound go far beyond what is usually encoded for written language). Among the writers of concern in this paper, there are numerous examples of the use of paralinguistic cues in speech to represent concrete information. One of the most obvious occurs when one late learner, in describing his house in Mexico, accompanied his speech with the communicative strategy of gesture by pointing to the surface of a bench while saying: *aquí está la sala* ("here's the living-room"), and then, moving his index finger to the right, he continued *y luego . . . pasas este cuarto y aquí está el baño* ("and then . . . you go through this room and here's the bathroom"). In writing, either the information that the *baño* is to the right of the *sala* must be expressed in linguistic form or it is lost.

In addition to the difference between speech and writing in the use of situational paralinguistic communicative cues, sociolinguists have proposed that the "online" processing demands on the addressee, as well as on the speaker, are a factor in how speakers organize information in speech. These demands are lessened in written communication, and writing is freer to employ strategies which would be burdensome to the addressee in speech. In approaching the design of the East Los Angeles writing study discussed in detail below, we return to the theme of the difference between the organization of discourse in speech and writing.

A specific empirical technique of comparing the organization of information in speech and writing has evolved in the sociolinguistic study of several monolingual English speaking communities. This involves the elicitation of spoken discourse units, especially narrative, and later written versions of the same units by the same performers, e.g., Ochs (1979), Tannen (1982), and Kroch and Hindle (1982). This allows empirical observation of how the differences between the spoken and written channels are actually used in the organization of information, and provides an instrument with which to test the extent to which learners avail themselves of the conventions and processing resources of writing which are not available in speech. This technique was used in the East Los Angeles writing study in order to investigate what advanced writing skills are independent of English and Spanish, and to what extent early and late learners differed in their ability to integrate these skills in their writing, given their differential experience in and command of spoken and written English.

The East Lost Angeles Writing Study

The site of the writing study reported below is the Hispanic bilingual community of Greater East Los Angeles. This area includes a central unincorporated area, adjacent incorporated townships, and some eastern sections of the city of Los Angeles, forming a continuous area which is well over 90% Hispanic, overwhelmingly Mexican-American. In view of the widespread use of both Spanish and English in the community, it may be viewed as a complex bilingual community, probably the largest bilingual community in the U.S. The adolescent writers considered in this study are all members of this community, either by birth or current residence.

By focusing on adolescents after the peak dropout point in high school (between 10th and 11th grade), the study sought to sample students with relatively highly developed literacy skills. Attention then focused on the difference between the literacy skills exhibited by the early and late learners. For purposes of comparison, the individuals whose speech and literacy skills were studied were categorized into two groups:

Early learners. These students entered the U.S. school system in the first grade at the latest, at a maximum age of 6 years. At the time of the study, they ranged in age from 16 to 18 years, with a majority 17 years old. They are all fluent speakers of English, but range in Spanish fluency from none to full.

Late learners. These students entered the U.S. school system as virtually monolingual Spanish speakers, no earlier than junior high school. They have the same age range as the early learners, and range in length of residence from 6 years to 3 months. They are all fluent speakers of Spanish, but range in English fluency from none to full.

As can be seen from the above descriptions, the composition of each group is far from homogeneous in terms of bilingualism, and the late learners are quite varied in exposure to U.S. education and English literacy. However, the two groups are quite distinct from each other. For our purposes, this lack of homogeneity within groups is desirable. In some cases, group comparisons will be sufficient to make a particular point. In other cases, the heterogeneity of both groups allows more detailed discussion of variety in individual performances.

The results reported will focus on the English results from a group of nine early learners and seven late learners. Three additional late learners had difficulty or rejected both the English speaking and writing performances in favor of Spanish. In contrast to the other late learners, these students had been in the U.S. for less than a year. Two of these students produced speech and writing only in Spanish. The third produced an English written narrative, but then, expressing dissatisfaction with the results of this performance (corresponding to difficulty he had in speaking English without the support of Spanish), requested permission to rewrite the narrative in Spanish. These three learners constitute a minor third group for whom we have Spanish performances. Consideration of this group will be useful in making inferences about differences between speech and writing which apply to Spanish as well as to English.

Using the technique of eliciting both spoken and written samples of the same content, the first stage of data collection consisted of obtaining samples of both *narratives* (oral versions of personal experience) and *dwelling descriptions*, in the course of guided taperecorded conversation among groups of self-selected peers, according to standard sociolinguistic techniques for obtaining extended discourse (e.g., Labov, 1972). The content of these units refer to personal experience directly accessible to the speaker, thus maximizing the speaker's expertise in the topic. On a later occasion, each speaker was requested to write the spatial tour and one of the narratives previously produced orally, thus controlling content across the spoken and written channels.

The purpose of eliciting both narratives and dwelling descriptions was to obtain some variety in the genres of discourse represented. These two genres, by the nature of their content, favor different syntactic resources with which to frame information, as discussed among the findings. In the case of either genre, the familiarity of the topic to each student avoids the problem of confounding difficulties in finding a linguistic means of expression with difficulties in selecting information for report on the part of the students.

Comparison of Spoken and Written Samples

This section will discuss several aspects of the relation between speech and writing, and how this relation interacts with the English language resources of early and late learners. The order of presentation will consider sentence complexity, the use of subject position, the English grammatical device of inversion, and then the mechanics of punctuation and spelling. Each aids in constructing a theory of how linguistic and literate knowledge interact in the development of literacy.

The aspects of sentence complexity investigated involve the number of clauses combined into a single sentence in speech and writing. Measures of sentence complexity are well known among studies of the development of spoken and written English (e.g., the T-unit studies of Hunt, 1977). Generally, it is found that the written language of educated English speakers exhibits greater complexity than the spoken language of the same speakers (e.g., Kroch & Hindle, 1982). The findings show that the norm of greater sentence complexity of writing when compared to speech is also characteristic of both the English and Spanish writings in the East Los Angeles writing study.

The use of position before the verb for full nominal subjects has been found to be more favored for written than for spoken narrative among adult monolingual English speakers. Kroch and Hindle (1982) propose that the different preferences in speech and writing for the use of subject position reflect information processing differences between the spoken and written channels. These differences are found among both early and late learners, but are greater for the late learners.

The English grammatical device of inversion, as discussed in more detail below, places a subject noun phrase after the verb, as in *next comes the livingroom* instead of *the livingroom comes next*. This device is favored in both speech and writing by early learners, but distinguishes the speech and writing among the late learners.

The mechanics of punctuation are explored through the specific case of the use of a period to separate independent sentences. It is found that early and late learners are equally likely to use or fail to use periods in this context, suggesting that this feature of punctuation is transferable from Spanish to English, and that difficulty in its use persists among individual speakers to a relatively late point in their school careers.

The mechanics of spelling are investigated through the analysis of spelling errors which spell graphically conventional words other than the word intended. It is suggested that the high frequency of errors of this type among total errors reflects anticipatory strategies in reading applied to the monitoring of spelling. It is found that, while individuals in both groups of speakers make spelling errors of this type, there are differences between early and late learners in the types of strategies used in spelling and monitoring spelling. This, in turn, reflects experience with written English.

In the specific discussion of the results of the study below, for each of the categories introduced above, an attempt is made to disentangle relatively high level language-independent writing skills from particular problems encountered by late learners in applying those skills to a language in which they are relatively inexperienced.

Sentence Complexity

Subordination and other grammatical connective devices are used in both speech and writing to organize clause-level information units, i.e., explicit propositions, into the larger text. Studies of speech and writing have shown that writing tends to be more syntactically complex than speech in terms of the number of clauses compressed into single sentences. As a point of departure, a first elementary measure devised to compare spoken and written versions of the same topics I call the *sentence complexity index*. It is an average of the number of tensed verbs per sentence, compared across speech and writing. As with the T-Unit, only one *and* clause was counted as belonging to the same sentence as the preceding clause. If there were a second *and* clause, it would be treated as the beginning of a second sentence, regardless of punctuation (which was often unconventional, as discussed later), e.g.,

> (2) . . . (a) I was in the bedroom (b) *and* the rocking chair is in the livingroom, (c) *and* I was asleep (d) *and* I heard this (makes a noise to represent a creaking chair) . . .
> Speech: Narrative (MG17fE)[1]

---

[1] Following a citation of speech or writing, the speaker is identified by two letters, standing for a name followed by age; sex; and E or L, standing for early or late learner, respectively. In the case of an L notation, age on arrival immediately follows, e.g., PL18mL16 means speaker PL was 18 at the time of citation, and is a late learner who arrived in the community at age 16 years.

Schematically, example (2) consists of C + *and* C + *and* C + *and* C, where C is a clause (containing a finite verb). Following standard counting procedure, only the first *and* C clause, the one signalled by (b) in the example, is counted as belonging to the first sentence. The *and* C clauses signalled by (c) in the example is treated as the beginning of a new sentence. The procedure for counting then repeats so that the *and* C clause signalled by (d) in the example is counted as part of the sentence beginning with clause (c). The resultant sentence complexity index for this segment is thus, 2 clauses + 2 clauses / 2 sentences, i.e., an index of 2.0.

Chains of *and* clauses, as in example (2), were not observed in writing. It appears that all writers were too sophisticated to directly transfer this spoken pattern to writing, where it is pedagogically discouraged. The closest equivalent to the content of example (2) in MG's writing consists of a main plus subordinate clause:

> (3) . . . The next night I would hear the rocking chair, like if someone was rocking in it. . . .
> Writing: Narrative (MG17fE)

(Note in passing that the subordinate clause is introduced by *like if* in (3), a vernacular equivalent to standard *as if* or *as though*. Although this vernacular norm has a transparent origin in Spanish *como si*, it is commonly used by monolingual as well by bilingual speakers in the community.) Note that the sentence complexity index of the segment represented in example (3) is also 2.0; C + *like if* C = 2 clauses/ 1 sentence, where *like if* is used as a subordinating conjunction.

Again following standard procedure for counting sentence complexity, in reported speech, only the clause immediately following the verb of reported speech was counted as belonging with it in the same sentence. An immediately following clause within the reported speech was counted as beginning a new sentence, e.g.,

> (4) . . . (a) I would ask my parents: (b) did you guys get up at—last night (c) or walk around the house? . . .
> Speech: Narrative (MG17fE)

(Notice that for counting purposes, the reduced conjoined clause (c) is restored to a full clause "or *did you* walk . . . ". In contrast, the written equivalent (5) below is reduced to a noun phrase, "or *something like that*". In the case of reduction to a noun phrase, the noun phrase is *not* restored to a full clause for counting purposes.)

Thus, in example (4) above, clause (b) is counted as belonging to the same sentence as clause (a), while clause (c) is counted as beginning a new sentence. Extended reported speech necessitating this counting rule was quite common in speech but very rare in writing. Thus, the written version of example (4) reduces clauses (b) and (c) above to a single clause with only one tensed verb:

(5) . . . (a) The next morning I would ask my parents (b) if they had gotten up in the night to go get something to eat or something like that, . . .

Writing: Narrative (MG17fE)

A comparison of examples (4) and (5) shows that the sentence complexity index is only concerned with registering the number of full clauses per sentence, only one aspect of sentence complexity. In addition, the counting rules for *and* clause chains and extended reported speech might be expected to favor a higher sentence complexity index for speech than for writing, since these structures are more common in the speech samples than in the writing samples. However, this is not the case. Table 1 below shows the observed trends for the two groups of learners, including the Spanish as well as the English samples. It immediately show that the amount of "true" subordination in the writing samples (i.e., adverbial and embedded clauses) more than makes up for whatever bias the above counting rules may cause in favor of raising the sentence complexity index of the speech samples.

In each sample, there are more clauses per sentence in writing than in speech. This is independent of both language and degree of experience with English. This suggests that the norm of greater sentential complexity of writing over speech may transfer from one language to another. In view of the observation that both linking *and* clauses and extended reported speech are rare in the writing samples, it can be more precisely suggested that a norm for greater subordination of clauses within single sentences distinguishes writing from speech in both languages, independently of experience with English. This suggestion is consistent with the interdependence hypothesis, which distinguishes some language

Table 1. Composite Sentence Complexity Indices for Speech and Writing Samples of Early and Late Learners.*

	Speech	Writing
Early	1.29 (18)	1.61 (27)
Late	1.18 (14)	1.37 (20)
Spanish	1.36 (7)	1.58 (5)

*N in parentheses refers to number of writing samples.

skills from others on the basis of an underlying competence which may be expressed in either language. While, on an elementary level, suggested examples of transferable literate skills include graphic sense (cf. Ferreiro, 1978; Hernandez-Chavez & Curtis, 1982) and the word decoding system, Table 1 suggests that at more advanced literacy levels the greater preference of writing for organizing clause-size units of information into single sentences is also transferrable.

However, there is another observation to be made from Table 1. The late learners function at lower levels of utilization of this skill than early learners, even though Spanish appears to be a more highly syntacticized language than English in terms of the number of clauses packed into a sentence in speech. It is evident, then, that language-independent skills cannot be transferred to English until the English-specific skills necessary to implement them are acquired. While this observation is, in fact, self-evident, it raises the question of when and how these English skills are best introduced into the process of English literacy instruction. We will return to this question later.

Subject Position

A more specific measure of the difference between speech and writing in organizing information is revealed in the use of subject position. Kroch and Hindle (1982), in a study of adult English monolinguals, observed that subject position tends to be utilized differently in speech and writing. Among their samples speech shows a greater tendency than writing to place new referents in the form of nouns (henceforth NPs) *following the verb* of the clause, and to reserve subject position *before the verb* for pronouns referring to entities already identifiable from the previous context.

Table 2 below looks at subject position before the verb in terms of a ratio of referential pronouns to lexical (full) nouns. By "referential" pronouns, I mean third person pronouns (i.e., he, she, it, they) which refer to a previously established entity in the discourse. Thus, for example, counted among referential pronouns is *it*, referring to, say, *the book*, indentifiable by previous context, but not "dummy" uses of *it*, as in *It's raining* or *It's hard to read this book*. Table 2 restricts attention to English narrative, the lengthier and informationally more complex of the two genres elicited. In narrative, entities, usually people, sustain recurrent reference in subject position, while in dwelling descriptions, entities, usually rooms, are newly introduced and rarely mentioned subsequently. Revealing syntactic features of dwelling descriptions are discussed in the next subsection.

According to the ratio, the higher the index in Table 2, the more often referential pronouns are used in subject position as compared to lexical nouns, and vice-versa for lower indices. The comparisons show that expectations conditioned by Kroch and Hindle's findings for adult monolingual English speakers are also satisfied by the present groups of speakers, regardless of experience with English.

It is interesting to note that the late learners are even more extreme in differentiating subject position in speech and writing than the early learners. The reasons for this difference are not entirely clear. However, the following may be suggested. The late learners may rely more than the early learners on the addressee to locate the referent of a subject pronoun in speech due to greater difficulty in audio-monitoring their speech. Under the more generous real-time monitoring conditions of writing they overcompensate for this processing difficulty by observing the writing norm of *explicitness* to a greater degree than the early learners. The use of an explicit lexical NP (full noun), in accordance with the explicitness principle, minimizes the reader's need to locate the referent of a pronoun which might have been used instead.

Since this difference in the use of subject position is quantitative rather than qualitative, it is difficult to illustrate with concrete examples. However, a comparison of (6) and (7) below gives an indication of how this principle applies to writing.

(6) . . . (a) She (= the teacher: BW) take my paper and give it to *the other guy*. . . . (b) but he pu - *he* write on my paper . . . (c) And the teacher said, hey . . . what the matter; qu- quiet. So *he* start telling me bad words . . .

Speech: Narrative (HG16mL13)

In (6), the spoken version of a narrative, the participant "the other guy" is first introduced in nonsubject position in clause (a). Thereafter, he is always referred to in subject position by the pronoun *he*, as in segments (b) and (c). In contrast, the written version of the same segments in (7), below, features the introduction of the participant in subject position (topicalized) in clause (b), and reintroduction of the referent in clause (c) as a full NP.

Table 2. Ratio of Referential (Third Person) Pronouns to Lexical (Full) Nouns in Subject Position by Residence Group in Spoken and Written English Narrative.*

	Spoken	Written
Early	2.9 (152)	1.8 (226)
Late	3.9 (170)	1.3 (157)

*N in parentheses refers to total number of nouns and referential pronouns in subject position.

(7) . . . (a) my teacher told all the students to change their papers (b) but *the boy* who get my paper He ride on it . . . (c) but my teacher said . . . but *the boy* told me a lot of things badworse (= bad words: BW) . . .

Written: Narrative (HG16mL13)

Also influencing the use of the explicit principle in writing may be the greater tendency in writing than in speech to focus on the sentence as an independent unit. This would account quite generally for the greater use in writing of the full NP reference in subject position as necessary to specify the fuller meaning of the sentence, as if its meaning were independent of the larger text. Of course, a consistent application of this principle could result in a totally bizarre text with no subject pronouns. This has not been observed for any writer. However, the principle of explicitness may be reinforced by the common instructional progression which concentrates on practice in the writing of autonomous sentences before proceeding to the writing of larger texts consisting of many sentences. Where a text consists of a single sentence, the use of a referential pronoun, rather than a full NP, will be devoid of referential meaning (who's "he"?). Late learners of English may have a greater tendency than early learners to "regress" to a focus on sentences rather than larger units in organizing their information due to greater difficulty in planning and producing local organization of information in second language text (i.e., clauses and sentences).

Inversion

It has already been noted in the discussion of subject position that, although early and late learners may follow the same trend in distinguishing speech and writing, the late learners may be more extreme in this trend. In the case of inversion, commonly used by the early learners in dwelling descriptions, the late learners further distinguish themselves from the early learners by making a distinction between speech and writing not found among the early learners.

Inversion is one of several strategies used by English speakers to introduce new rooms in the description. A common alternative in the community is the *existential* clause, e.g.

(8) *Inversion:*   to the left *is* my room. (ED17fE)
                      LOC   BE   NP

     Existential: to the left *there's* the bathroom. (ED17fE)
                          LOC   THERE BE   NP

Here both devices are used by the same writer, an early learner. Now consider Figure 1 below.

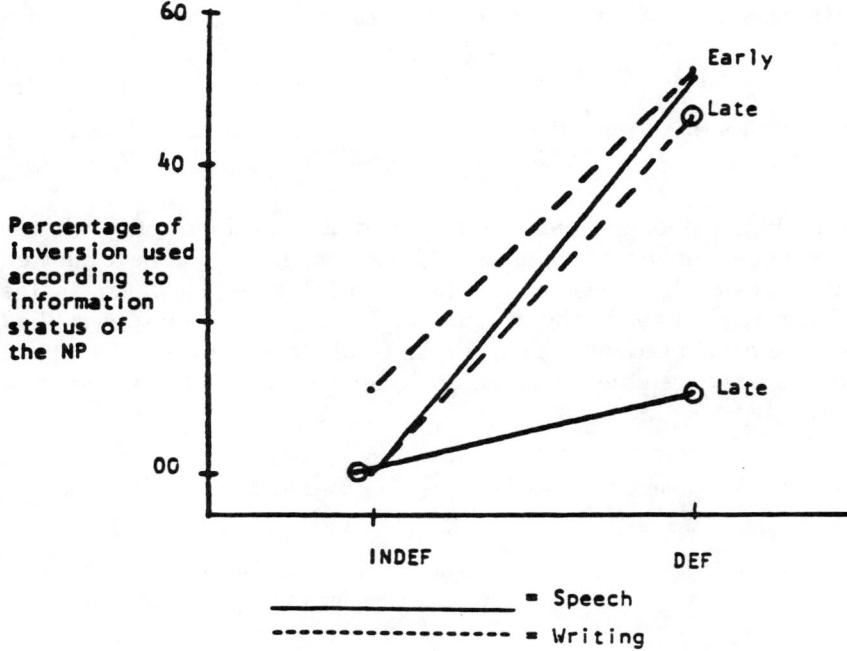

Figure 1. Percentage of inversion out of all first mentions of rooms according to definite and indefinite determination of the Noun Phrase in the speech and writing of early and late learners.

The figure shows that, among the early learners, there is no difference in the frequency of inversion between speech and writing, but that the late learners seem to avoid it in speech. Why? As in the case of the exaggeration of the explicitness principle applied to subject position among late learners, discussed above, a difference in the monitoring of speech and writing can be offered by way of explanation. In the case of inversion, however, the argument is more complex, since it involves explaining an *avoidance* strategy in speech. A basis for the avoidance strategy can be offered in the lack of congruence between the conditions in which inversion is used in Spanish and English. In Spanish, inversion of subject and verb is of much wider application than in English, and applies to all verbs and tenses. English is more restricted in its use of inversion, and uses the existential construction under many conditions in which Spanish uses inversion. Inappropriate transfer of inversion from Spanish to English is observed occasionally among the late learners, restricted to those least experienced in speaking English. Thus, compare the following utterance by a late learner with the fluent English version.

(9) *Inversion*:   At the corner *were coming* two cholos.
                                  BE   V-ING   NP
         (PL18mL16)

   Existential: (From the corner,) *there were* two cholos *coming*.
                   LOC   THERE BE   NP   V-ING

Interestingly enough, in an earlier period of its evolution, English was more similar to Spanish in its use of inversion, and would have allowed utterances of the type exhibited by PL in (9) above. However, by the Middle English period the insertion of *there* as a "dummy subject" had become usual in contexts such as (9)a, resulting in a transitional type of structure between the earlier use of pure inversion and the modern existential type, e.g.,

   (9)a Whylom *ther was dwelling* at Oxenford/ a rich gnof . . .
                THERE BE V-ING

   (i.e. once *there was dwelling* at Oxford a rich ignoramous . . .
                              Chaucer: Miller's Tale, lines 1–2)

By the modern period, it became usual for the subject to migrate to a position between the auxiliary (*be*) and the participle (*V-ing*), e.g., ". . . *there was* a rich gnof *dwelling* at 0." Thus, earlier varieties of English would have more easily facilitated "positive transfer" from Spanish with respect to inversion, probably obviating the need for an avoidance strategy, while Spanish speakers figured out the principles for inversion in English.

As the learners come to recognize that English does not use inversion as generally as Spanish, they may adopt the strategy of avoiding it in speech, lest they use it inappropriately (cf. Schachter, 1974). The data suggest that, even as the late learners acquire knowledge of the English use of inversion, they retain the avoidance strategy in speech. Under the extended time for monitoring production available to writing, inversion emerges more easily than in speech.

To summarize so far, distinct strategies for organizing information in writing appear to be among the interdependent (i.e., language-independent) literacy skills which transfer from one language to another. In addition, the case of inversion serves to illustrate that, where there is difficulty in acquiring linguistic patterns neutral to the written and speech channels, writing, due to its reduced real-time monitoring demands, allows for more practice than speech in the acquisition of linguistic patterns. Consequently, native-like English patterns may emerge sooner in writing than in speech.

Mechanics of Writing

The mechanics of writing present a different set of skills from those discussed above, in that no useful comparison can be made with speech. In turn, discussion will focus on a basic aspect of punctuation, and on spelling. Spanish and English display great similarity in the aspect of punctuation to be discussed, the use of the period to mark the end of a written sentence. Consequently, transfer of skill in use of the period from Spanish to English is possible. In contrast, English spelling is highly idiosyncratic. Consequently, a great deal of language-specific knowledge of written English is necessary in order to spell English words correctly. It will be seen that the similarities and differences between the spelling and monitoring strategies used by early and late learners are revealing of their differential experience with written English.

Punctuation. Among devices specific to writing for organizing discourse is punctuation. One of the most basic punctuation devices, similarly used in Spanish and English, is the period. The major function of the period is to separate consecutive sentences. Among the sample, both "run-on sentences" with no punctuation, and commas, were often observed where the period is conventional. There was no difference between early (22% of 96) and late learners (23% of 80) in failure to use punctuation between sentences in the dwelling descriptions.

Whether due to monitoring difficulty in editing writing, or to a more fundamental difficulty in distinguishing relations among various clause sequences, the problem which exists in punctuating sentences appears to be independent of experience with English literacy. It is expected to be a totally transferrable skill from Spanish to English—and one which remains difficult, even at a relatively advanced stage of public education.

Spelling. In contrast to punctuation, spelling tests the limits of transfer possibilities. English and Spanish spelling rest on a common alphabetic base with some similarity in the uses of particular letters to represent sounds. However, much more striking is the idiosyncratic conventionality of English spelling, derived from a logic which makes sense only in the light of the history of individual words.

The "phonetic" principle, associating sound with visual symbols, is easily transferred from written Spanish. Late learners show a generalization of the phonetic principle in "creative spellings" similar to that observed for young monolingual English children (cf. Read, 1980), and young bilingual Spanish and English speaking children (cf. Edelsky, 1981a). However, there are greater differences between the spelling strategies used by neoliterates and the strategies used by adolescent late learners. Consider the following segment from HG's written narrative, shown in Figure 2a.

Note first the use of the grapheme /a/ in *lat(')s* (i.e., *lots*) and *gad* (i.e., *got*) to represent the English "short o." This is a transparent use of the

(a) He was crying in the Flour but I can't stop He told me lats of thing. and them He gad a nifht I can't

Writing: Narrative (HG16mLAOA13)   (reduction to 77%).

Transliteration:

He was crying in the Flour but I can't stop He told me lats of thing. and them He gad a nifht I can't

(b) 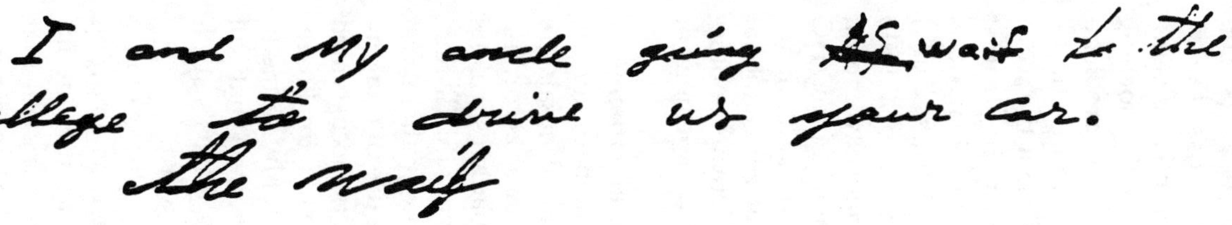 *[handwritten: I and My ancle going ~~its~~ waif to the college to drive us your car. the waif]*

Writing: Narrative (SM16mL16)   (reduction to 77%).

Transliteration:

I and My ancle going (illegible deletion) AS waif to the
college to drive us your car.
   the waif

Figure 2. Example of (a) HG's spelling and (b) SM's narrative writing in English, plus transliterations.

phonetic principle to transfer the phonetic value of the Spanish grapheme /a/ to English. Even more interesting, however, is the influence of conventional English spelling on HG's unconventional spellings. Setting aside the words spelled conventionally, note that HG uses the digraph /ou/ in spelling the word "floor" (as *flour*). The digraph /ou/ is not used in modern Spanish orthography. Now note further the spelling /nifht/ for the word "knife." An explanation of this spelling is problematic. HG recognizes that the grapheme /i/ can be used to represent the diphthong /ay/ in English, as indeed his use of /I/ to represent the word "I" attests. Spanish orthography would insist on /ai/ for the nearest equivalent to this English vowel. Most plausibly, the use of final /ht/ is based on conventional spellings of words such as "night," "right," etc., so that HG has abstracted a strategy on the basis of English spelling to the effect that /ht/ can be used at the end of words phonetically ending in a consonant to make the internal vowel *i* "long.". (In point of fact, HG produced the conventional spelling for /right/ as in "right hand" in another context.) It is evident that HG is indeed aiming at conventional English spelling, and creating spelling strategies of much greater sophistication than anything found in the literature on the creative spellings of monolingual (or bilingual) neoliterates.

Finally, note in this example HG's clear use of the spelling /them/ for the word "then." One may, of course, deduce a phonetic basis for the use of final /m/ rather than /n/ in this spelling. That is, final nasals are indistinct in Spanish, so that their point of articulation varies according to dialect and phonetic context.[2] Consequently, native Spanish speakers inexperienced in English have great difficulty in recognizing the distinction between English words ending in different nasals, e.g., "them" vs. "then." At such a stage in the acquisition of English, the use of final /m/ in English spelling is quite mysterious to Spanish speakers, accustomed to the invariable use of final /n/ as the only representation of a final nasal in Spanish. The absence of final /m/ in Spanish orthography immediately shows that HG is aiming at an English spelling strategy. What will concern us now is not simply the Spanish phonetic basis of HG's spelling strategy, but the fact that /them/ spells an English word.

As an isolated instance, HG's use of the spelled English "word" /them/ for the English word "then" cannot be interpreted as anything but a coincidental spelling of an English word other than the one intended, cf. *flour* for *floor*, mentioned above. However, it turns out that many of the phonetic spellings of English words among the late learners

---

[2] Indeed the pronunciation of word-final *-m* where standard Spanish uses /n/ is a well-known feature of the Mayan language area of Southern Mexico and adjacent Guatemala; cf. Lope Blanch, 1983.

spell conventional words other than the word intended. I will call any spelling which is conventional, but not for the word intended, a *sight spelling*. Sight spellings may be due to chance, or they may be due to visual familiarity with the word actually spelled. Confusion of words with similar visual or phonetic shapes is observed even among highly skilled writers, e.g., *there/their* or *to/too*. In order to control the likelihood that the learners had been exposed to the sight spellings in print, words counted as sight spellings were restricted to those listed by Harris and Jacobson (1982) in their study of English reading primers from first through eighth grade. This ruled out some plausible sight words such as *flour* (as a spelling for *floor* in (10) above).

Table 3 gives an analysis of all sight spellings in the sample, except for those involving the past–present distinction, e.g., *look:looked* or *give:gave*, which were reserved for separate analysis.

The frequency of sight spellings out of total nonconventional spellings (for the intended word) is not significantly different between early and late learners. This, in itself, may suggest that both groups tend to use the sight spelling strategy to the same degree. By this strategy, shapes of words are memorized as wholes, rather than deduced from phonological principles applied to constituent letters. The difference between early and late learners does not appear in the utilization of this strategy. Like the "phonetic principle" it appears to be language-independent and transferrable.

However, a highly significant difference appears in the proportion of *partials* among sight spellings between the groups. By *partials*, I mean spellings of words which are not semantically or phonologically identical to the intended word, e.g., *now* for *know* or *through* for *thought* (but not *their/there* or *thing/things*). Partials, then, are conventionally spelled words which partially resemble the intended word, but more visually than semantically or phonologically. An explanation for the greater occurrence of partials among the early learners suggests greater experience in English reading, according to the following proposal.

The difference between the types of unconventional spellings of the early and late learners suggests how anticipatory strategies, discussed above, and developed among both early and late learners, interact with experience with English spelling. For both groups of speakers, the monitoring of spelling appears to rely to the same extent on recognizing a word shape which is familiar, because it represents a conventionally spelled word. In monitoring spelling, the anticipatory strategies of reading deduce the meaning of a word even if it is unconventionally spelled. These strategies are language-independent, and thus apply to Spanish as well as English. Therefore, they may easily transfer from one lan-

Table 3. Percentage of Sight Words and Partials Out of Total Number of Unconventional Spellings (Excluding Past Tense Forms) Among Early and Late Learners.*

	All Sight Words	Partials	N
Early	45	23	120
Late	52	09	93

*$x^2 = 0.9$ p = n.s. for total sight words out of total unconventional spellings at 1df. $x^2 = 13.8$ p 0.005 for partials out of total sight words at 1df.

guage to the other. An unconventional spelling of a word is most easily recognized by readers of any degree of experience if it does not spell any familiar word at all. If it does spell a familiar word, although not the intended one, it may be passed over as correct because it is recognized as a legitimate word shape, and its meaning is clear in context. It is somewhat ironic that the use of anticipatory strategies, which represent a relatively high level of skill in reading, detract in this way from the monitoring of spelling. For the early readers, it appears that a cursory and only partial visual resemblance between the word intended and the word spelled is sufficient to allow the incorrectness of the spelling to be overlooked. However, the tendency for the late learners to require more precision in the phonological identity of the word intended and the word actually spelled suggests that, in monitoring the spelled word for accuracy, the late learners fall back more on the earlier strategy of phonological decoding.

Two points emerge from this discussion. First, both early and late learners show a sophistication not evident among poor and incipient readers, in the use of anticipatory strategies for monitoring spelling. In addition, the late learners' capacity for storing conventionally spelled words appears to be well developed in that they are not significantly more likely to "invent" spellings than are early learners. That is, they are no less aware than early learners that spelling is conventionalized in English (as in Spanish). Second, the connection between the way a word is spelled and the way it is pronounced exerts greater influence among late learners than among early learners. This suggests that early learners more often bypass pronunciation in the recognition of words, and simply associate the visual shape of the spelled word directly with its meaning. The difference between the early and late learners in this respect suggests that the process of bypassing pronunciation in the recognition of written words is a cumulative skill which proceeds from word to word, and builds up over an extended period of time. In this skill, late learners are at a disadvantage compared to early learners, since their experience with reading English and accumulating a store of written word shapes and their meanings is less than that of the early learners.

Implications

As stated in the introduction, this study has been concerned with the deduction of relatively high level literacy skills which are independent of particular languages, and how those skills interact with language-specific knowledge of English in the development of English writing skills. In exploring the implications of the findings of the East Los Angeles writing study among students approaching the end of their public school careers, I will resume discussion of the theories of literacy arising in the context of educating U.S. language minority students.

The great bulk of recent research has focused on the language of initial literacy and the development of low level literacy skills. This research effort is logical, given the large size of the language minority population entering the educational system in the early grades and the overarching educational goal of English literacy. Admitting inevitable simplification here, early debate over educational procedures which might be most effectively used toward attaining the goal of English literacy may be polarized under the labels *speak-first* and *read-first* theories.

The *speak-first* theories emphasize the connection between *English* and English literacy. Consequently, they stress English oral skills as a route to English literacy. It is safe to state that speak-first theories derived largely from the resistance of the U.S. educational system to the use of languages other than English in school systems. These theories were not based on a body of research, but reflected a longstanding tradition in most districts limited to the literacy training of students who had already developed skills in spoken English. It would be more accurate to refer to the principle of "English speech before literacy" as a dogma rather than a scientific theory.

The *read-first* theories emphasize the connection between *literacy* and English literacy. Consequently, they stress the development of literacy skills in whatever language is most appropriate as a route to English literacy, given the social and individual circumstances of the students. Arising largely in reaction to the speak-first dogma, read-first theories have drawn for supporting evidence on immersion (e.g., Lambert & Tucker, 1972) and "language-shelter" (e.g., Skuttnabb-Kangas & Toukomaa, 1976) programs. More recently, read-first theories have additionally drawn on age and literacy training differences in the rate of acquisition of English literacy among speakers with a non-English mother tongue first exposed to non-English literacy. For example, Cummins' (1981a) reanalysis of the Wright data on immigrant students in Toronto suggests that older students acquire English literacy skills faster than younger students. An implicit assumption in interpreting these data as supporting read-first programs is that, the older the speaker on arrival in the Toronto school system, the more likely the student was to have acquired certain general literacy skills which were rapidly transferrable to English literacy. As mentioned in the introduction, a more recent study supporting this assumption is the Seattle study of the English literacy achievement of students of Cantonese language-background. This study reports that training in Cantonese literacy had a significant correlation with literacy level achieved in English among the students who had training in Cantonese literacy prior to immigration to Seattle.

Read-first theories have achieved their goal of refuting the speak-first dogma. However, serious problems remain. The primary question is: if initial literacy training may or should begin with a language other than English, when and how is English to be introduced toward the goal of English literacy? In this context, the results of the same studies which have refuted the speak-first dogma have made further observations to the effect that, naturally, literacy training in a language other than English may be necessary but is not sufficient toward a goal of English literacy. Thus, for example, Cummins' reanalysis of the Wright study suggests that, even though older students make more rapid progress toward English literacy than younger students in the same amount of time, they remain behind grade level, since the amount of material they need to learn in order to reach grade level criteria increases even more rapidly with each grade. Similarly, the Seattle study reports that performance in selected oral English skills also highly correlates with English reading achievement, but, in this case, students with literacy-training in Cantonese had no advantage, presumably due to the lack of experience with English oral skills among the Cantonese students first schooled abroad. The conclusion to be drawn from studies such as these is that both English skills, whether oral or literate, and first language literacy skills contribute toward the goal of English literacy.

The aspects of the East Los Angeles writing study presented above provide further support for this conclusion, particularly in identifying ways in which general English language skills (such as knowledge of syntactic devices for organizing information) and cross-language literacy skills (such as strategies for organizing information in writing) interact in the acquisition of English literacy. By beginning to distinguish those advanced literacy skills which transcend language and those which are language-dependent, the study carries implications for a literacy program aimed at distinguishing skills which need specific knowledge of English and those which need specific knowledge of literacy.

It is important to note that the East Los Angeles writing study cannot directly address the question of when and how the transition from literacy in a first language to a second language should be made. Instead, it specifically addresses a language minority population which, prior to immigration, may be inferred to have advanced well beyond the initial stages of literacy in a first language, and which has attained a high placement in an educational system which promotes literacy in English. Nevertheless, the study contributes to the general problem of characterizing the general principles of the problems which may be anticipated in the transfer of interdependent literacy skills from a more familiar to a less familiar language. From the discussion of the literacy skills shared by early and late learners, it should be evident that the strategies used by late learners in acquiring English literacy will not be of the same kind as those which would be used by neoliterates, whether younger or older.

Among the skills which appear to transcend specific English and Spanish language skills by the late high school years are the different strategies accorded to the written and spoken channels in ways of organizing information in coherent discourse, and experience in using a holistic word recognition strategy in reading, which bypasses phonological decoding and also applies to the visual monitoring of spelling.

Among language-specific devices which are necessary for the implementation of these strategies in English are specific syntactic forms for the organization of information, and experience in the recognition of English words. The latter appears to result from practice in English readings, and the former from reading, writing, and explicit teaching of English grammatical devices and their functions in writing (e.g., on the college level, the sentence-combining devices discussed by Amastae, 1981, and Lawlor, 1981).

It does not seem to be the case that the types of cross-language skills identified in this paper are directly and overtly taught. Instead, they appear to come with experience in writing and reading. However, it appears that they imply a certain level of literacy skills, and that, once they have been acquired in one language, they will be transferred to the other languages. This suggests that, in designing a program for developing English literacy skills, a means should be developed to assess these skills in the first language, and to ascertain the level of language-independent development to which they apply. This will avoid the wasteful and retarding types of instructional programs observed by, for example, Moll (1981), in which students were being trained in language-independent skills in English, e.g., word decoding and simple sentence reading, which they had already mastered in Spanish. At the same time, where weaknesses in language-independent skills are found, for example, in punctuation, it seems reasonable to consider parallel training in both English and Spanish. In this way, encouragement to develop the skills further in both languages is facilitated, so that the skills may transfer as they develop from the stronger to the weaker language.

On the other hand, the types of language-specific skills identified in this paper need as much practice as possible in English. Among them are spelling and practice in the use of English complex syntax. For spelling a great deal of English reading and writing appear to be necessary. Specific practice in English reading and writing appears to be necessary to acquire word shapes for long-term storage in memory. It may also be useful to review those partial regularities in spelling which are usually taught in early grades, e.g., *igh* words and other sets of words which represent long vowels, etc. However, it is important to note that, for high school students, these skills are separable from language-independent skills. Therefore, explicit teaching of these skills, usually associated with the primary school level, should not be taken to imply a primary school set of language-independent skills.

The devices for complex syntax may also be explicitly taught in order to accelerate the transfer of these resources from Spanish to English, in the case that they have already developed in Spanish. The recognition and use of different conventions for the organization of information in writing are transferrable across Spanish and English. However, the linguistic means for organizing and packaging information must be acquired in L2 in order for students to utilize this insight. Considerations of explicit teaching of this sort have not been evaluated positively among the discussions of instructional strategies for preliterate or neoliterate students. Many current theories generally emphasize the extent to which what must be acquired must be deduced by the learners under favorable conditions without explicit instruction in details. This relates to an instructional strategy which de-emphasizes form in favor of content. Without denying the wisdom of this approach for beginning literacy, at which time establishing confidence in learning to read is paramount, by the late high school years, students are approaching adult maturity and are increasingly judged on ability to control form as well as content. Thus, for example, the hold that conventional spelling has on judgments of competence, either in continuing education or in the job market, is evident in the staunch resistance of the business community, as well as the educational system, to spelling reform (cf. *Wall Street Journal* front-page article "Organizashun urjez chanjez in speling to simplify English," July 28, 1982). Similarly, there is much sociolinguistic evidence that nonstandard English uses in syntax are negative factors in the judgment of job suitability and educational achievement (cf. Shuy & Fasold, 1973). To the extent that the public schools are held responsible for providing resources to enable students from non-English backgrounds to compete with students from monolingual English communities, matters of form cannot be dismissed. If they are to be challenged as improper criteria for judgments of literacy achievement (cf. Edelsky, 1981b), or whatever other purposes they may serve in the competition for economic survival, this challenge must not be limited to the schools alone but extended to the society at large which reinforces these formal criteria.

As a final consideration suggested by some observations made during the East Los Angeles writing study, a second language *write-first* (i.e., before speaking) theory looks like a useful component to a program concerned with developing adolescent linguistic skills applicable to both speech and writing in a new language.

There are two possible reasons for this. First, monitoring of performance is easier for literates in the written than in the spoken channel. Second, as discussed in detail elsewhere as well as in the case of very recent arrivals in the study who refused to speak English (e.g., Wald, 1985), writing English is less stressful than speaking English among those unpracticed in speaking English—and the embarrassment of speaking English in public increases with age and sense of projected public image of oneself as a communicatively competent social actor.

In this context, the example of 16-year-old SM, with less than a year's experience in an English dominant social setting, is instructive. SM totally refused to speak English in the conversational phase of the study. However, upon completion of the narrative writing task in Spanish, he was willing to try to rewrite the narrative in English. The total result is shown in Figure 2b.

Using the Spanish text as a guide, it is evident that he is trying to say that he and his uncle had taken his aunt to a college (parking lot) to teach her how to drive a car. Although his English is extremely limited, he is willing to try it in writing, a situation allowing more privacy and less stress than speech. His English writing reveals his problems are not so much with writing as with English. The joint revision of such texts by the writer and a bilingual instructor can be instrumental in increasing SM's English resources not only for writing but for speech.

To conclude, the polarization of approaches which oppose development of L1 literacy skills to the development of English oral skills as prerequisites for English literacy is misguided, where U.S. Hispanic communities are involved. A program reconciling both methods must be instituted, taking into account the distinction between those components of literacy which are relatively language-independent and those which depend on specific knowledge of literate English conventions. Only a program of this type will help students acquire the highest levels of English literate skills which they are capable of attaining.

The East Los Angeles writing study has not been offered as conclusive demonstration that particular aspects of writing are language-independent and other aspects are language-specific. The samples of languages, students, writings and analyses have been far too limited to warrant such conclusions. Rather, the study and the discussion contained in this paper have been intended to draw attention to the problems which remain for further advances in our knowledge of the ingredients of English writing among language minority students, and to illustrate, in a programmatic way, what some of the basic issues are and some of the directions that may be taken toward solving these problems.

References

Amastae, J. (1981). The writing needs of Hispanic students. In B. Cronnell (Ed.), *The writing needs of linguistically different students* (pp. 99–128). Los Alamitos, CA: SWRL Educational Research and Development.

Cummins, J. (1981a). Age on arrival and immigrant second language learning in Canada: A reassessment. *Applied Linguistics, 2*(2), 132–149.

Cummins, J. (1981b). *Linguistic interdependence among Japanese immigrant students*. Paper presented at the Language Proficiency Assessment Symposium, Warrenton, Virginia.

Cummins, J. (1984). Wanted: A theoretical framework for relating language proficiency to academic achievement among bilingual students. In C. Rivera (Ed.), *Language proficiency and academic achievement,* (pp. 2–19) Clevedon, Avon, England: Multilingual Matters Ltd.

Edelsky, C. (1981a). From "Jimosal (c)sco to "7 narangas se calleron y el-arbolest-triste en lagrymas": Writing development in a bilingual program. In B. Cronnell (Ed.), *The writing needs of linguistically different students* (pp. 63–98). Los Alamitos, CA: SWRL Educational Research and Development.

Edelsky, C. (1981b). Semilingualism and language deficit. *Applied Linguistics,* 4,(1), 1–22.

Ferreiro, E. (1978). What is written in a written sentence?: A developmental answer. *Journal of Education, 160,* 25–39.

Fillmore, C., & Kay, P. (1980). *Progress Report: Text semantic analysis of reading comprehension tests*. Unpublished manuscript, UC Berkeley Depts. of Linguistics and Anthropology.

Goodman, K., & Goodman, Y. (1978). *Reading of American children whose language is a stable rural dialect of English or a language other than English*. (NIE Final Report C-00-3-0087.)

Gumperz, J.J. (1982). *Language and social identity*. Cambridge, England: Cambridge University Press.

Harris, A. J., & Jacobson, M. D. (1982). *Basic reading vocabularies*. New York: Macmillan Publishing Co., Inc.

Heath, S. B. (1983). *Ways with words: Language, life and work in communities and classrooms*. Cambridge: Cambridge University Press.

Hernandez-Chavez, E., & Curtis, J. K. (1982). *Study of graphic sense and its effect on the acquisition of literacy*. Berkeley, CA: Instituto de lengua y cultura.

Hunt, K. W. (1977). Early blooming and late blooming syntactic structures. In C. R. Cooper & L. Odell (Eds.), *Evaluating writing: describing, measuring and judging* (pp. 91–104). Buffalo, NY: NCET.

Kintsch, W., & van Dijk, T. A. (1978). Toward a model of text comprehension and production. *Psychological Review, 85,* 363–94.

Kroch, A., & Hindle, D. (1982). *A quantitative study of the syntax of speech and writing*. (NIE Final Report G-78-0169.)

Labov, W. (1972). *Sociolinguistic patterns.* Philadelphia, PA: University of Pennsylvania Press.

Lambert, W. E., & Tucker, G. R. (1972). *Bilingual education of children: The St. Lambert experiment.* Rowley, MA: Newbury House.

Lawlor, J. (1981). *Sentence combining: Scope and sequence for instruction.* Paper presented at the Annual Meeting of the NCTE. Boston.

Lope Branch, J. M. (1983). *El estado actual del español: observaciones sobre las investigaciones.* Talk presented at the conferences on "Research needs in Chicano Spanish," University of Texas at El Paso.

Mace-Matluck, B. J., Dominguez, D., Holtzman, W. Jr., & Hoover, W. (1983). *Language and literacy in bilingual instruction.* Austin, TX: Southwest Educational Development Laboratory. (NIE Final Report 400-80-0043.)

Michaels, S. (1981). Sharing time: Children's narrative style and differential access to literacy. *Language in society 10*(3), 423–442.

Moll, L. (1981). The microethnographic study of bilingual schooling. In R. V. Padilla, (Ed.), *Ethnoperspectives in bilingual education research* (Vol. 3, pp. 430–446) Ypsilanti, MI: Eastern Michigan University.

Ochs, E. (1979). Planned and unplanned discourse. In T. Givón (Ed.), *Syntax and discourse* (pp. 51–80). New York: Academic Press.

Olson, D. (1977). From utterance to text: The bias of language in speech and writing. *Harvard Educational Review, 47,* 257–281.

Olson, D. R., & Torrance, N. (1981). Learning to meet the requirements of written text: Language development in the school years. In C. H. Frederiksen & J. F. Dominic (Eds.), *Writing: The nature, development, and teaching of written communication* (Vol. 2, pp. 235–256). Hillsdale, NJ: Erlbaum.

Read, C. (1980). Creative spelling by young children. In T. Shopen & J. M. Williams (Eds.), *Standards and dialects in English* (pp. 106–135). Cambridge, MA: Winthrop Publishers Inc.

Sanford, A. J., & Garrod, S. C. (1981). *Understanding written language: Explorations of comprehension beyond the sentence.* Chichester, England: John Wiley & Sons.

Schachter, J. (1974). An error in error analysis. *Language Learning 24,* 205–14.

Schank, R. & Abelson, R. (1977). *Scripts, plans, goals and understanding.* Hillsdale, NJ: Erlbaum.

Shuy, R. W. & Fasold, R. A. (Eds.). (1973). *Language attitudes: Current trends and prospects.* Washington, DC: Georgetown University Press.

Skutnabb-Kangas, T., & Toukomaa, P. (1976). *Teaching migrant children's mother tongue and learning the language of the host country in the context of the sociocultural situation of the migrant family.* Tempere, Finland: University of Tempere. Report on a UNESCO project.

Tannen, D. (1982). Oral and literate strategies in spoken and written narratives. *Language, 58*(1), 1–21.

Vygotsky, L. S. (1978). *Mind in Society.* Cambridge, MA: Harvard University Press.

Wald, B. (1985) Motivation for the language choice behavior of elementary school Mexican American children. In E. E. Garcia & R. V. Padilla, (Eds.) *Advances in Bilingual Education Research.* (pp. 71–95) Tucson: University of Arizona Press.

8

Metapragmatic Knowledge of School-Age Mexican-American Children

Louise Cherry Wilkinson

Graduate School of Education
Rutgers-The State University of New Jersey

Celia Genishi

The Ohio State University

Language development consists of two related but distinct dimensions, basic language skills and metalinguistic awareness, and it involves multiple levels of linguistic forms and functions, including the rules of phonology, syntax, semantic, and pragmatics. We are concerned with metalinguistic awareness and pragmatics. Metalinguistic awareness is the ability to reflect on language itself as an object of knowledge, while basic language skills are comprehension and production. Pragmatics refers to the rules and conventions involved in communicating in social situations.

Pragmatic development reflects the acquisition of the speech conventions of a speaker's community. Previous research on pragmatic development has focused on Anglo middle class, monolingual, English speakers (Wilkinson, Wilkinson, Spinelli, & Chiang, 1984; Ervin-Tripp, 1978; Garvey, 1975; Read & Cherry, 1978). The present study, however, enables a comparison between the speech conventions of the majority (Anglo) speech community and a specific minority community. The Mexican-American children in the present study lived in a city in Texas, near the Mexican border, and is characterized as both bilingual (Spanish–English) and bicultural. Both Mexican and American social and linguistic conventions influenced speakers' communicative behavior.

Pragmatic knowledge is a particularly critical skill for students entering school. Knowing the rules of how to get things done in the classroom is a skill that is not usually taught by teachers, and which may be in part an aspect of the "hidden curriculum." We believe that it is necessary to understand children's concepts for using language, particularly those of children for whom English is not a first language and whose concepts about how to use language with peers and with teachers may be different from the norm in middle-class classrooms in the United States.

The specific aim of the study discussed in this chapter was to examine English-speaking Mexican-American children's metalinguistic awareness of one aspect of pragmatics: the request function. This function was chosen because it is one of the earliest language functions to appear, and because it has been the object of both theory and empirical research. We are concerned with what these children know about use of language in classroom situations. In the present study, several new measures were devised to examine first and third grade English speaking Mexican-American children's metapragmatic knowledge of the use of requests in the classroom.

The Development of Metalinguistic Awareness

Children's metalinguistic knowledge develops with age (Saywitz & Wilkinson, 1982; Van Kleeck, 1982; Wilkinson et al. 1984), and it appears after the development of language useage (Hirsh-Pasek, Gleitman, & Gleitman, 1978). A full awareness of language structure, as measured by multiple tasks, is not found until 7 or 8 years, even though primitive types of metalinguistic awareness are evident as early as 2 years (Clark, 1978). Children are able to focus on language as an object, and manifest this skill in a variety of tasks once they have entered school. In contrast, during the preschool period, children are unable to focus on language separated from communicative function. The metalinguistic skills that emerge during this period focus on the communicative success of messages, rather than on the language itself (Van Kleeck, 1982). In general, the findings concerning emergence of metalinguistic awareness are in accord with the view that the child's metacognitive abilities are limited and fragile during the preschool years, and that they become extensive and durable after the child enters school (Brown, Bransford, Ferrara, & Campione, 1984; Gleitman, Gleitman & Shipley, 1972; Van Kleeck, 1982).

School-Age Children's Metapragmatic Knowledge of Requests

With the exception of a study by Mitchell-Kernan and Kernan (1977) and Wilkinson et al. (1984), no studies have examined school-age children's metapragmatic knowledge of the function. Mitchell-Kernan and Kernan used a role-playing task to elicit requests for action/object with black American children aged 7 to 12 years, and found few age-related differences.

Wilkinson et al. (1984) investigated developmental differences in English-speaking first and third graders' metalinguistic knowledge of the use of requests, using two tasks, comprehension and production, and examining the following differences among requests: directness versus indirectness, politeness through the use of please, and the bases for understanding these differences. The meta-production task involved a role-playing task with dolls where requests were elicited in hypothetical classrooms. The meta-comprehension task involved eliciting judgments of the appropriateness of requests in hypothetical classroom situations, and explaining the bases for the judgments.

The results showed that age differences tended to be of two kinds. First, the politeness of a request, as indicated by the presence or absence of "please," was more prominent for younger children than for older ones. This age difference was consistent over studies in the judgment task and was also evident in the production task. Second, while the child's concern with politeness tended to decline with age, the richness of the child's understanding of indirectness increased considerably with age. Indirectness involves *not* using a direct form in production of requests (e.g., direct imperative, tag question, wh- or yes/no question forms). Indirectness emerged as a more important factor for older than for younger children in their explanations of inappropriate requests.

Equally important were the kinds of metalinguistic awareness of pragmatic rules that were evident in the children regardless of age. No age difference was found for production of indirect forms. Previous research has shown a preference for production of indirect forms in preschool children aged 4½–5½ (Garvey, 1975). The data reported here showed that this preference persists over the age range of 5–8 years, and that the degree of preference remains constant over these years. Another effect that was constant over age concerned the object of the request. Whether the object was action or information affected the directness of a request, and the explanation given for judging a request to be inappropriate. These results are consistent with a sociolinguistic view, since the type of request produced depends on whether the object of the request is action or information.

Methods for the Study of Metalinguistic Knowledge

Since many of the extant studies have employed a single task to assess metalinguistic awareness, it may be useful for us to consider some methodological issues in the study of metalinguistic awareness. Use of but one task can provide a limited view of children's knowledge.

In previous research, four kinds of tasks have been used to examine children's metalinguistic awareness: production, comprehension, reflection, and inference. Meta-production tasks most typically elicit behavior in conditions that resemble "real-life" situations in which the behavior typically occurs. The meta-production tasks are less concrete than simple production tasks. They often involve imaginary settings and provide less internal motivation for communication. An example of this type of task is given by de Villiers and de Villiers (1974), who requested subjects to repair inappropriate, unacceptable, or inadequate statements made by puppets.

Metacomprehension tasks are less concrete than the meta-production tasks. Judgment tasks are most often used, in which the subject is required to evaluate the behavior produced by another speaker along dimensions such as accuracy, well-formedness, and appropriateness, among others. For example, Bates (1976) asked her subjects to evaluate the politeness of the speech generated by puppets to an elderly female puppet.

In a third type of task, subjects are required to reflect about the behavior under study, and to provide information about their own internal processing of it. Both this reflection task, and the fourth type of task, which involves the experimenter making inferences about the subject's internal psychological state, have been more commonly used in assessments of meta-cognitive abilities, not specifically concerned with language (e.g., Meichenbaum & Butler, 1980; Sternberg, Conway, Ketron, & Bernstein, 1981).

In the present study, Mexican-American school-age children's metapragmatic knowledge of the request function was examined with three tasks: production, comprehension, and reflection. The metaproduction task involved a role-playing task with dolls, where requests were elicited in an imaginary classroom. The metacomprehension task involved eliciting judgments of the appropriateness of requests in hypothetical, classroom situations. Explanations of the reasons for the judgment were also elicited. The reflection task consisted of an open-ended interview, which provided subjects an opportunity to talk about the use of requests in the classroom. In this study, we wanted to discover whether the finding of Wilkinson et al. (1984) could be replicated with a sample of children whose first language was not English but for whom English was the only language of instruction provided in school.

Methods

Subjects

Twenty English speaking Mexican-American, middle-class, children aged 6 to 9 years participated in the study. There were 9 males and 11 females, of whom 10 were in first grade and 10 were in third grade.

Data Collection

Each child was tested individually at school by one female experimenter. All tasks were audio-taped.

Prior to administering the tasks, the experimenter conversed with the child for several minutes and briefly explained the activities that would follow, including the four tasks: metalinguistic production, judgment, and interview tasks and the Peabody Picture Vocabulary Test. The interview was administered first for all subjects, because pilot testing showed that rapport between the experimenter and the subject could best be established early in the testing session with the interview. The remaining tasks were administered in a counterbalanced order for the subjects.

The *interview* (Appendix A) consisted of 12 questions (see Appendix A) concerning the use of language and, specifically, the use of requests in the classroom. The questions were paraphrased if the subjects did not respond appropriately or requested clarification. Subjects were asked to expand their responses occasionally, with prompts such as: "Can you tell me more?", "What's cool talking?", "Can you show me?"

Each of the remaining tasks contained two types of requests for information (procedures, academic information) and one type of request for action. Each task also contained one segment for a student-listener, and one for a teacher-listener.

The *judgment* task required subjects to evaluate the appropriateness of various requests. The subject was shown a picture of two students seated at a table in a classroom and a picture of a student seated at the table with a teacher standing beside him or her. The experimenter described a situation about one of the students at the table who needed directions for a worksheet, a pencil, and help spelling a word. The subjects were required to judge the adequacy of five requests directed to another student-listener, and of the same requests directed to a teacher-listener for each of the three types of requests (procedures, academic information, action). The judgment task was administered according to the following script:

"This is Pat." (Show picture of student sitting at a table with a pencil and paper in front of her/him.) "S/he just got back from the library and missed the instructions on how to do the worksheet. So s/he needs some help. You will hear some ways that Pat asks her/his classmate Chris and a teacher, Mrs. Garcia, for help. I want you to tell me if you think that that is a good way to ask for help."

(Show picture of a teacher-listener or student-listener standing beside Pat.) Pat will ask each of the following to the teacher-listener, and the student-listener:

1. How do I do this page?
2. Can you tell me how to do this page, please?
3. I missed the instructions for the worksheet.
4. You tell me how to do this worksheet right now.
   (For each segment ask): "Was that a good way to ask for help from _____?"
   (If the child responds "no" ask): "Why not?" (followed by) "What would be a better way to ask?"

In other words, if the subject judged a request as inappropriate, then he or she was asked to provide an explanation and a more appropriate form. Thus, the appropriateness judgment differs from a right or wrong judgment. The alternative forms of requesting varied along directness and politeness dimensions and of interest were age-related differences in the judged appropriateness for each form as well as explanations for inappropriateness judgments.

The requests were produced by a tape-recording of either a male child's voice or a female child's voice.

The *production* task consisted of two scripted narratives about a student who needed help with worksheet procedures, academic content, and a colored marker, all of which the student in the script needed to complete the assigned work. In one script, the student directed requests to a teacher, and, in the other script, the student directed requests to another student. The experimenter related the narrative to the subject, stopping at various points in the script to give the subject an opportunity to produce the appropriate request. Props used with the narrative included wooden dolls to represent actors in the script, markers, and worksheets. Following is a sample of the instructions.

E: "We're going to act out a story with dolls. Let's pretend this is Tony (Toni). S/he is a kindergarten/first/second/third grader, and this is a kindergarten/first/second/third grade teacher. The children in Tony's class are supposed to do this worksheet. Pretend that Tony is at the school library and is not in the room. The teacher is going to tell the class what to do. She says, 'Find the pictures that

go together. Draw a circle around them. Use an orange marker.'
The first picture is some potato chips. The second is lemonade with
a straw. And the last is a cake. Now Tony comes in. The teacher
gives Tony a worksheet. Tony doesn't know what to do. How can
s/he find out what to do?

S: (Ask the teacher)
E: "Ok, show me a good way for Tony to ask the teacher for help."
S: (Asks teacher what to do)
E: (Repeats instructions)
E: "Pretend that Tony needs an orange marker. Show me what he would do."
S: (Asks teacher)
E: "Pretend that Tony doesn't know which pictures go together. What would Tony say to get help from the teacher?"
S: (Asks teacher)
E: "Pretend that Tony doesn't know the next answer either. Make her/him get help."
S: (Asks teacher)

English language knowledge was assessed with the Peabody Picture Vocabulary Test (Dunn & Dunn 1981) and the Loban (1976) analysis. The latter assessment was based on the informal conversation between the experimenter and the subject, which provided scores on two scales of grammatical complexity: the mean number of words, and the mean number of dependent clauses in a communication unit. For purposes of statistical analysis, we derived a single composite measure of English language knowledge by (a) standardizing the vocabulary (PPVT) score and the two scores of grammatical complexity, and (b) computing the first principal component of the three standard scores.

Data Analysis

All of the data were transcribed within two weeks of collection. The data base consisted of: 20 sets of responses to the 12 questions in the interview; 480 judgments; 320 requests.

Different coding systems were employed with the different kinds of data. The subjects' responses to the questions in the interview were analyzed qualitatively, without statistical tests.

The subjects' judgments were first separated into "appropriate" and "inappropriate" categories. Secondly, the explanations were coded for adequacy. Inadequate explanations included no explanation, "because" standing alone or noncompletion, an example of a different request, and an explanation irrelevant to the dimension of appropriateness (e.g., "it's too sad"). Adequate explanations included the following: those with evaluative content (e.g., "That was bad"); with formal violation (e.g., "No please"); with pragmatic violation (e.g., too direct); with pragmatic violation in the nonverbal domain (e.g., the observation that one does not just take material, but has to request it; this only applies to the request for materials).

The requests produced by the subjects were coded according to the indirectness of the form employed in the request. Indirect requests were defined as those that contained a declarative statement with the intent of eliciting a response, or an embedded request with or without "please (questions or modal verb)." Direct requests were defined as those that included the direct syntactic form for the request (e.g., the imperative of the Wh- question), or a request for confirmation. "Please" could be appended to the direct form, without any alteration in coding.

Results

The Interview

The purpose of the interview was to collect information about the metapragmatic knowledge that was assessed in the two subsequent experimental tasks. Interview data were first analyzed according to *themes*. The criterion for a theme was the frequency of occurrence in the subjects' responses. There were two frequent themes, *speaking when called upon* and *indirectness* as a "good way" to ask for help. A less frequently occurring theme was the *teacher as a source of help for information*. A fourth theme, *politeness*, was established, not by the students' responses, but by the interview questions.

With respect to the first theme, 16 students (eight in each grade) said that they *speak when called upon*, in response to question 3, "When do you talk at school?" Seven subjects (six first graders and one third grader) said that they speak in a lesson context, for example, reading or language. Further, four children (two in each grade) said that one talks at school in case of emergency, such as when a child is hurt on the playground.

The second theme of *indirectness* in asking for help appears in 18 students' (nine at each level) responses to questions 5 and 9. When they articulate a good way to ask for help, they used question forms. Fourteen students (six first graders and eight third graders), in response to questions 6 and 10, used an imperative as an example of a bad way to ask for help. Not offering the listener a choice or forcing him/her to do something was bad. One third grade subject used an imperative with a clear threat to illustrate a bad way, "Help me or I'll beat you up," and "Give me your book or I'll shoot you." For him and six other subjects, the least indirect, not verbally mediated, act was the worst way to ask for something.

A third theme is that of the *teacher as source of help*. Five first graders and eight third graders answered questions 4 and 7 by saying that one should get help from the teacher. The underlying sociolinguistic rule might be, "Don't ask another child for help; ask the teacher." This suggests that these children's view of learning in the classroom is a traditional one in which the teacher is the primary source of information and the only legitimate source of help.

With respect to *politeness*, there was no consensus within grade levels, but there was a marked difference between them. Five first graders equated politeness with niceness, kindness, or talking about pleasant topics, whereas third graders focused on politeness forms—for example, please, thank you, saying you're sorry. Four first graders seemed not to understand the word *polite*. In contrast, all third graders responded as if they knew the word and its meaning. Although the children seemed to revere the authority of the teacher, 11 of them (seven first graders and four third graders) responded to questions 7 and 11 by saying that they would talk to children and the teacher in the same way.

Closely related to politeness and how one speaks to peers and teachers are questions 1 and 2, about "good" and "bad" talking. Five students in each grade said "bad" talking is mean, bad, or without manners. Rudeness seemed to constitute "bad" talking. The definition of "good" talking seemed to present problems to many children at both levels, as they appeared to be puzzled by the question and the answers varied. Five third graders gave the most frequent response: good talkers talk with manners and are polite. Another group of answers was related to the mechanics of talking, for example, moving one's mouth or not stuttering, and to paralanguage (e.g., good talkers don't shout; talk softly and gently).

The third graders seemed to be more proficient English speakers than the first graders. The older children took less time to respond to questions, and their answers were at times elaborate. Two first graders said almost nothing in response to the questions, although they were later able to respond to questions about themselves in the language sample. Although English proficiency could explain some of the subjects' responses, we believe it was not a major factor. The consistency of responses to questions regarding when to speak and how to ask for something demonstrated adequate English proficiency.

A more plausible explanation for some subjects' difficulty with the task may be the nature of the task. First, talking about good and polite talking may have been an unfamiliar activity to these children. Interviews of this type were generally uncommon, since little research was done in the school system. Second, some of the interview questions may not have reflected these children's classroom experiences. For example, when asked questions about helping a classmate, many subjects said that one asks the teacher, not a classmate, for help. In response to question II, about asking a classmate versus the teacher for a book, one first grader said, "I'd ask the teacher because they have the books."

Language Knowledge

The results of the assessment of aspects of structural knowledge of English showed that the children in this study seemed to be functioning below grade level in their knowledge of structural aspects of English, in comparison with standardized norms of the monolingual population. The 20 children were from 7 months to 1 year behind their grade equivalents. We note that the children's knowledge of structural aspects of Spanish was not measured. Assessment of their structural knowledge of English is, therefore, only a partial measure of their general language ability.

The composite measure of language knowledge emerged as a significant predictor of some aspects of metalinguistic knowledge, and these results will be discussed in relation to the results in the metalinguistic production and judgment tasks.

Production Task

Discriminant function analyses were performed on data from the production task.[1] The independent variables in the analysis were Age (the linear trend), Object (a dummy variable contrasting requests for information vs. actions), Type of Information (a dummy variable contrasting academic vs. procedural requests for information), and interactions of Age x Type and Age x Object. The dependent variable in one analysis was the classification of a response as direct/indirect. In a separate analysis, the dependent variable was the classification of indirect responses as modal, embedded-please, yes/no question, or declarative. The data were responses pooled over all children. Since each child contributed a number of responses, the observations were not independent, and the significance levels were not entirely trustworthy. One solution to this problem is to select a statistic that measures the effect of interest, in this case the log of the F value, and to jackknife that statistic by individual

---

[1] Discriminate function analysis, like multiple regression, uses a set of predictor or independent variables. Unlike regression, the predicted or dependent variables are discrete, not continuous.

children (Mosteller & Tukey, 1977). This method assesses the degree to which the effect estimated from the pooled data of all subjects persists when an individual subject is deleted from the analysis.

The upper part of Table 1 shows F statistics from the discriminant function and jackknifing analyses of the production task. The table shows only the effects that reached statistical significance in both types of analysis.

For the production data, there were main effects of both Age and Information/Action, but no significant interaction. Tables 2 and 3 present the frequencies and percentages for the main effects.

Older subjects produced more indirect than direct requests, compared with younger subjects. All subjects were more likely to produce indirect requests, replicating a finding in the literature that in the transition from the kindergarten to first grade years, there's an increase in the production of indirect request forms. These children used indirect forms to request action more often than information.

Table 1. F Values for Discriminant Function Analyses and for Jackknifing Analyses

		Pooled Discriminant Function		Jackknife	
		F	df	t	df
Production Task					
Indirectness	Age	31.17**	1,298	6.49**	19
	Object	9.79**	1,298	5.30**	19
Type of Indirectness	Object	4.82**	2,452	4.71**	19
	Type	4.24*	2,452	2.41*	19
Judgment Task					
Appropriateness	Age	10.55**	1,457	2.72*	19
	Object	17.30**	1,457	7.70**	19
	Type	3.93*	1,457	3.26**	19
Explanation	Age	17.56**	1,457	3.26**	19
Kind of Explanation	Age	8.05**	2,628	2.68*	19

**$p < .01$
*$p < .05$

Table 2. Production Task: Effect of Age on Frequency of Direct and Indirect Requests

	Age	
	6–7	8–9
Request		
Direct	52(35%)	15(9%)
Indirect	96(65%)	145(91%)

Table 3. Production Task: Effect of Object of Request on Frequency of Direct and Indirect Requests

	Object of Request	
	Information	Action
Request		
Direct	59(26%)	8(10%)
Indirect	171(74%)	70(90%)

Embedded forms plus please were the most frequent form used for indirectness, followed by modal forms and declaratives, as indicated by the frequencies and percentages given in Table 4. Within requests for information, the data in Table 5 show that embedded forms plus please were most often used for both academic and procedural requests. For procedural requests, modals were second in frequency, followed by declaratives, whereas declaratives were used more frequently than modals for indirect requests for academic information.

Judgment Task

For the judgment task, discriminant function and jackknifing analyses were performed, as had been done for the production task. The independent variables were the same, but the dependent variables were different. One dependent variable was whether the request form was

Table 4. Production Task: Effect of Object of Request (Information/Action) on Type of Indirectness

	Object of Request	
	Information	Action
Type of Indirectness		
Modal	30(18%)	17(25%)
Embedded + please	110(65%)	51(75%)
Declarative	29(17%)	0(0%)

Table 5. Production Task: Effect of Type of Information (Academic/Procedure) on Kind of Indirectness

	Type of Information	
	Academic	Procedure
Type of Indirectness		
Modal	17(15%)	13(23%)
Embedded + please	70(63%)	40(70%)
Declarative	25(22%)	4(7%)

judged appropriate or inappropriate. A second dependent variable was whether explanations for judgments of "inappropriate" were adequate or not. A third dependent variable focused on the types of explanations reflected in those that were adequate (evaluative content, "please," pragmatic-verbal, pragmatic-nonverbal). Results of these analyses are shown in the bottom part of Table 1.

Age, Object, and Type emerged as statistically significant and consistent main effects for judgments of appropriateness. Older subjects were more likely than younger subjects to judge any given request as inappropriate ("no"). Table 6 shows this effect, which represents a change in response bias over age. Although the linear trend in age is significant, there is some vacillation and the trend may have been attributable to a few subjects. Children were more likely to provide a "no" judgment for requests for action (67%) than information (48%), and they were more likely to provide a "no" for requests for academic (53%) than procedural (42%) information.[2]

The adequacy of subjects' explanations varied by Age (see Table 1). Table 7 shows that older children were more likely to provide inadequate explanations than younger children. Table 8 indicates that both older and younger children's explanations referred most often to politeness violations ("please"). Their second most frequent explanation relied on evaluations of the content of the request.

Table 6. Judgment Task: Effect of Age on the Frequency With Which Requests Were Judged as Appropriate

	Age	
	6–7	8–9
Judged as Appropriate		
Yes	123(53%)	90(38%)
No	109(47%)	145(62%)

Table 7. Judgment Task: Effect of Age on Whether an Explanation Was Adequate

	Age	
	6–7	8–9
Explanation Adequate		
Yes	182(78%)	143(61%)
No	50(22%)	92(39%)

---

[2] These are percentages of the following frequencies: Requests for action = 157; requests for information = 310; requests for academic information = 156: and requests for procedural information = 154.

Table 8. Judgment Task: Effect of Age on the Frequency With Which Each Kind of Explanation Occurred

	Age	
	6–7	8–9
Kind of Explanation		
Evaluative Content	75(41%)	37(26%)
Politeness	100(55%)	86(60%)
Pragmatic	7(4%)	20(14%)

When we add in the factor to the discriminant analyses of the knowledge of structural aspects of English, there is an interaction effect involving knowledge of English in the production of the type of indirectness (Tables 9 and 10). The data show that children who have a higher level of knowledge of structural aspects of English tend to produce a greater variety of indirect forms in their request for information (Table 9). In contrast, the children who have low and medium levels of knowledge of structural aspects of English tend only to produce the one form, that is, the embedded imperative plus please, and there seems to be a routinized aspect of their production in contrast to the higher ability children.

Children of low and medium language knowledge based their explanations on politeness, whereas the children with greatest knowledge of English language structure based their explanation on evaluative content (Table 11).

Table 9. F Values for Discriminant Function Analyses and for Jackknifing Analyses (With Language Knowledge)

		Pooled Discriminant Function		Jackknife	
		F	df	t	df
Production Task					
Indirectness	Age	29.57**	1,293	6.23**	19
	Object	9.36**	1,293	5.08**	19
Type of Indirectness	Object	5.64**	2,442	4.64**	19
	Type	4.84*	2,442	2.89**	19
	Language/Type	6.12**	2,442	2.37*	19
Judgment Task					
Appropriateness	Age	11.81**	1,452	3.00**	19
	Object	18.06**	1,452	8.07**	19
	Type	3.87*	1,452	3.02**	19
Explanation	Age	17.70**	1,452	2.92**	19
Kind of Explanation	Age	10.31**	2,618	3.66**	19
	Language	11.93**	2,618	3.47**	19

**$p < .01$
*$p < .05$

Table 10. Production Task: Effects of Type of Information (Academic/Procedure) and Language Knowledge on Type of Indirectness

	Type of Information					
	Academic			Procedure		
Language Knowledge	Low	Medium	High	Low	Medium	High
Type of Indirectness						
Modal	10(24%)	1(2%)	6(22%)	5(29%)	3(14%)	5(28%)
Embedded + please	28(68%)	31(71%)	11(41%)	11(65%)	12(73%)	13(72%)
Declarative	3(7%)	12(27%)	10(37%)	1(6%)	3(14%)	0(0%)

Conclusion

To summarize the major findings from this study: (a) Relative to their age and grade counterparts, this sample of 20 children seems to have less knowledge of the structural aspects of English than their monolingual counterparts. (b) The second major finding is that the older children tended to produce more indirect requests than younger children. (c) Older children tended to have both polite and indirect bases for their explanations, while younger children tended to use politeness and explanations based on evaluative content. (d) Children who had a high level of knowledge of structural aspects in English tended to show more variety in their production of indirect forms, and they also showed that same variety in their production of different types of explanations. The variety for the higher ability children stood in sharp contrast to the low and medium ability children, who tended to produce only one indirect form and provided only the explanation of politeness for their judgments. This variety may be an indication of instability, however, and these children may be on their way to a greater reliance on one or two indirect forms and to the predominance of pragmatic bases for explanations rather than the production of all three types of explanations.

It appears that, with these Mexican-American children, we may have captured the transition between first and third grades in the greater production of indirect forms as the children become older. The study suggests that there are age-related differences in metalinguistic awareness

Table 11. Judgment Task: Effect of Language Knowledge on Type of Explanation

	Language Knowledge		
	Low	Medium	High
Type of Explanation			
Evaluative Content	15(13%)	50(45%)	47(45%)
Politeness	85(76%)	57(52%)	44(43%)
Pragmatic	12(11%)	3(3%)	12(12%)

of pragmatic rules between the time when the child enters school and the third grade. This knowledge appears to emerge when the child enters and becomes elaborated and differentiated within that 2-year period.

This study reveals that these Mexican-American children placed a greater emphasis on politeness, as opposed to directness, than their monolingual counterparts in earlier studies (Wilkinson et al., 1984). Because we were unable to observe the children's classrooms, we do not know whether their teachers valued politeness or whether the community at large emphasized it. The experimenter's informal observations during the data collection period supported the conclusion that the emphasis on politeness was a cultural difference between these Mexican-American children and our previous monolingual subjects. The Mexican-American children behaved in a more restrained and formal manner with the experimenter than monolingual age-mates in other communities in which we have conducted research. If teachers expected restrained and respectful behavior from their students, the Mexican-American subjects were behaving in ways appropriate to their particular educational setting. We expect the same kind of restraint in children from other, non-Mexican-American, communities where teachers' expectations for behavior are similar.

The children's responses to the interview questions suggested that politeness and asking permission of the teacher were highly valued. Thus, another important difference between this study and earlier work is that in this elementary school, peer interaction may not have been encouraged. Primary reliance on the teacher for information and help may explain why the children, particularly the younger ones, gave explanations that responded to the content of requests rather than to pragmatic bases. For example, one child's answer to the question, "How would you ask a friend for a book?" was, "I'd ask the teacher." Since their interaction with peers, at least about academic content, was limited, the experimenter's questions required the children to produce requests for hypothetical situations, not ordinarily encountered in their classrooms.

References

Bates, E. (1976). Language and context. *The acquisition of pragmatics.* New York: Academic Press.

Brown, A. L., Bransford, J. Ferrara, R., & Campione, J. (1984). Learning, remembering and understanding. In J., Flavell & E. Markman (Eds.), *Carmichael's manual of child psychology* (Vol. 1 pp. 77–166). New York: Wiley.

Clark, E. (1978). Awareness of language: Some evidence from what children say and do. In A. Sinclair, R. Jarvella, & W. Levelt (Eds.), *The child's conception of language* (pp. 17–44). New York: Springer-Verlag.

de Villiers, J., & de Villiers, P. (1974). Competence and performance in child language: Are children really competent to judge? *Journal of Child Language, 1*, 11–22.
Dunn L. & Dunn L. (1981). *Peabody Picture Vocabulary Test Revised.* Circle Pines, MN: American Guidance Service.
Ervin-Tripp, S. (1978). Wait for me roller-skate. In S. Ervin-Tripp & C. Mitchell-Kernan (Eds.), *Child discourse* (pp. 165–188). New York: Academic Press.
Garvey, C. (1975). Requests and responses in children's speech. *Journal of Child Language, 2*, 41–63.
Gleitman, L., Gleitman, H., & Shipley, E. (1972). The emergence of the child as grammarian. *Cognition, 1*, 131–163.
Hirsh-Pasek, K., Gleitman, L., & Gleitman, H. (1978). What did the brain say to the mind? A study of the detection and report of ambiguity by young children. In A. Sinclair, R. Jarvella, & W. Levelt (Eds.), *The child's conception of language* (pp. 97–132). New York: Springer-Verlag.
Loban, W. (1976). *Language development.* Champaign, IL: National Council of Teachers of English.
Meichenbaum, D., & Butler, L. (1980). Cognitive ethology: Assessing the streams of cognition and emotion. In K. Blankstein, P. Pliner, & J. Polivy (Eds.), *Advances in the study of communication and affect: Assessment and modification of emotional behavior* (pp. 2–25). New York: Plenum.
Mitchell-Kernan, C., & Kernan, K. (1977). Pragmatics of directive choice among children. In S. Ervin-Tripp & C. Mitchell-Kernan (Eds.), *Child discourse* (pp. 189–210). New York: Academic Press.
Mosteller, F., & Tukey, J. (1977). *Data analysis and regression.* Reading, MA: Addison-Wesley.
Read, B., & Cherry, L. (1978). Preschool children's production of directives. *Discourse Processes, 1*, 223–245.
Saywitz, K., & Wilkinson, L. Cherry. (1982). Age-related differences in metalinguistic awareness. In S. Kuczaj (Ed.), *Language development: Language, thought, and culture* (pp. 229–250). Hillsdale, NJ: Erlbaum.
Sternberg, R., Conway, B., Ketron, J., & Bernstein, M. (1981). People's conceptions of intelligence. *Journal of Personality and Social Psychology, 41*(1), 37–55.
Van Kleeck, A. (1982). The emergence of linguistic awareness: A cognitive framework. *Merrill-Palmer Quarterly, 28*(2), 237–265.
Wilkinson, L. Cherry, Wilkinson, A. Cherry, Spinelli, F., Chiang, Chi-Pang. (1984). Metalinguistic knowledge of pragmatic rules in school-age children. *Child Development, 55*, 2130–2140.

Appendix A: Interview Questions

1. If a person is a good talker how does (s)he talk?
2. If a person is not a good talker how does (s)he talk?
3. When do you talk at school?
   Can you think of some more times when it is important for you to talk?

4. Suppose some one in your class needs help with an assignment. Are some ways to ask for help better than other ways?
5. What would be a good way to ask for help?
6. What would a bad way to ask for help?
7. Suppose someone in your class needs help with an assignment. Would they ask a teacher for help in the same way that they would ask a classmate? (If no,) how would they be different?
8. Suppose someone in your class wanted to borrow a book. Are some ways to get the book better than others?
9. What would be a good way to try and get the book?
10. What would be a bad way to try and get the book?
11. Suppose someone in your class wanted to borrow a book. Would they ask a teacher in the same way that they would ask a classmate? (If no,) how would the ways be different?
12. What is polite talking?

9

Teacher Language Use in a Chinese Bilingual Classroom

Larry F. Guthrie
Grace Pung Guthrie
Far West Laboratory for Educational Research and Development

Recent research has shown that the ways children and teachers use language in classrooms can contribute to children's acquisition of both social and academic skills (Cazden, John, & Hymes, 1972; Green, 1982; Green & Wallat, 1981; Trueba, Guthrie, & Au, 1981; Wilkinson, 1982).

This study involved a sociolinguistic examination of the language use of two different teachers interacting with a group of Chinese-American first-graders. The class of limited-English speaking students alternated each half-day between a Chinese bilingual teacher and a non-Chinese-speaking teacher. Our goals were, first, to describe, quantitatively and qualitatively, the interactions between teachers and their students; and, second, to uncover what differences knowing the students' first language (Cantonese) made in the way teachers organized and conducted instruction. In the first section, we discuss theoretical and methodological issues specific to cultural and linguistic minorities, and review relevant research in the area of classroom language use.

Language Use in Classrooms

In instructional contexts, teachers are responsible for orchestrating their interactions with students, including, not only the presentation of academic content, but also the distribution of student turns and the overall maintenance of order (Green, 1982). Teachers determine the rules for questioning and answering, rules for turn-taking, the types of questions asked, and which behaviors are sanctioned. Research has also examined the possible effects of teacher differences, variation in students' communicative competence, student group status, and so on.

In general, the focus of recent research on language use in classrooms had been less on the strictly linguistic aspects of language than on the uses to which language is put and the functions it serves. The traditional notion of second language proficiency held that knowledge of a language involves the mastery of particular phonological and grammatical features. Hymes (1974) and others, however, have pointed out that the ability to manipulate linguistic rules or mimic native-speaker phonology does not insure effective communication in the second language. How teachers and students *use* language, rather than particular linguistic aspects of their speech, may have more to do with the way children learn, and the miscommunication, misunderstanding, and educational difficulty students encounter (Guthrie & Hall, 1983; Hymes, 1972; Gumperz, 1981).

A major focus of research from the perspective of language *use* has been on the possible mismatch between how language, is used at home and at school. If there is a discontinuity between the students' home language use and that required for success at school, then the opportunities for success for those students are reduced (Guthrie & Hall, 1983; Hall & Guthrie, 1981; Heath, 1983). Students of different cultural and linguistic backgrounds, for example, act and use language according to the rules of their community and culture while at home; in the school, a different set of rules is operative.

Even learning to read in school is in many respects an interactional process. Whereas reading for adults is usually a solitary endeavor—they read silently to themselves—reading for children most often takes place in a group (Cazden, 1979; Guthrie & Hall, 1984). If interactions within that group are compatible with the students' native ways of communicating and organizing interactions, then learning should be facilitated. The degree to which miscommunication is minimized should also contribute to student success.

Theoretical and Methodological Issues in Studying Language Use

The study of language use in classrooms has in recent years become an interdisciplinary endeavor engaging scholars from a variety of fields: anthropology, education, linguistics, psychology, and sociology. Cross-fertilization of ideas and approaches has become so pervasive that some researchers span several disciplines in their work. While they may differ somewhat in scholarly background, perspective, and method, certain themes run through most of their work.

A common assumption of research from this perspective is that the functions and uses of language and other communicative means are relative to particular cultures, and even subcultures. Languages vary, for example, in the amount and way in which they are integrated into a culture (Hymes, 1974), and ways of speaking, gestures, songs, touching, and other means of communication may occupy different positions in one culture or another, so that the nature of communicative competence varies. What we use *speech* to communicate, another culture may communicate with *gesture*, or what is an appropriate way of speaking in a given context for one culture may be unacceptable in another.

This theoretical perspective has several implications for the research methodology. Ervin-Tripp and Mitchell-Kernan (1977) have identified five common themes affecting method; studies of language use should take these into account.

Natural Language in Context. First, the data source for studies of conversation or children's language should be natural language in context. Traditional methods of language study, such as interviews and introspection, have proved inadequate. Research has shown that, for children (and adults), the interview situation tends to cause the subject's speech to shift toward a more formal register (Labov, 1972; Ervin-Tripp & Mitchell-Kernan, 1977). Self-report is also suspect. In a recent example cited by Legarretta-Marcaida (1981), for instance, teachers were asked to estimate the relative amounts of English and Spanish they used in the classroom. They reported using each language to an equal degree, but subsequent observations showed English was actually used nearly 75% of the time.

Researchers have two alternatives. The first is to observe language in use and make use of on-the-spot coding or note-taking. The most popular observational system for classrooms is that of Flanders (1970), but a wide variety of observational schemes are used in educational research and evaluation. Most of these, however, do not focus on language and language use per se. The Flanders system has been used in modified form for bilingual classrooms (Legarretta, 1979). More recently, structured observation instruments for the specific purpose of examining language use have been developed, such as those used in the Significant Bilingual Instructional Features Study (Tikunoff, 1983). In the Time Allocation Procedure (TAP), for example, the observer codes instances of language change, recording the addressee (individual, small group, or whole group) and the ostensible function of the first statement (discipline, procedures, or instruction). While such a system may be useful for describing turn-taking, relative amount of language use, and their relation to various instructional variables, it has serious limitations when it comes to describing discourse. Chief among them is the basic fact that all information-gathering is done on-the-spot and restricted to a fixed set of categories. These schemes are thus inadequate for capturing the more subtle aspects of language-in-use and multiple functions of language. The complexities of social interaction are so great that no observer, no matter how astute, can see everything; he can take note of even less. For these reasons and others, the use of structured observations as a means for describing discourse has been widely criticized (Labov & Fanshel, 1977; Mehan, 1979).

A second alternative is to utilize some sort of recording device, either audiotape, videotape, or film (see Erickson & Wilson, 1982). In this way, a permanent record of an interaction is produced which will allow repeated viewing or listening. In Erickson and Schultz's method (1981), for instance, researchers may view videotapes scores of times in the course of the analysis. In addition, by using more than one microphone or camera, different perspectives on the same interaction can be made available. This is not to say, of course, that the use of mechanical devices represents a perfect method; the process is time-consuming and the data sample is thereby necessarily limited. For the study of discourse, however, it appears that the use of recordings to some degree is required.

In the present study, a combination of research techniques was employed. Descriptive fieldnotes were taken in the first phase of the study in order that students and speech events for later recording could be identified. Then audio-tape recordings of the natural speech of target children and teachers were made and supplemented by fieldnotes. While one researcher operated the recording equipment and noted speakers, another described the contexts of actions and activities.

Beyond the Sentence Level. The second theme identified by Ervin-Tripp and Mitchell-Kernan (1977) was that the study of discourse includes elements of language beyond the sentence level. Traditional linguistic studies saw no particular reason to look at stretches of language longer than the sentence; neither did the early transformational grammarians (Chomsky, 1965). More recently, however, it has become apparent that multiple constraints beyond the sentence level operate on the production of speech. Sociolinguistic study, for example, has moved to a focus on the speech event or speech act. As Hymes (1974) put it, "in seeking structures, Saussure is concerned with the word, Chomsky with the sentence, the ethnography of speaking with the act of speech" (p. 90).

In this study, the focus was on both the speech event and the speech act. Typical speech situations in the two classes were identified through naturalistic observation. Then, through more structured observations, the participant structures of various speech events (lessons) were determined and selections were made for study. Finally, by using the Conversational-act system (Dore, 1977; Guthrie, 1981; Guthrie, 1983), we were able to consider elements of discourse beyond the sentence or utterance level. While this system (to be described in more detail later) codes individual utterances, the coding is done in context, both linguistic and situational.

Social and Situational Constraints. This brings us to the third theme in the study of children's discourse. Most current research on language use recognizes that features of the social and situational context affect linguistic rules and output (for a detailed discussion, see Guthrie & Hall, 1983). In the mutual construction of their discourse, actors make selections about what they want to say next (semantic options), about how to say it (social options), and about the form it will take (linguistic options). At the basis of all these choices, and impinging upon them, is a series of factors which can act as constraints. At the most general level, these include social and cultural facts such as social status and cultural norms. At the most narrow level are facts within the interaction itself, such as particular prosodic or phonological variations.

The various constraints do not operate in isolation, however; all are interdependent and interacting. The influence of broader constraints like culture, in a sense, is filtered through every other level, and is simultaneously experienced in terms of the situation, social context, and task. In the process of interaction, the actor makes lexical, grammatical, phonological, and prosodic selections for each instance of a speech act. All these together are made within the confines of the interaction as established by the actor's own interpretations and definitions of the ongoing environment, and in accordance with his knowledge of interactional facts and rules. As suggested earlier, actors also have at their disposal a wide variety of ways in which to say what they mean and thereby carry out their purposes.

It is at the discourse level that the effects of these selections and the constraints upon them are realized—and meaning is conveyed. Once again, in the present study, by coding utterance in context, the influence of these various constraints is captured.

Variable Rules. The fourth theme is that linguistic rules are variable. For example, as shown definitively by Labov (1966), phonological rules vary according to the situation. It should not, however, be assumed that there is any regular one-to-one correspondence between particular constraints or rules and particular discourse features. Constraints may operate singly or in combination and across the various discourse and linguistic levels. Factors of social status, for example, can just as well influence code choice as phonological variation; a contextualization cue as subtle as rise in intonation can result in a change in code, definition of the situation, or phonological choice. It is not possible to specify exactly how these factors constrain interaction, primarily because they are all filtered through the perception and interpretation of interactants and are, in addition, out-of-awareness. As mentioned earlier, one can never be absolutely certain which factor constrained a particular interaction in a particular way, though an educated guess or approximation is possible. Even in the most ritualized or controlled of cases such as a wedding, a religious ceremony, or an experiment, there is room for flexibility and variation at one level or another.

Multiple Functions in Context. The fifth theme suggested by Ervin-Tripp and Mitchell-Kernan is that conversational utterances can serve multiple functions in context, and that particular functions do not map on to structural features. For example, philosophers recognize two types of meaning, literal (sentence) meaning and nonliteral (utterer's) meaning (Grice, 1975). The former is the meaning which an utterance has regardless of context; the latter is the meaning a speaker imputes in a certain situation. Indirect speech acts are examples of nonliteral language use that occur in everyday conversations. In the right context, for example, when someone says "it's hot in here," he or she is not just commenting on the room temperature, but is indirectly telling someone to open a window. Teachers make frequent use of such devices as when they say, "I like the way Johnny is sitting." This comment not only serves to compliment Johnny, but at the same time reminds all the other students that they had better be still.

In the present study, we have tried to account for the multiple functions of language in two ways. First, we have coded utterances in context—relying on the tapes, transcripts, fieldnotes, and the memory of the coders who were also the data collectors. Second, the Conversational-act coding system allows for double coding so that two functions may be represented.

Teachers' Language Use with Limited-English-Speaking Children

Effective use of language by teachers with limited-English-speaking children (LES) has been the subject of considerable debate. Much of the discussion has focused on the relative amounts of English and the students' first language a teacher should use. Some have attempted to prescribe the relative amounts of each language.

Legarretta-Marcaida (1981), for example, has suggested that for limited- and non-English-speaking children in grades K-2, teachers should use the students' primary language approximately 70% of the time. The English proportion can then be gradually increased to about 50% in later grades. Milk (1981, p. 13) advocated that:

> If a particular classroom is aiming toward truly equal development of both languages, then each language must be used by both teachers and

students more or less equally for the full range of classroom functions. It is not sufficient, therefore, for the languages to be used an equal amount of time—they must also be used to an equal extent to accomplish the principal pedagogical functions of the class.

It has also been suggested that the use of students' first language and English in the same lesson should be avoided. Still others have recommended the almost exclusive use of English (Baker & deKanter, 1982).

Research has in some cases compared teachers' instruction and language use across different student groups. Much of this work has concentrated on the differential treatment of students in lower groups (Good & Brophy, 1974; McDermott, 1976; Rist, 1973). Cherry (1978) conducted a comparative study of teachers' expectations across student communicative competence levels. Her finding was that, while teachers' language use varied with student groups, between-teacher effects were greater. This finding has been supported in the work of Enright, Ramirez, and Jacobs (1981–82), who compared the language use of two teachers with the same group of students in a Hebrew-English bilingual situation.

In a study of Hispanic Americans, Moll, Diaz, Estrada, and Lopes (in press) examined the language use of two teachers, only one of whom spoke Spanish, with the same group of children. They found that the teacher who did not speak the students' first language provided lessons at a lower level of difficulty than did the Spanish speaking teacher. Apparently, the Anglo teacher underestimated the Spanish-speaking students' abilities because he himself did not speak Spanish.

Mohatt and Erickson (1981) compared the cultural congruence of two teachers with their Native-American students. One teacher was of the same culture as the students; the other was not, and had little prior experience in teaching children from that culture. Both, however, were regarded as experienced and competent teachers. Mohatt and Erickson videotaped and analyzed a number of school lessons in each class. One focus of their analysis was pacing, "doing the right things at the right time" (p. 112). Their conclusion was that the Native-American teacher and her students revealed a "shared sense of pacing" in their behavior that was at first absent in the other teacher's class (p. 112).

With the exception of work by Fillmore (1982), Guthrie (1984), and Pung Guthrie (1982, 1985), language use of Chinese students and their teachers has been largely ignored. Further, the work that has been done has been at a more general, descriptive level. It is often assumed that because Asian-Americans have a reputation for high achievement, their children experience little educational difficulty. This attitude obscures the fact that large numbers of recent immigrants from Asia face serious problems in communicating and learning to speak and read English.

Language Use in a Chinese-English Bilingual Classroom

At present, very little is known about how Chinese-speaking children and their teachers mutually construct interactions. In our study, we examined the communicative acts of a group of such children and their teachers, so that we might be able to describe what happens in their lessons and identify instructional and interactional approaches which are particularly effective.

Two basic questions directed the research. The first of these sought an in-depth description of the classroom interaction between Chinese-American children and their teachers. How do teachers orchestrate lessons and how, in turn, do students respond? What variation, in both teacher and student language, is found across English proficiency groups?

Second, we compared the language use of the two teachers. What differences occur between the ways in which the two teachers orchestrate lessons? What effect did knowing Cantonese have on the bilingual teacher's instruction and interaction with students? What are the implications for these differences across linguistic proficiency groups?

Context

The setting for the study was an elementary school with a predominantly Chinese population, located in the heart of a Chinatown community on the West Coast. There were approximately 644 students enrolled in Chinatown Elementary at the time of this study, and almost half of these were Chinese; the remainder of the students were largely Spanish-surnamed, other Oriental (primarily Vietnamese), and black. The school population is relatively stable, but there are periodic influxes of new immigrant and refugee students from the Oriental Education Center where most new immigrants are first enrolled.

Of the 330 Chinese students at Chinese Elementary, 242 (73%) were classified as either limited-English-speaking (LES) or non-English-speaking (NES), and placed in either a bilingual or regular class. Twenty-seven students were enrolled in the first grade bilingual class studied. Of these, all were Asian except for two black students and one East Indian. Prior to data collection, each teacher was asked to rank all students in the class on a four-point scale of oral English proficiency (Fuentes & Wisenbaker, 1979). The bilingual teacher also provided similar information on students' Chinese proficiency. Results of these ratings are given in Table 1. These judgements were then verified through observations of potential target students.

As mentioned above, the two participating teachers in the study taught in a half-day alternation bilingual program. Each teacher met with the stu-

Table 1. Language Proficiency Ratings of Target Class

	Rating			
Language	1 None	2 Some	3 Lacks Fluency	4 Fluent
English	0	6	9	12
Chinese	5	0	6	16

dents in the target class for half of each school day, alternating between mornings and afternoons. One teacher was bilingual and biliterate in Chinese and English, and of the same cultural background as the students; a woman in her early twenties, she had immigrated to the U.S. at the age of nine, and both her Cantonese and English were native-like. We call her Mrs. Wu. The other teacher was an Anglo male who had taught in Spanish-English bilingual programs, but had little prior experience with Chinese students. He spoke no Chinese. We refer to him as Mr. Martin. Both teachers had several years of teaching experience.

Two types of lessons were selected for analysis in this report: Reading with the bilingual teacher and Oral Language in the Anglo teacher's class. Although the lesson context and focus differed somewhat across the teachers' lessons, they were in many respects comparable. For 2 weeks prior to taping, classroom observers took descriptive fieldnotes and coded for activity structures (Bossert, 1978). These two lessons were found to be compatible in that they were both teacher-directed, student membership was approximately the same, and both teachers organized lessons around a basic question/answer format. Descriptions of the typical organization of each teacher's lessons follow.

Reading. The bilingual teacher, Mrs. Wu, divided students into four instuctional groups for Reading: Flintstones, Roadrunners, Bugs Bunnies, and Snoopies. Each group met with her for 15 to 20 minutes during each reading period, rotating according to the schedule she set up.

Reading lessons were conducted in much the same way with each group. The teacher usually began by writing a list of vocabulary words on the board near the reading table. She then introduced each word and asked students to read and say the words as a group. Individual students then were called on to read all the words aloud. The next task often involved using the accompanying story posters, which contained a picture on the top and a brief story below. The teacher asked the students to look at the picture first, and then she asked them to describe it. They would then read the story on the poster together. At other times, she used the student textbook, but adopted the same approach as with the poster, beginning with a description of the picture, followed by reading. The final step in a typical reading lesson was to ask the children to read the text silently, after which the teacher asked them comprehension questions. In answering, students were allowed to read an appropriate phrase or sentence from the text.

Oral Language. The Anglo teacher, Mr. Martin, divided his class for Oral Language into three instructional groups on the basis of oral English proficiency. The Low group consisted of six students, the Middle, nine, and the High, twelve. In the analyses, the Middle and High groups have been collapsed. For Oral Language, Mr. Martin often held up cards depicting animals, occupations, or means of transportation, which students were required to identify, describe, and answer questions about. The overall procedures employed with each group were much the same.

Data Collection

Audiotape recordings were made through the use of a Marantz recorder, with two Lavaliere microphones placed in the middle of each group's table. Two data collectors were present during each taping session, both fluent speakers of Cantonese, Mandarin, and English. One data collector took fieldnotes on the activities of the focal group, recording important nonverbal behaviors, the text and/or materials used, and other contextual information. The other data collector, meanwhile, monitored the audiotape through earphones. Because of incidental noise in the class and the voices of students in other groups, the earphones enabled the data collector to hear much better the speech of the teacher and target students. This data collector wrote down names and utterance fragments of speakers throughout the interaction to aid in subsequent transcription.

Transcription

The audiotape recording of each lesson was transcribed by the data collector who monitored that taping session. The handwritten transcript was then entered into an IBM Personal Computer used for the analysis. Those utterances in Chinese were transcribed in Chinese, and an English translation was provided in brackets. Descriptions of nonverbal behavior were included in parentheses.

Coding

Utterances were coded using a system of Conversational-acts (C-acts) developed by Dore (1977) and employed in several studies of children's language use (Cole, Dore, Hall, & Dowley, 1978; Dore, Gearhart, &

Newman, 1978; Guthrie, 1981; Hall & Cole, 1978). C-acts represent a taxonomy of speech act types which code utterances according to (a) the grammatical structure of the utterance, (b) its illocutionary properties, and (c) its general semantic or propositional content. Because of the different nature and focus of the present research, some modifications were made in the system as used in previous studies. These included both the addition and deletion of certain codes. The revised list of codes, definitions, and examples is presented in the Appendix.

Forty-nine separate speech acts, each assigned a three-letter code, comprise the Conversational-act system employed here. These are grouped into six broad function types: (a) *Assertions*, which solicit information or actions; (b) *Organizational Devices*, which control personal contact and conversational flow; (c) *Performatives*, which accomplish acts by being said; (d) *Requests*, which solicit information or actions; and (e) *Responses*, which supply solicited information or acknowledge remarks (Dore et al., 1978, pp. 372–73). An additional category of *Special Speech Acts*, which codes microphone talk, laughing, singing, etc., is also included. Each function type may include several Conversational-acts. Conversational-acts which function as Requests, for example, include Requests for Action (QAC), Products Requests (QPR), and Requests for Permission (QPM). Responses include Agreements (RAG), Acknowledgements (RAK), Product Answers (QPR), and so on (See Appendix).

Coding proceeded as follows. First, the grammatical form and its literal semantic meaning were determined. Then a judgement was made as to the conventional force, or purpose, of the utterance. In this step, sequencing, reference, and other conversational cues, such as marked illocutionary devices and intonation, were taken into consideration. Utterances were thus placed first within the six broad function types, and then categorized as an individual Conversational-act. Throughout the coding, the contextual information contained in fieldnotes provided an additional check for the validity.

Initial coding was conducted by the data collector who observed a particular lesson. To ensure inter-coder agreement, each taped session was then coded a second time by another member of the research team, all of whom had engaged in 2 weeks of training and practice. Discrepancies were resolved through discussion. Although utterances in Chinese were translated into English and entered as data, all coding was done on the original Chinese in order that no meaning was lost in translation. Throughout the coding process, inter-coder agreement for individual lessons ranged from .90 to .96. It should be noted that Conversational-act coding has been shown to be highly reliable in other studies as well. In both the Cole et al. (1978) and Hall and Cole (1978) studies, inter-rater reliability approached .90.

The speech act approach to discourse analysis has been criticized (Cicourel, 1980) on the grounds that it cannot easily account for (a) organizational features of interaction; (b) participant's strategies, e.g., plans for elaboration; (c) the contextualized nature of discourse and the role of situated meanings; and (d) the multiple functions of utterances. In this study, we attempted to overcome these weaknesses by incorporating the following methods:

First, organizational features of interaction, e.g., participant structures, were identified in initial observations and guided the selection of episodes (lessons) for taping. All coding and analysis was then done with regard to the participant structures. Second, attention was given to participants' local strategies and plans for elaboration in ways of speaking. Because coding was done not on isolated sentences or utterances, but on stretches of discourse, taking the course and development of the conversation into consideration, it was sensitive to speaker's strategies and intentions. In the subsequent qualitative analysis, special attention was given to the questioning strategies each teacher employed in conducting their lessons. Third, since all coding was done on relatively large stretches of language, situational meanings were taken into account. Speakers' utterances were considered in context. Finally, the present study was sensitive to the multiple functions of utterances in context. The C-act system allows for multiple coding so that important meanings and intentions are not lost. Because Conversational-acts are sensitive to grammatical form, semantic content, and illocutionary force, and not just one of these, they provide a link between form and function. Further, in this study, the observers' fieldnotes provided a running description of the context which contributed to the coder's knowledge of and sensitivity to the interaction. The fact that the data collectors conducted the coding also contributed to its validity.

Quantitative Data Analysis

We began with a large corpus of data, nearly 6 hours (340 minutes) of tape recordings consisting of 15,753 coded utterances. Analyses were conducted at the level of the function type (assertion, request, response) and individual C-act. For each speaker, we examined the relative frequency of each function type and C-act within lessons. In this way, we could see what percentage of a speaker's C-acts in reading lessons, for example, were requests, responses, or particular kinds of requests and responses. From the investigation of function type differences, we were able to determine that certain of these, notably Special Speech Acts, occurred so infrequently that data on them could tell us little. We thus focused our attention on these function types: Assertions, Organizational Devices, Performatives, Requests, and Responses. Within each, C-acts having especially high or low usage relative to the teacher and the instructional group were examined further.

Frequency analyses of the 49 different C-acts showed that a large number of these were used very little. Following Green and Harker (1982), we thus established an arbitrary criterion for the investigation of differences in teachers' C-act use. Only C-acts of relatively high frequency, 5% or more of the speaker's contribution to an episode, were considered. The 5% level eliminated all but eight or ten C-acts for each speaker; these were the C-acts through which most of his or her speech was conducted. In comparing C-act use across speakers, only differences of more than 2% were considered significant.

Comparisons were made to determine whether teachers' language use differed in interaction with the same sets of children. These were conducted across each of two groups, High and Low (Table 2). If the proportion for one teacher did not meet the 5% criterion for a particular C-act, that proportion is enclosed in parentheses.

High Group Comparisons. With the High group, the two teachers used similar sets of C-acts and only three of the C-acts in Table 2 (PPR, QCH, and RAK) did not meet the frequency criterion for both teachers. They used Boundary Markers (OBM) and Speaker Selections (OSS) in practically the same proportion, which suggests that they organized the lessons in similar ways.

Table 2. Teachers' Use of C-acts: Proportions

	C-act	Low Group		High Group	
		Wu	Martin	Wu	Martin
Total Coded Utterances		1950	1376	2022	2594
Assertives					
Description	(ADC)	0.09	0.11	0.13	0.09
Organizational Devices					
Attention Getter	(OAG)	(0.02)	0.06	(0.01)	(0.02)
Boundary Marker	(OBM)	0.08	0.10	0.08	0.07
Speaker Selection	(OSS)	0.06	(0.02)	0.07	0.07
Performatives					
Protest	(PPR)	(0.03)	0.07	(0.01)	0.05
Requestives					
Action Request	(QAC)	0.11	0.13	0.06	0.09
Choice Question	(QCH)	0.07	0.06	0.08	(0.04)
Product Question	(QPR)	0.12	0.10	0.09	0.11
Responsives					
Agreement	(RAG)	0.10	0.05	0.09	0.11
Acknowledgment	(RAK)	(0.02)	0.07	(0.02)	0.05

Boundary Markers may have much to do with a teacher's personal speaking style, e.g., the use of "okay" or "now" to set off lesson segments. Speaker selections, on the other hand, indicated the type of turn-taking routine operative in the exchange. When a teacher verbally nominates speakers, a very different way of allocating turns is in force than when students bid for turns, or turns are automatically distributed. For the high group, 7% of the C-acts in each teacher's lessons were Speaker Selections (OSS).

Low Group Comparisons. Comparisons across teachers' language use with the low group revealed both similarities and differences in the C-act frequencies, as shown in Table 2. Consider first those C-acts which were used in similar proportions by both teachers, i.e., which differ by 2% or less. These include Complete Descriptions (ADC), Boundary Markers (OBM), Requests for Action (QAC), Choice Requests (QCH) and Product Requests (QPR). Similar frequencies in these categories suggest that the overall questioning strategies of the two teachers were comparable, and that the task demands for the students were much the same. The rate with which Mr. Martin employed Requests for Action (QAC), however, was over 200 per hour, or nearly 3.5 per minute. In the sample data, this is the highest rate for either teacher with any C-act. By comparison, one teacher in the Enright et al. (1982) study used "directives" at a rate of 2.8 per minute, but that coding system would presumably include other C-acts such as Suggestions (QSU) and Requests for Verbal Action (QVB).

The greatest differences in proportion appear more in regard to the ways of organizing and managing the group, and in responding to student answers. The bilingual teacher, for instance, showed higher proportions of Speaker Selections (OSS) and Agreements (RAG), while Mr. Martin used relatively more Attention Getters (OAG) and Protests (PPR). Requests for Action (QAC) could be an indication of management difficulties on the part of Mr. Martin. In coding the data, Requests for Action, for instance, could include both procedural instructions (Turn the page) and behavioral sanctions (Be quiet and listen). An examination of Mr. Martin's Requests for Action in one lesson revealed that sanctions outnumbered procedures almost three to one.

Differences also emerged in the responses to student answers made by the two teachers. As can be seen in Table 2, both teachers used a combination of Acknowledgements (RAK) and Agreements (RAG), and, interestingly enough, the total proportion of RAG and RAK for each teacher was 12%. Acknowledgements (RAK) and Agreements (RAG) are common ways in which teachers react to student responses. Acknowledgements coded those teacher reactions which were noncommittal, e.g., "yeah," "okay." Agreements, on the other hand, provide the student with an evaluation: "right," "yes," or "no." In the coding of these, distinctions frequently had to be made on the basis of the speaker's intonation. Mr. Martin used a much higher proportion of Agreements (RAG) with the High group (11%) than with the low (5%). This suggests that students in the high group received more feedback on their answers. Over half of the responses Mr. Martin gave to the low group were Acknowledgements (RAK), and thus little information regarding correctness. Mrs. Wu, on the other hand, showed a preference for Agreements (RAG) with both groups, using them at a ratio of more than four to one over Acknowledgements (RAK). Notice that, with the Low group, she employed a much higher proportion of Agreements (RAG) than did Mr. Martin; these constituted fully 10% of her overall speech to the group. This difference suggests that the bilingual teacher provided more informational feedback to the students than did the Anglo teacher. Good examples appear in the passage quoted below. Here, the teacher is asking the students in the group to describe the illustration in their text.

Speaker	C-act	Utterance (9:389-401)
Student 11	RVB	The man is looking.
Mrs. Wu	RAG	Oka-ay.
	QPR	Who is the man looking at?
	OSS	Harriet (Student 52).
Student 52	RPR	The girl.
	RPR	The man is looking at the girl.
Mrs. Wu	RAG	Right.
	QPR	And what is the girl doing?
	OSS	Hieu-Nan (Student 24).
Student 24	RPR	The girl said, "Hi."
Mrs. Wu	RAG	The girl said, "Hi."
	OEX	*Aiya*. [Cantonese exclamation.]
	RAG	That's right!

The use of Speaker Selections (OSS) or Attention Getters (OAG) represent complementary strategies in the organization of interaction within an instructional group. When students are on task and attending to what the teacher says, Speaker Selections may be used to allocate turns; when students are off task, Attention Getters must be employed. These data suggest that Mr. Martin was forced to follow the latter route more often than was Mrs. Wu. With the low group, 6% of his talk was composed of Attention Getters (OAG).

Finally, consider the teachers' use of Protests (PPR) with the low group. The higher frequency of protests in the talk of Mr. Martin are a further indication of the management difficulties he experienced. Protests occupied 7% of Mr. Martin's total speech to the group, and were used at a rate of nearly 117 per hour, nearly two per minute. Mrs. Wu used Protests only 3% percent of the time and at a rate of only 30 per hour.

Mrs. Wu revealed a remarkable consistency in her language use across the groups; indeed, the only C-acts which were significantly different in proportion were Complete Descriptions (ADC), Requests for Action (QAC), and Product Requests (QPR). All other high proportion acts were found to be more or less equivalent. These included Organizers (OBM and OSS), Requests (QCH), and Response (RAG).

Similarities and differences in C-act use across the two instructional groups for Mr. Martin were also examined (Table 2). Language use patterns for Mr. Martin were quite different. Most of the differences in proportion were not particularly great (the largest was 0.06), but six C-acts showed a difference of 0.03 or more across the groups. C-acts favored in the High group included Speaker Selections (OSS), Product Requests (QPR), and Agreement Responses (RAG). With the Low group, Mr. Martin used more Complete Descriptions (ADC), Attention Getters (OAG), Boundary Markers (OBM), Protests (PPR), Requests for Action (QAC), Choice Requests (QCH), and Acknowledgements (RAK). Mr. Martin's language use with the High group, then, was similar to that of Mrs. Wu with her groups. Turns were allocated through Speaker Selection, and feedback was given with Agreements (RAG).

Several of the C-acts used in greater proportion with the Low group have implications for the way in which the group was organized, e.g., Speaker Selections and Attention Getters. Others related more to instruction. In terms of organization, Mr. Martin seemed to have had difficulty managing the Low group. There were higher frequencies of Attention Getters, Protests, and Requests for Action. With regard to instruction, he provided them with more information, and did relatively less questioning. Interactions with the High group, on the other hand, were orderly. Instruction was conducted in a basic Question–Answer– Evaluation format, turns were allocated through Speaker Selections, and there were few calls for attention or protests by the teacher.

Selected Qualitative Findings

The most important findings of the qualitative analyses, as they relate to the development of English language proficiency, concerned the ways in which the bilingual teacher used the student' first language (L1) in instruction. As reviewed above, the use of L1 in classrooms has been widely studied and discussed (Duran, 1981; Gumperz, 1982; Gumperz & Hernandez-Chavez, 1972; Valdes-Fallis, 1978). Gumperz (1982) and others (e.g., McClure, 1981) have proposed typologies of the functions of code-switching. Little attention, however, has been directed to the particular instructional purposes to which teachers might put their limited English speaking students' first language (L1).

In qualitative analysis, we focused on the practical functions which Cantonese served for Mrs. Wu. First, instances in which she used L1 in reading lessons were identified and examined in context. Using the audiotape transcripts, the Conversational-act coding, and observers' fieldnotes, we were able to assign instructional functions to passages with some confidence. In some more ambiguous cases, we listened once again to the original tapes. Potential functions were assigned to each occasion of L1 use, and, following the constant comparative approach (Glaser & Strauss, 1967), these original categories were reduced to a set of five functions. Our interpretations were then triangulated with the teacher. The teacher was shown samples from the transcripts and asked to speculate on possible motivations for language changes.

The analysis reported here was conducted on data from Mrs. Wu's English reading lessons. In contrast to her choice of language throughout the school day, when she made frequent use of Cantonese, Mrs. Wu employed Cantonese in less than 7% of the sampled lessons. Even with a class of limited-English-speaking first graders, her emphasis was on the English language. The students' first language served a definite function, however. Research has shown that code-switching or language alternation among bilinguals is seldom random and usually purposeful, however unconscious. Mrs. Wu, in fact, told us she tried to avoid the use of Cantonese during reading lessons; when she did, she chose those occasions carefully.

This analysis of the teacher's use of Chinese revealed that she employed it for at least five distinct purposes: (a) for translation, (b) as a "we-code," (c) for procedures and directions, (d) for clarification, and (e) to check for understanding. While there may have been others, these appeared to be the most frequent and consistent.

Translation. Mrs. Wu used Chinese to translate particular words which students appeared not to know or which were clearly beyond the range of their vocabulary. Once, for example, she inadvertently used the words "aisles." Sensing a lack of understanding, she followed immediately with a Cantonese translation, which at least one student acknowledged (18:404). On another occasion, she gave a quick, one-word equivalent for the word "country" for a student who stumbled over it while reading aloud. In this manner, Mrs. Wu reduced the students' uncertainty and assured herself that they understood without taking up a lot of class time to explain. While we recognize the *concurrent* translation is ultimately self-defeating, since students learn to screen out their weaker language, the occasional, unplanned translation can be effective. At those times when the goal is overall comprehension rather than vocabulary development, selective translation may be a more expedient approach than trying to explain or demonstrate a word's meaning in English.

We-code. Gumperz (1982) has used the term "we-code" for a language which indicates group membership and personal connection. While Mrs. Wu did not make frequent use of Cantonese for this purpose, she did occasionally appeal to the students' sense of group solidarity, as in the following example when the reading group was becoming disruptive.

Speaker	C-act	Utterance (21:137-144)
Student 91	QAC	Get over.
Student 52	PPR	Stop it!
Mrs. Wu	OAG	Hieu Ngat,
	ADC	she's not doing anything.
	PPR	*Mhsai gam* (Don't be like this.)

A second example is taken from a lesson in which the students had been given flashcards to study. After practice in reading the words aloud, the teacher asked if anyone had lost any cards. Going down the list, she determined that one student had lost them all. Loss of the cards is embarrassing to the student, and the use of Chinese is perhaps mitigating.

Speaker	C-act	Utterance (12:545-552)
Student 15	ADC	*Ditsaai laak.* (I lost them all.)
Mrs. Wu	QPC	*Dimgaai a?* (Why?)
	ADC	*Neih faam ukkei taihah yawhmouh bindouh. Bin. Bin go jih mhgeidak?*
	QAC	*Mhginjo. Gong bei ngoh teng.*
		(You go home and check to see which word you have forgotten, you have lost, then you let me know.
	ORQ	Okay?)

Procedures and Directions. Mrs. Wu also sometimes used Cantonese when giving procedures and directions. In a lesson on declaratives and interrogatives, for example, we recorded the exchange below. Here the teacher wanted students to distinguish between statements (telling sentences) and questions (asking sentences). By providing examples in Cantonese, she was able to ensure that the students understood the task.

Speaker	C-act	Utterance (11:54-64)
Mrs. Wu	ADC/QCH	I can run.
Student 23	RCH	Telling.
Mrs. Wu	RAG	Telling you something.
	RAG	*Mhhaih mahn a.* (It's not asking.)
	ADC	*Ngoh gong bei neigh teng.* (I'm telling you.)
	OBM	Okay.
	ADC	Can you run?
	QCH	*Mahn dihnghaih gong?* (Asking or telling?)
Student 23	RCH	Telling.
Student 25	RCH	*Mahn.* (Asking)
Mrs. Wu	ADC	I can run.
	QCH	*Mahn dihng gong?* (Asking or telling?)
Student 25	RCH	*Gong.* (Telling.)
Mrs. Wu	RAG	*Gong.* (Telling.)

Clarification. One of the new vocabulary words introduced to the Middle and High groups was the word "lost." Mrs. Wu took care to make sure the groups understood what the word meant and in what ways it contrasted with the Cantonese words for the same thing. In one lesson, two of the students appeared to confuse the transitive and intransitive uses of the English word ("I lost my book." vs. "I was lost in the woods."). The students said, for example, "I lost one day" (18:332). In Chinese, this confusion is not possible, since there is a different lexical item for each meaning. Mrs. Wu paused at one point to help the group map these meanings onto the two forms in English.

Speaker	C-act	Utterance (18:451-468)
Mrs. Wu	QPR	What does "I lost my pencil" mean?
Student 23	RPR	*Ngoh mhginjo ngohge bat.* (I don't see my pen.)
Mrs. Wu	RAG	Okay.
	OFS	Where does, uh . . .
Student 25	TRA	*Mhgin yuhnbat.* (Don't see pencil.)
Mrs. Wu	ADC	I was lost in the park.
	QCH	*Haih mhhaih mhginjo neih jinhgei a?* (Does it mean you don't see yourself?)
	QCH/RPC	Does it mean that?
Student 23	RPC	*Ngoh mhginjo hai hai* park. (I can't be seen in the park.)
Mrs. Wu	AEX	*Mhginjo jikhaih dohng-sat-louh gam gaai.* ("Can't be seen" means "got lost".)
	ORQ	Okay?
	AEX	*Mhhaih wah mhginjo.* It doesn't mean "don't see".)

Check for Understanding. Mrs. Wu also used Cantonese to check for understanding. Both the observers' fieldnotes and the audiotapes revealed that Mrs. Wu sometimes sensed that one or more of the group did not quite understand. She told us that the looks on students' faces often gave her a clue. She then either switched to Cantonese or asked for a Cantonese equivalent from the students. In the following excerpt, students were reading English vocabulary words off the board. Suddenly, she stopped and asked in Cantonese for the meaning of "likes." The way the students responded revealed they had confused "likes" with "lights." The teacher then attempted to clarify using English: "He likes the dog."

This example points up an additional benefit of the teacher's facility with Cantonese. By using the students' first language, she was able to ferret out those areas of confusion and misunderstanding. By asking directly for the equivalent word in Cantonese, she quickly and efficiently assessed how well the students understood.

This strategy is not available to the monolingual English speaker. Sensing the same lack of understanding, a teacher who did not speak Cantonese could of course ask for an English synonym (what does "lights" mean?) or for the student to use the word in a sentence (Can you make a sentence with "light"?). He might also conduct a demonstration, turning on and off the lights, for example. For Student 11, however, it is unlikely that these approaches would have been effective. As Mrs. Wu put it, he needed a lot of "language support"; he was uncomfortable using English and insecure about it. He probably could not have used "likes" or "lights" in a sentence, or come up with *any* response in English, much less an appropriate one. His level of understanding would still have been a mystery.

Speaker	C-act	Utterance (16:230-245)
Student 11	RVB	Little . . .
	RVB	Like . . .
	RVB	Likes . . .
Mrs. Wu	QPR	Likes *dim gaai a?* (What does "likes" mean?)
Student 11	RPR	*Dang.* (Light.)
Mrs. Wu	OCQ	*Ha?* (What?)
Student 13	RPR	*Hoi dang.* (Turn on lights.)
Student 11	RPR	*Dang.* (Lights.)
Mrs. Wu	RAG	No. *Mhhaih.* (No.)
	AEX	It's not lights.
	QVB	Likes.
	ADC	He likes the dog.
Student 11	RPR	*Ngoc Jungyi.* (I like.)
Mrs. Wu	RAG	Okay.
	RAG	*Ngoc Jungyi.* (I like.)

These examples point up the value of a teacher's knowing students' first language. Even though Mrs. Wu employed Cantonese only a small portion of the time in her reading lessons—less than 7%—the fact that she had it available as an alternative code appeared to be an important strategy in the lessons observed. Mrs. Wu made a conscious effort to avoid using Cantonese in her reading lessons, because she wanted the students to concentrate on English. When we asked her to try to explain her language choices, she was surprised to see she had used Cantonese as much as she did. By introducing the students' first language when she did, however, Mrs. Wu was able to keep students engaged and facilitate their understanding. The use of Cantonese as a we-code and for procedures and directions enabled her to effectively manage and direct the lessons. Her sensitivity to the variable meanings in Cantonese and English made it possible for her to pick out likely sources of confusion.

Without Cantonese available as an alternate code, Mr. Martin could do none of these. The data from his class reveal just how difficult teaching limited-English speaking children can be for teachers who do not speak their first language. When students did not understand, he was often unable to either make himself understood or to get at the source of the students' confusion, simply because of the language barrier. In the course of one lesson, for example, he suddenly changed the focus, setting up a hypothetical situation. "Let's play a pretend game," he said, asking the group to imagine they got separated from the group during their fieldtrip to the aquarium. "What would you do?" he asked. The students were confused as to the task and its purpose, however. Student 12, for instance, appeared to misunderstand completely the conditional aspect of his request.

Speaker	C-act	Utterance (6:410-415)
Mr. Martin	QCH	Could you go up to the policeman and tell him that you were lost?
Group	RCH	No-o-o.
Mr. Martin	QPC	Why?
Student 12	RPC	I didn't lost.

A brief translation of his statement of the task could have been quite effective in this situation.

In a comparable way, confusion frequently arose because students had difficulty making themselves understood and lacked the English skills necessary to rephrase what they wanted to communicate. In an extended exchange, Mr. Martin sought desperately to figure out whether they were trying to say they had seen a shark, shack, or snake at the aquarium. The prolonged mutual lack of understanding resulted in a situation in which Mr. Martin no longer controlled the direction of the lesson.

Another unfortunate outcome of this situation was that Mr. Martin often sanctioned students when they used Cantonese during lessons. Unable to tell whether what they said was related to the task or not, Mr. Martin often shushed them, assuming they were not paying attention. Our data show, however, that what students said in Cantonese frequently was about the lesson. Sometimes they clarified directions for each other. At other times, they made comments about the lesson or provided answers in Cantonese. In discussing the seal they had seen on a fieldtrip to the aquarium, for example, one student remarked in English that the seal was fat, and Mr. Martin agreed. When another student repeated, "*Hou feih* (so fat)" in Cantonese, however, he quieted her. It was not that Mr. Martin had established an "English only" policy, but during lessons when students spoke to each other in a code he could not understand, he sanctioned them.

Mr. Martin was of course also unable to employ the "we-code" to establish rapport with the students. Like Mrs. Wu, when several students became noisy, he sometimes appealed to them to behave, but without the same result. At one point, he asked a student to sit down, only to learn that she had changed her name to Helen. "Ah-Gnat is not Ah-Gnat now," a classmate explained. Starting to joke, one student announced he had changed his name to Banana and another to Ah-Gnat. Soon all were laughing and shouting. "Oh come on . . . give me a break," Mr. Martin finally pleaded. "Okay, give me a break."

The way in which turns were distributed in Mr. Martin's groups also seemed to contribute to his management problems. Both observations and lessons transcripts showed that the High group was required to raise their hands for a turn, but the Low group was not. In that group, any student could call out an answer. As long as only one or two students responded, this procedure worked, but, as more sought a chance to speak, near chaos broke out.

Other research (e.g., McDermott, 1976; Eder, 1982) has shown that clearly set rules for turn-taking can facilitate reading lessons. Taking turns in a round-robin fashion, one after the other, ensures an equal number of turns for each student. When students bid for turns, turns have to be constantly renegotiated. In Mr. Martin's Low group, turns were not even bid for and renegotiated, but simply claimed. As several students sought to claim a turn simultaneously, the order of the group fell apart and the teacher lost control. Judging from the procedures used with the other group, it is likely that a more structured turn-taking mechanism had been used previously and had simply broken down. If, because of limited English proficiency, students in the Low group were unable to respond individually to the teacher's questions, and he was unable to clarify further, he might have relaxed the rules so that he would at least get an answer from someone.

Discussion

Sociolinguistic studies such as this one are both labor intensive and time consuming. Collection of language samples, coding, analysis, and interpretation require hundreds of hours to complete; and, in the end, one still has data on only a small sample of speakers. Drawing implications from this data is no less difficult, therefore. While the unit of analysis may be the lesson, not the teacher or class, the fact remains that only two teachers and one group of children participated in the study. This reservation notwithstanding, we come away from the study knowing a great deal about how these two teachers used language in their lessons, and how their students responded. This knowledge of how language was used in the two classes suggests clear implications for practice, especially in the area of staffing and training.

The teachers in this study were part of a half-day alternation program, which had the advantage of exposing students to native speakers of both languages. From a practical perspective, such a program is also a way to avoid displacing regular teachers when a bilingual program is established. The importance of specific training for the program, both for regular and bilingual teachers, cannot be overemphasized, however. As the data from Mrs. Wu's lessons show, the effective use of L1 in instruction, even in English reading lessons, requires a high level of sophistication in the use of both L1 and L2.

There are specific ways in which teachers use the students' first language that seem to facilitate instruction. When Mrs. Wu used Cantonese, for example, it was for brief translations, to clarify instructions and as a we-code. In preparing bilingual teachers, therefore, attention must be given to those specific ways in which the students' first language can be used to facilitate instruction, create understanding, and build rapport. Prospective and practicing teachers should be provided with examples of the various functions that L1 may serve in instruction. Mere use of L1 is not the issue; it is *how* the bilingual teacher uses the students' language that is important.

Prescribing the relative amounts of L1 and L2 to be employed in instruction is useful at only the grossest level. Whether to use L1 or English should be decided on the basis of the situation and the specific purpose, not because of some aimed-for percentage. It might, however, make sense to recommend using more English in some lessons (reading) and less in others (math). Mrs. Wu, for example, consciously avoided using L1 during the reading lessons, but was less careful about which language was used in math, social studies, or in transitions. Information such as this could easily be incorporated into preservice and inservice training programs.

The picture of instruction in Mr. Martin's class derived from this study is one of difficulty and frustration. More than anything else, what seemed to be lacking in his interactions with the low group students were specific strategies for confronting the special needs of those students. He needed ways to make procedures and directions clear, to maintain order, and to deal with the students' use of L1. As as first step, Mr. Martin might be encouraged to concentrate on clear and simple instructions along with a more structured turn-taking routine. These and other techniques could easily be made part of an in-service program for monolingual English teachers faced with instructing LES/NES students.

Instruction of LES/NES students may be improved if language use strategies such as those described here, both for bilingual and monolingual teachers, are incorporated into actual preservice and inservice training. Additional work will be required, however, to make these strategies more explicit and to identify other strategies that are equally promising.

References

Baker, K., & deKanter, A. (1981). *Effectiveness of bilingual education: A review of the literature.* Final draft report, Office of Technical and Analytical Systems, Office of Planning and Budget, U.S. Department of Education, Washington, D.C.

Bossert, S. (1978). *Tasks and social relationships in classrooms.* Cambridge, England: Cambridge University Press.

Cazden, C. B. (1979). Learning to read in classroom interaction. In L. Resnick & P. A. Weaver (Eds.), *Theory and practice of early reading: Vol. 3* (pp. 295–306). Hillsdale, NJ: Erlbaum.

Cazden, C., John, V., & Hymes, D. (1972). *Functions of language in the classroom.* New York: Teachers College Press.

Cherry, L. (1978). A sociolinguistic approach to the study of teacher expectations. *Discourse Processes, 1,* 373–393.

Chomsky, N. (1965). *Aspects of a theory of syntax.* Cambridge, MA: MIT Press.

Cicourel, A. (1980). Three models of discourse analysis: The role of social structure. *Discourse Processes, 3,* 101–132.

Cole, M., Dore, J., Hall, W., & Downley, G. (1978). Situation and task in children's talk. *Discourse Processes, 1,* 119–176.

Dore, J. (1977). Children's illocutionary acts. In R. Freedle (Ed.), *Discourse production and comprehension: Vol. 1* (pp. 227–244). Norwood, NJ: Ablex.

Dore, J., Gearhart, M., & Newman, D. (1978). The structure of nursery school conversation. In K. Nelson (Ed.), *Child language* (Vol. 1) (pp. 337–395). New York: Gardner Press.

Duran, R. (Ed.). (1981). *Latino language and communicative behavior.* Norwood, NJ: Ablex.

Eder, D. (1982). Differences in communicative styles across ability groups. In L. Cherry Wilkinson (Ed.), *Communicating in the classroom* (pp. 245–264). New York: Academic.

Enright, D. S., Ramirez, A., & Jacobs, J. (1981–82). Language use in an English/Hebrew bilingual preschool classroom. *NABE Journal, 6,* 69–88.

Erickson, F., & Schultz, J. (1981). When is a context?: Some issues and methods in the analysis of social competence. In J. Green & C. Wallat (Eds.), *Ethnography and language in educational settings* (pp. 147–160). Norwood, NJ: Ablex.

Erickson, F., & Wilson, J. (1982). *Sights and sounds of life in schools: A resource guide to film and video for research and education* (Research Series No. 125). East Lansing, MI: Michigan State University, Institute for Research on Teaching.

Ervin-Tripp, S., & Mitchell-Kernan, C. (1977). Introduction. In S. Ervin-Tripp & C. Mitchell-Kernan (Eds.), *Child Discourse.* New York: Academic Press.

Fillmore, L. Wong. (1982). Instructional language as a linguistic input: Second-language learning in classrooms. In L. Cherry Wilkinson (Ed.), *Communicating in the classroom* (p. 283–296). New York: Academic Press.

Flanders, N. A. (1970). *Analyzing teaching behavior.* Reading, MA: Addison-Wesley.

Fuentes, E. J., & Wisenbaker, J. M. (1979). *The use of teacher rating of oral English proficiency as a covariate in the analysis of reading scores.* Paper presented at the AERA annual meeting, San Francisco, CA.

Glaser, B., & Strauss, A. (1967). *The discovery of grounded theory.* Chicago, IL: Aldine Publishing Co.

Good, T. L., & Brophy, J. E. (1974). *Looking in classrooms.* New York: Harper and Row.

Green, J. L. (1982). Teaching as a linguistic process. In E. Gordon (Ed.), *Review of research in education* (Vol. X) (pp. 151–252). Itasca, IL: F. E. Peacock.

Green, J. L., & Harker, J. O. (1982). Gaining access to learning: Conversational, social, and cognitive demands of group participation. In L. Cherry Wilkinson (Ed.), *Communicating in the classroom* (pp. 183–221). New York: Academic Press.

Green, J. L., & Wallat, C. (1981). *Ethnography and language in educational settings.* Norwood, NJ: Ablex.

Grice, H. P. (1975). Logic and conversation. In P. Cole & J. Morgan (Eds.), *Syntax and semantics III: Speech acts* (pp. 41–58). New York: Academic Press.

Gumperz, J. J. (1981). Conversational inference and classroom learning. In J. L. Green & C. Wallat (Eds.), *Ethnography and language in educational settings* (pp. 3–23). Norwood, NJ: Ablex.

Gumperz, J. J. (1982). *Discourse strategies.* Cambridge, England: Cambridge University Press.

Gumperz, J. J., & Hernandez-Chavez, E. (1972). Bilingualism, bidialectalism, and classroom interaction. In C. Cazden, V. P. John & D. Hymes (Eds.), *Functions of language in the classroom* (pp. 84–108). New York: Teachers College Press.

Guthrie, L. F. (1981). *The task variable in children's language use: Cultural and situational differences.* Unpublished doctoral dissertation, University of Illinois, Champaign-Urbana.

Guthrie, L. F. (1983). *Learning to use a new language: Language functions and use by first-grade Chinese Americans.* (Final Report). Washington, DC: National Institute of Education. (ERIC Document Reproduction Service No. ED 236 945).

Guthrie, L. F. (1984). Contrasts in teachers' language use in a Chinese-English bilingual classroom. In Handscombe, J., Orem, R. A., & Taylor, B. P. (Eds.), *On TESOL '83* (pp. 39–52). Washington, DC: Teachers of English to Speakers of Other Languages.

Guthrie, L. F., & Hall, W. S. (1983). Language continuity/discontinuity and schooling. In E. Gordon (Ed.), *Review of research in education* (Vol. X) (pp. 55–77). Itasca, IL: F. E. Peacock.

Guthrie, L. F., & Hall, W. S. (1984). Ethnographic approaches to reading research. In P. D. Pearson (Ed.), *Handbook of reading research* (pp. 91–110). New York: Longman.

Hall, W. S., & Cole, M. (1978). On participant's shaping of discourse through their understanding of the task. In K. Nelson (Ed.), *Children's language* (Vol. 1) (pp. 445–466). New York: Gardner Press.

Hall, W. S., & Guthrie, L. F. (1981). Cultural and situational variation in language function and use: Methods and procedures for research. In J. Green & C. Wallat (Eds.), *Ethnography and language in education settings* (pp. 209–228). Norwood, NJ: Ablex.

Heath, S. B. (1983). *Ways with words.* Cambridge, MA: Cambridge University Press.

Hymes, D. (1972). Introduction. In C. B. Cazden, V. P. John, & D. Hymes (Eds.), *Functions of language in the classroom* (pp. xi–lvii). New York: Teachers College Press.

Hymes, D. (1974). *Foundations in sociolinguistics.* Philadelphia, PA: University of Pennsylvania Press.

Labov, W. (1966). *The social stratification of English in New York City.* Washington, DC: Center for Applied Linguistics.

Labov, W. (1972). *Language in the inner city: Studies in the Black English Vernacular.* Philadelphia, PA: University of Pennsylvania Press.

Labov, W., & Fanshel, D. (1977). *Therapuetic discourse: Psychotherapy as conversation.* New York: Academic Press.

Legarreta, D. (1979). The effects of program models on language acquisition by Spanish speaking children. *TESOL Quarterly, 13,* 521–534.

Legarreta-Marcaida, D. (1981). Effective use of the primary language in the classroom. In *Schooling and language minority students: A theoretical framework.* Los Angeles, CA: Evaluation, Dissemination and Assessment Center, California State University.

McClure, E. (1981). Formal and functional aspects of the code-switched discourse of bilingual children. In R. P. Duran (Ed.), *Latino language and communicative behavior* (pp. 69–94). Norwood, NJ: Ablex.

McDermott, R. P. (1976). *Kids make sense.* Unpublished doctoral dissertation, Stanford University.

Mehan, H. (1979). *Learning lessons.* Cambridge, MA: Harvard University Press.

Milk, R. (1981). An analysis of the functional allocation of Spanish and English in a bilingual classroom. *CABE Research Journal, 2,* 11–26.

Mohatt, G., & Erickson, F. (1981). Cultural differences in teaching styles in an Odawa school: A sociolinguistic approach. In H. T. Trueba, G. P. Guthrie,

& K. H. Au (Eds.), *Culture and the bilingual classroom: Studies in classroom ethnography* (pp. 105–119). Rowley, MA: Newbury House.

Moll, L., Diaz, E., Estrada, E., & Lopes, L. (in press). Making contexts: The social construction of lessons in two languages. In M. Saravia-Shore & S. Arvizu (Eds.), *Cross-cultural and communicative competencies: Ethnographies of educational programs for language minority students*. Washington, DC: Council on Anthropology and Education.

Pung Guthrie, G. (1982). *An ethnography of bilingual education in a Chinese community*. Unpublished doctoral dissertation, University of Illinois, Champaign-Urbana.

Pung Guthrie, G. (1985). *A school divided: An ethnography of bilingual education in a Chinese community*. Hillsdale, NJ: Erlbaum.

Rist, R. (1973). *The urban school: A factory for failure*. Cambridge, MA: MIT Press.

Tikunoff, W. (1983). *An emerging description of successful bilingual instruction: An executive summary of Part I of the Significant Bilingual Instructional Features Study*. San Francisco, CA: Far West Laboratory for Educational Research and Development.

Trueba, H. T., Guthrie, G. P., & Au, K. H. (Eds.). (1981). *Culture and the bilingual classroom: Studies in classroom ethnography*. Rowley, MA: Newbury House.

Valdes-Fallis, G. (1978). Code switching and the classroom teacher. *Language in education: Theory and practice* (No. 4). Washington, DC: Center for Applied Linguistics.

Wilkinson, L. Cherry (Ed.). (1982). *Communicating in the classroom*. New York: Academic Press.

Appendix
Codes, Definitions, and Examples of Conversational Acts

Codes, Definitions, and Examples of Conversational-Acts

Code	Definition and Examples
Assertives report facts, state rules, convey attitudes, etc.	
AAT	*Attributions* report beliefs about another's internal state: "He does not know the answer."; "He wants to."; "He can't do it."
ADC	*Descriptions* predicate events, properties, locations, etc. of objects or people: "The car is red."; "It fell on the floor."; "We did it."; "We have a boat."
AEV	*Evaluations* express personal judgments or attitudes: "That's good."
AEX	*Explanations* state reasons, causes, justifications, and predictions: "I did it because it's fun."; "It won't stay up there."
AID	*Identifications* label objects events, people, etc.: "That's a car."; "I'm Robin."
AIR	*Internal Reports* express emotions, sensations, intents, and other mental events: "I like it."; "It hurts."; "I'll do it."; "I know."
APR	*Predictives* states expectations about future events, actions, etc.: "I'll give it to you tomorrow."; "It'll arrive later this week."
ARU	*Rules* state procedures, definitions, "social rules," etc.: It goes in here."; "We don't fight in school."; "That happens later."
Organizational Devices control personal contact and conversational flow.	
OAC	*Accompaniments* maintain contact by supplying information redundant with respect to some contextual feature: "Here you are"; "There you go."
OAG	*Attention Getters* solicit attention: "Hey!"; "John!"; "Look!"
OBM	*Boundary Markers* indicate openings, closings, and shifts in the conversation "Okay"; "All right"; "By the way."
OCQ	*Clarification Questions* seek clarification of prior remark: "What?"
OEX	*Exclamations* express surprise, delight, or other attitudes: "Oh!"; "Wow!"
OFL	*Fillers* enable a speaker to maintain a turn: ". . . well . . ."; ". . . and uh . . ."
OFS	*False Starts* indicate aborted utterances: "We . . . they"
OPM	*Politeness Markers* indicate ostensible politeness: "Please"; "Thank you."
ORQ	*Rhetorical Questions* seek acknowledgment to continue: "Know what?"
OSS	*Speaker Selections* label speaker of next turn: "John"; "You."
OVP	*Verbal Play* indicate language in which meaning is secondary to play.
Performatives accomplish acts (and establish facts) by being said.	
PBT	*Bets* express conviction about a future event: "I bet you can't do it."
PCL	*Claims* establish rights for speaker: "That's mine"; "I'm first."
PJO	*Jokes* cause humorous effect by stating incongruous information, usually patently false: "We throwed the soup in the ceiling."

233

PPR	*Protests* express objections to hearer's behavior: "Stop!"; "No!"
PTE	*Teases* annoy, taunt, or playfully provoke a hearer: "You can't get me."
PWA	*Warnings* alert hearer of impending harm: "Watch out!"; "Be careful!"

Requestives solicit information or actions.

QAC	*Action Requests* seek the performance of an action by hearer: "Give me it!"; "Put the toy down!"
QCH	*Choice Questions* seek either-or judgments relative to propositions: "Is this an apple?"; "Is it red or green?"; "Okay?"; "Right?"
QMA	*Requests for Mental Action* seek specific mental activity by the hearer: "Think"; "Remember."
QPC	*Process Questions* seek extended descriptions or explanations: "Why did he go?" "How did it happen?"; "What about him?"
QPM	*Permission Requests* seek permission to perform action: "May I go?"
QPR	*Product Questions* seek information relative to most "WH" interrogatives: "Where's John?"; "What happened?"; "Who?"; "When?"
QSU	*Suggestions* recommend the performance of an action by hearer or speaker or both: "Let's do it!"; "Why don't you do it?"; "You should do it."
QVB	*Verbal Action Requests* seek performance part of an instructional routine such as reading aloud, conducting language-learning exercises, repeating, or spelling: "Read this word"; "Repeat after me"; "I go, you go, he . . ."

Responsives supply solicited information or acknowledge remarks.

RAG	*Agreements* agree or disagree with prior non-requestive act: "No, it is not!"; "I don't think you're right."
RAK	*Acknowledgments* recognize prior non-requestives and are non-commital: "Oh"; "Yeah."
RCH	*Choice Answers* provide solicited judgments of propositions: "Yes."
RCL	*Clarification Responses* provide solicited confirmations: "I said no."
RCO	*Compliances* express acceptance, denial, or acknowledgment of requests: "Okay"; "Yes"; "I'll do it."
RPC	*Process Answers* provide solicited explanations: "I wanted to."
RPR	*Product Answers* provide Wh-information: "John's here"; "It fell."
RQL	*Qualifications* provide unsolicited information to requestives: "But I didn't do it"; "This is not an apple."
RVB	*Response to Requests for Verbal Action* provide solicited speech, such as reading aloud, repeating in chorus, or spelling.

Special Speech Acts are prescribed utterances expressed in a special way.

SAC	*Counting* indicates naming numerals or counting objects.
SAL	*Laughing* codes laughter.
SAS	*Singing* indicates singing, either words or sounds.
MKE	*Microphone talk* codes speech directed at the tape recorder microphone, often silly or nonsensical.
NVB	*Nonverbals* code important nonverbal acts.
TRA	*Translation* codes conscious, direct translations.
UNT	*Uninterpretables* indicate uncodable utterances.

10

Organizing Classroom Instruction in Specific Sociocultural Contexts: Teaching Mexican Youth to Write in English

Henry T. Trueba

Graduate School of Education University of California, Santa Barbara

The acquisition of oral proficiency in English as exhibited by second and third generation Mexican children is not, in itself, sufficient for the students to achieve academically at the level of their mainstream peers. Students from language minority backgrounds, whether monolingual in English or fluent bilinguals in Spanish and English, often have serious difficulty writing and thinking in English. Scholars who have explored the relationship between reasoning and writing suspect that certain kinds of written language emphasize the use of precise definitions and adherence to rules of logic and to particular forms of language structure. Applebee (1984, p. 583) for example, has recently stated:

> The process studies claim, virtually without exception, that writing is a learning process. . . . Planning processes can involve generating new ideas, as well as making new connections among old ones; reviewing (or monitoring) processes can involve attention to the consistency of an argument . . . and revising can involve changes in the meaning of what has been written. Yet none of the process studies provides useful evidence of how—or even whether—any such learning actually takes place.

Literacy in general, and writing in particular, have recently received a great deal of attention from boards of education and the public in general. Two main factors have contributed especially to attract the interest of the mass media:

(1) The report of the recent National Commission on Excellence in Education (NCEE) stated "some 23 million American adults are functionally illiterate by the simple tests of everyday reading, writing and comprehension, . . . and about 13 percent of 17-year olds in the United States can be considered functionally illiterate," 40 percent of whom are minority students (by Clifford, 1984, p. 478).

(2) The maintenance and development of the industrial and technical superiority of the United States will become critically dependent on the contribution of language minority populations, and this contribution will be conditioned by their ability to acquire English literacy and to achieve highly in schools.

It seems that students, both minority and mainstream, are increasingly less competent to analyze text, defend a point of view, explain criteria for selected linguistic and conceptual structures; in brief, they are less capable of dealing with the deeper meaning of scientific and humanistic disciplines. Writing activities in high schools have emphasized language skills and sentence structure, routine repetition of subject-matter information, and the organization of text for particular audiences. These activities have conspicuously neglected the cognitive and metacognitive strategies for the revision and restructuring of text, and the exploration of new meanings and relationships (Applebee, 1984).

It seems that in organizing reading and writing instructional activities we are neglecting reflective and creative thinking while we emphasize routine repetition of factual information. Teachers argue that students are not prepared for critical reading and reflective writing, and that their lack of reasoning skills prevents instructors from engaging in exercises requiring creative thinking.

Two interrelated factors appear to be responsible for the failure of schools in developing the reasoning skills of children: (a) the lack of an adequate learning environment in the class, in which both the learner seeking assistance, and the teacher offering it, fail to establish a smooth and effective "interactional system of social and cognitive support" (Erickson, 1984, p. 533); and (b) the tendency to disregard the sociocultural context of instruction and, consequently to misjudge students' academic ability and motivation to learn (Carrasco, 1981; McDermott, 1974; McDermott & Roth, 1978; McDermott & Gospodinoff, 1981; McDermott & Hood, 1982; Au & Jordan, 1981; Moll & Diaz, 1982; Erickson, 1984; Michaels & Collins, 1984; Anderson & Stokes, 1984; Jacob, 1984; Leichter, 1984).

Naturally, if these factors affect the entire student population, they severely limit the learning opportunities of the low-income and language minority student populations. Thus, for example, the reading levels of minority students in high school are consistently lower than those of the nonminority students, and are associated with low achievement and higher school attrition rates. Consequently, it is not surprising to find that the writing skills of language minority students lag further behind those of mainstream students. This fact is still less surprising if we consider that minority students:

(1) often do not master oral language skills in English;
(2) have difficulties reading in English, especially in areas in which their academic background, cultural or historical knowledge, and personal experience are of little help to interpret meaning; and
(3) lack the cognitive and metacognitive skills to make appropriate inferences and handle microtextual and macrotextual difficulties.

These considerations are particularly relevant to the situation in California. By the year 2000, 53.3% of the school-age population in that state will be composed of minority students. The 2.5 million Hispanic school-age children (35% of the projected total school-age population) for the year 2000 will continue to increase more rapidly than any other population. The 1984 distribution of language minority students in California was: 73% Hispanic, 6% Vietnamese, 4% Cantonese, and 17% others (totalling 487, 835). These populations are concentrated in Southern California (61% in Los Angeles, Orange, and San Diego counties alone). Inevitably, a major segment of the U.S. population (especially in the Southwest) will be composed of Hispanics. Their active contribution to agricultural, industrial, and specialized technical developments will demand English literacy.

The purpose of the study reported here was to monitor the process of skill acquisition in writing instruction. The larger research project included ethnographic field data collection for close to 2 years, both in the homes and community of the junior high school student population under study. This study is based on the work of 12 junior high school teachers who were first trained in ethnographic data collection, then guided to develop six new writing modules which would be implemented in their own classrooms. The researchers monitored the implementation and helped analyze the results in each of the classes. In the process of module implementation, teachers were forced to reorganize the instructional process and to let students play a more active role. The results were recorded by the teachers and are the basis for this paper.

After a brief description of the teachers and students, I will present the research outcomes and discuss possible explanations for the encouraging results. Finally I will

(1) draw some implications for current thinking on literacy and the need to understand the relationship between the home sociocul-

tural environment of language minority students and its implications for the organization of instruction in school, and
(2) raise some issues related to the conception of functional literary required of high school students.

Research Setting

As with other ethnographic studies, this one focused on a small sample and consequently is of limited generalizability. It was meant to provide a better understanding of the nature of writing instruction as a process, the conditions for its effectiveness, and the relationship between actual instruction and learning outcomes. It was conducted in the South Bay area near the border with Tijuana.

The San Diego South Bay area, California, consists of 60 square miles along the U.S.–Mexican border. There are large numbers of resident ethnolinguistic minority families recently arrived from Mexico and Central America, Vietnam, and the Phillipines. These families form barrios, or ghettoes, but they are neither cohesive nor ethnically homogeneous; rather, they keep residential pockets of higher or lower quality according to the social status and income of the ethnic families. The shops, markets, churches, and homes reflect the ethnic character of, and often display decorations unique to the Mexican, Vietnamese, or other cultural groups.

The Anglo population lives in the more affluent northern and northeastern areas of the South Bay region. The proximity to Tijuana and Ensenada, Mexico, makes this area a "revolving door," resulting in a genuine binational region with respect to its social, economic, and political institutions, as well as its linguistic patterns. The peso devaluation has had devastating consequences for the South Bay economy, and has contributed to the increase in undocumented migrants. Spanish is used as part of the daily life in the homes, stores, and church activities. Street names, newspapers, radio broadcasting, and the physical presence of a large Mexican population give the region a unique character.

The schools where our study took place were Southwest Junior High School (with 60% minority students, 43% Mexican) and Castle Park (with 62% minority, and 46.3% Mexican). These two schools have the lowest achievement levels in the Sweetwater Union High School District. Southwest has a larger proportion of monolingual Spanish speaking students and the better share of state and federal monies for creating new programs; Castle Park remains relatively isolated and unchanged.

A brief study of the forms and functions of the literary activities used in the home, and the values placed on literacy by several local families whose children were attending the two Junior High Schools (Trueba, 1984), revealed that the use of English text in the homes was very limited and that there was an incongruence between the high value attached to literacy by the families and the lack of actual engagement in reading and writing activities in the home. It also showed a low level of skills in the use of text at home. After this brief study, the research team approached several teachers to invite them to participate in an ethnographic research seminar designed to improve the teaching of writing in English.

Teachers recognized the critical needs of their students, particularly when confronted with the results of the competency examinations. Their response was enthusiastic.

An initial face-to-face interview with the 12 teachers selected for the seminar and research project revealed the following (Table 1):

Table 1. Profile of Twelve Teachers

	Spanish Language Proficiency	Class Taught	Significance of Writing for Class	Training in Writing
1.	Limited	English 8	High (critical analysis)	Minimal
2.	Limited	ESL	High (grammar, sentence)	Adequate
3.	Minimal	ESL/English	Some (sentence)	None
4.	Minimal	English 9, P.E.	High (paragraph)	None
5.	Minimal	Reading	High (paragraph)	Minimal
6.	Limited	Math	None	None
7.	Adequate	Math	None	Minimal
8.	Limited	English 6, P.E.	High (paragraph)	Minimal
9.	Minimal	ESL	High (grammar, sentence)	Minimal
10.	Adequate	ESL/Reading	Some (sentence)	Limited
11.	Adequate	ESL	Some (sentence)	Adequate
12.	Limited	Special Education	Some (sentence, paragraph)	Minimal

(1) Most teachers were outsiders to the South Bay area community, and unaware of the significance of social and cultural factors affecting students' achievement.
(2) All teachers were eager to improve their teaching skills and relatively untrained in writing instruction, except for two.
(3) Most teachers felt that students' ignorance and lack of skills prevented the teacher from being effective.
(4) All teachers were looking for quick and easy recipes to remedy the writing problems of their students.
(5) Only three of the twelve teachers had adequate Spanish language skills.
(6) Five of them taught English as a Second Language (ESL) to students classified as monolingual in Spanish or near monolingual, five others taught English and reading to students with some English proficiency (insufficient for full participation in regular classrooms and requiring remediation), and two were assigned to Math and Physical Education classes.
(7) Teaching styles were varied, and ranged from the use of traditional textbooks and curriculum guides to an eclectic combination of methods used with some modifications with different subgroups and/or individuals.
(8) Most teachers kept instruction at the very elementary level of sentence construction, emphasizing grammatical and syntactic norms, insisting that with such types of students nothing else was possible.

The Ethnographic Seminar was used as a vehicle to confront teachers with their basic ignorance about the actual social, linguistic, and cultural background and environment of their students, and to involve them in some creative thinking about possible experimentation with new instructional modules. The basic structure of the modules was originally agreed upon as consisting of five 50-minute sessions, consisting of pre-writing and writing activities in small groups of five or six students each.

The pre-writing time allowed students to negotiate topics, coverage, brainstorming, and inventorying of possible strategies to articulate ideas for a particular audience. It also allowed them to negotiate distribution of work if additional information had to be gathered. Writing time consisted of a series of steps in going from oral to written speech. The compositions were at times negotiated, and the teacher provided active support and valuable inputs to each student. As compositions began to circulate, role differentiation was based on skill level. More capable students became consultants and editors. Once the piece was finished, all students of the small group read it, and then it was finally brought to the teacher. The actual use of time in pre-writing and writing activities was flexible and negotiated from module to module.

Towards the end of the project, there were important qualitative changes in the use of pre-writing time; students structured serious inquiries in order to obtain specific data according to a plan of research. Their written pieces were more sophisticated, and reflected the effective distribution of work in gathering information. The overall structure of the module was accommodated to the topics chosen and the circumstances of each class: subject-matter, teacher's preference and abilities, students' concerns and organization, and, finally, their motivation to engage in each module.

An important concern throughout the entire research project was the development of effective means of communicating the ethnographic information gathered in the homes and community to the teachers involved in classroom writing instruction. Teachers, for example, were invited to meet with parents and other community representatives. Some of the seminar sessions for the teachers were held in the homes of community persons. Parents organized some informal gatherings they called "Cafes de Amistad," to which teachers were also invited. The above efforts began to develop in the teachers special sensitivity for topics of high priority to their students.

By the second module (all five modules were implemented over a period of 6 months), teachers had learned to elicit topic priorities and to handle the small group structure in their classes. The topics listed by students corresponded to the parents' perceptions of concerns manifested by the local youth. Thus, writing activities began to center around the following themes: violence, gang organization, drugs, immigration, parents and parenting, sex, love, Chicanas' roles, Chicanos' roles, career aspirations, ethnic relations, police brutality, bilingual education, teachers, schooling, achievement, and teacher–student relations.

It was well understood by all teachers participating in the experimental writing instructional modules that the main purposes were:

(1) To increase the quantity and quality of the written production,
(2) To facilitate students' abilities to manipulate text, revise meaning, and express themselves effectively, and
(3) To measure and analyze progress made by the students.

Each teacher, with approximately 30 students, was responsible for monitoring the writing process, under the guidance of one of the researchers involved in the project, and for analyzing the outcomes. Thus, ethnographic research methods were used to train teachers to observe their own classrooms and to internalize the sociocultural and linguistic background of their students, as well as to assess the wealth of human experiences students had in the community.

Ethnographic data gathered prior to teacher training suggested the existence of specific literacy events in the home and the relative difficulty of students in interpreting and generating English text (Trueba, 1984). With this information, researchers and teachers developed the specific strategies to create more effective writing instruction. Ultimately, teachers became more sensitive to the views, perceptions and abilities of their students. Teachers understood better the motivation behind specific writing activities, and the relationship between rate of progress and motivation to continue writing on subjects truly meaningful for students.

Modules were scored holistically using the district test, which was conducted in English. A comparison of the pre- and post-test scores for the total sample of students (both Spanish-surname and non-Spanish-surname) suggests that there was a statistically significant gain over the period of the study (see Table 2). One must keep in mind that the students whose scores were analyzed represented diverse groups and levels in ESL, math, English, and special education classes. The intervention documented in this study, however, was effective even from the standpoint of producing higher scores. Considering only the Spanish-surname students, the results are also positive (see Table 3). The significance of a positive result for these students is that Hispanics have consistently scored low in the district tests of writing competency, despite previous efforts.

While these test scores are important, what we wanted to do was to obtain a better understanding of the conditions in which Hispanic children could learn to write more effectively, and to help teachers learn to teach more effectively. In presenting the qualitative analysis based on ethnographic methods, the intent is to provide the reader with some of the insights and understandings gained in the process of documenting the intervention. Specifically, the following discussion summarizes our findings on the perceptions of teachers relative to: (a) classroom organization and the structure of interaction resulting in better writing, (b) role

Table 2. Comparison of Pre- and Post-Writing Test Scores for Total Sample (N = 205)**

	Pre	Post	t
mean	9.05	10.20	−2.60*
SD	2.88	6.18	

*p < .01 df = 204
** students who took both tests

Table 3. Comparison of Writing Pre- and Post-Test Scores for Spanish Surnamed Students (N = 121)**

	Pre	Post	t
mean	8.65	9.27	−2.92*
SD	2.99	2.52	

*p < .004 df = 120
** students who took both tests

of students in the production of text, and (c) role of teachers during the various phases of the process ultimately resulting in text production.

Ethnographic Analysis of the Instructional Process

Not every teacher thought that the modules were a great success, but most of them did. Much of the success had to do with the relative investment of time and effort made by each teacher, and the extent to which the teacher successfully internalized the role of researcher and innovator. The ethnographic journals of teachers reveal important changes in their overall perceptions of what the instructional process was all about. One of the teachers, for example, decided to face students about the fact that they showed no interest in writing on "safe" topics such as the cafeteria food, or a happy weekend story. The teacher writes:

> I wrote on the board the topics: killing, fear, fighting, hate, sadness, drugs, guns, revenge, anger, confusion, depression, loneliness, rejection, jealousy, feelings. . . . A recent sad experience had triggered their emotional topics. The teacher's adult aid, well known to the students, had just been killed by her husband. *Students freely discussed their feelings* and organized their groups to plan the writing of their first module. (Trueba, Moll, Diaz, & Diaz, 1984, p. 128)

The initial turn of events for the teacher was to use the actual experience of the students (their emotional charge) to: (a) discuss freely their feelings, (b) express their feelings in specific written linguistic forms, and (c) analyze the correspondence between their feelings and the linguistic form. Thus, the process was geared at achieving successful transitions from oral to written language. The motivation was based on the emotional need of students to share their shock, frustration, and confusion caused by the sudden loss of a dear teacher's aide. The teacher comments are most eloquent: "They were slow in starting. . . . I knew this would be the case due to the powerful emotions involved. . . . The writing began. Many wrote frantically to pour it out" (Trueba et al., 1984, p. 128).

In order to have the teachers become more conscious of the structural changes in the writing of individual students, researchers suggested a more systematic comparison and contrast of the compositions students were producing for each of the modules. This was done in the ethnographic seminar attended by the teachers. To her surprise, the teacher who had initiated the discussion of topics genuinely concerning students pulled out a composition written by one of the poorest students. Here is a fragment:

> A couple of years ago, I found out my Uncle and Aunt had a divorce. My Aunt got the kids. Candy and Tammy were their names. She had an affair with the chauffeur. After it was over, she was going to get married to another man. The chauffeur was still in love with her, *so he stabbed her*! After a while I asked my cousins how they felt about the whole thing. Tammy said she saw her mom dead on the floor and *she started laughing*! That has affected me very much. *How can her daughter feel that way. I felt confused about the whole thing. What triggered it was jealousy. The more I think about it the more I'm glad I'm alive and treasure my life.* (Trueba et al., 1984, p. 130)

For a student who had been considered a poor writer, this piece shows substantial control of linguistic structures and critical thinking about a subject of great personal significance. The tragic incident is described succinctly. Its impact on Tammy as a nonsensical response to the tragic death of Tammy's mother is used by the writer to highlight, in contrast, her own personal reaction and the analysis of this reaction: confusion, frustration, and condemnation of violence. She talks about the destructiveness of unrestrained feelings such as jealousy. She ends her piece with a discussion about the gift of life, the happiness of being alive.

The articulation of ideas and the reflective thinking demonstrated here is a nontrivial accomplishment for someone whose mother tongue is Spanish and who has not been exposed previously to systematic writing activities. This student is only one of many examples. The teacher impressed her peers with similar examples from her class. In her personal journal she wrote that night:

> I was impressed with the results. As I went around and discussed each paper with the students I got interesting statements. . . . Virginia, who wrote about a close call in a gang fight stated: "Don't they know it's easier for us to tell how we feel when we've been there?" *This was a very successful lesson for me in many ways. It also furthers my belief that if what is taught is important in the mind of the learner, much more will truly be learned.* (Trueba et al., 1984, p. 131)

Teachers were surprised by success, but they recognized it when they saw it. This teacher went further; she also recognized the reason for the success when she quoted her student: "Don't they know it's easier for us to tell how we feel when we've been there?" Finally, this teacher analysed the important lesson she had learned earlier in her previous experience: "if what is taught is important in the mind of the learner, much more will truly be learned." However, one can ask: what did the teacher teach in this instance? Teachers neither internalized nor fully analyzed their role at this stage of the training. This particular teacher realized that she was in control of the teaching time, and that, by facilitating a writing activity perceived as important by the student, she obtained good results. But she had not yet analyzed any specific intervention strategies used to motivate or guide students attempting to write well about a personally important matter.

In the examples examined for the first module, teachers and students were more concerned with sharing their personal experiences than with structuring their writing for a specific audience. Presumably, the audience was vaguely perceived as consisting of the teacher and peers. In the subsequent modules, students became consciously aware of the teacher as an audience and of the need to organize their arguments to persuade her.

One of the students' continuous concerns was with grades. They had been talking about grades with their teacher, and wanted to explain to her why they had had bad grades. Here is an example of a fragment from a composition consisting of a series of arguments structured to convince the teacher that bad grades are sometimes inevitable despite all reasonable efforts made by a responsible student:

> My worst grade was a "D" in math for several *good reasons*. First, *they change me from math to consumer math* and I can't understand that class. Secondly, *the teacher didn't explain clearly and he always spoke English* and that class was supposed to be bilingual. Also, *I didn't understand my homework because I couldn't understand in class*. Finally, *the test was too hard for me to understand it*. As you see my worst grade was a "D." (Trueba et al., 1984, p. 143)

The reasoning was powerful indeed. A change from an easier to a more difficult math class placed the student (in his perception) at a disadvantage. The implication is that there is math and there is consumer math (a tough one that this student claimed not to understand). To compound the problem, the consumer math teacher "didn't explain clearly." It must have been confusing for a number of reasons, not the least of which was that "he always spoke in English" when he should have used Spanish and English ("was supposed to be bilingual"). The student could not do the homework because he did not understand the class. Finally, "the test was too hard for me to understand" (it might not have been too hard to answer if the questions had been clear—so the argument goes). Thus, having presented all these factors beyond the student's controls, he can rest his case: "as you see my worst grade was D."

The student's mastery of rhetorical argumentation is indeed an example of above average reasoning skills applied to a real-life good cause: the exoneration of oneself by convincing the teacher (a specific audience) of the inevitability of a bad grade and the total innocence of a poor student placed in such a predicament! As we might expect, this student did not succeed in persuading the teacher about his grade, but he did persuade her about his ability to write. The teacher wrote the following comment that night in her ethnographic journal: "I'm pleasantly surprised at the control my kids have over the language. The assignment is showing me a very positive improvement already in their English abilities" (Trueba et al., 1984, p. 143).

As the teachers who had been initially skeptical about experimentation with the modules began to witness genuine progress, they also began to articulate some of the most important lessons they themselves had learned: (a) Motivation to learn was vitally linked to the students' understanding of the reasons that something was worth learning, and of how learning efforts would pay off; (b) If the motivation is high, the more challenging a learning task is, the better the performance of students will be. Most teachers agreed on the above. Here is, for example, the comment written by a teacher in her journal:

> *The more controversial and relevant I can make the topic, the more willing the students are to unite and write well.* Also it seems, and this is just a feeling, the more complicated the assignment is, the better the responses.

Relevant and controversial writing tasks are perceived by this teacher as triggering a motivation response which other assignments fail to do. However, both relevance and controversy are determined by the students' experiences and from their sociocultural perspective. Implied in this statement is the teacher's judgement that, if we permit students to play an active role in selecting topics and suggesting structural classroom arrangements, relevance and motivation will be insured. The follow-up thought is intriguing, and makes sense: given adequate motivation, the difficulty of the task may become a positive factor in challenging students intellectually and inviting them to invest higher levels of effort and learn more.

The investment of energy in learning when students are highly motivated is explained by another teacher, who became increasingly aware of the active role students need to play in learning tasks:

> In class, *there was a lot of constructive communicating going on*. Students asked each other "how to say" this and that, and asked me (usually) "How do I do it?". After I had already explained the questions they had a difficult time getting going, but I decided not to hand-feed them this time, but instead to let them muddle through. I answered specific questions today, but I didn't volunteer the questions. Students returned Monday with their papers in different stages of completion, *they selected one for editing purposes* and to clarify the previous instruction. The quality and *the sophistication of the papers is impressive if compared with the pieces these students were producing a few short months earlier*. (Trueba et al., 1984, pp. 164–165)

In a regular classroom, that "lot of constructive communicating" may well look like lack of discipline deserving a reprimand from the principal. This teacher felt she had to take her chances by being flexible. Not to explain in detail some matters, or to omit the anticipation of questions, may also be perceived as poor teaching. And yet, this teacher knew that students needed to take a more active role, thinking critically before writing: "I decided not to hand-feed them this time, but instead to let them muddle through." It surely paid off, and the enthusiasm of the teacher's comments is obvious: "The quality and sophistication of the papers is impressive."

The last two modules seemed to have raised some anxiety in the teachers. The modules had been designed to challenge students by involving them in an active research project and face-to-face interviews structured by them to obtain specific kinds of information; then students would reconvene in small groups and discuss findings, analyze them, and write the results. One of the teachers wrote in her journal: "This module was really tough to plan! I decided to use the questionnaire or interview format discussed in our last class session [the ethnographic seminar]." Students had selected the topic of "Cheating." Students worked on developing a series of questions they would ask adults about cheating. The teacher continued: "We wrote them on the board. I typed all the questions on a ditto master and gave the survey to them Tuesday." Students were to interview at least five individuals, two of which had to be adults. Students eagerly completed their assignment. Here are the teacher's comments on the results:

> I was really apprehensive about this assignment. I was afraid the skill level required would be too advanced for my students. Was I ever surprised! . . . I pointed out to them that they had gathered a great amount of facts. . . . I asked them to focus on the adult interviews only. . . They compared the answers the adults gave to question #1: "Is cheating ever right?" After five minutes I explained they were to take several more questions from the adults' interviews and summarize the responses." (Trueba et al., 1984, p. 152)

This teacher had discovered the art of intervention without killing learning initiatives, and of allowing for maximum personal involvement of students in the learning process. The compositions were indeed the best reward the teacher ever received. The difficulty of the task, and the complexity of the analysis, were compounded by the intrinsic ethical questions intertwined in the problem of "cheating." Furthermore, adults speaking to youth about this problem had to take a stand and offer an acceptable moral position. The actual writing of the answers obtained from adults, and the summaries used by students in order to produce a single composition, reflect a rapid development of cognitive skills in these students. Here is a fragment of one of the compositions:

> The adults I interviewed thought that cheating was sometimes good but not right or fair, because you have to be honest. They thought that *it could be beneficial but not right*. One of the adults said he had never cheated. The other one said he may have cheated some time. The ways they thought that adults could cheat were at their work, in business, etc., almost any way. One of them had never seen anyone cheat, and the other one said he had seen some people. They wouldn't do nothing if they saw someone cheating, it's their problem and none of their business. *People, they said, cheat because they think that what they obtain from it, it's better than the truth, than being honest. Generally, they thought that cheating was a dishonest and dangerous thing to do.*

The following is a student's summary of students' interview on cheating:

> However, the students I interviewed had some different opinions. One of them thought that it was completely wrong to cheat, like the adults. But the others said that it was good some times but dangerous if you got caught. They said it could help you with your grades. They had seen people cheat and cheated themselves, to get good grades in the way that adults could cheat, their answers were, in their tax report, doing traffic infractions, and at their work. They wouldn't do any thing if they saw someone cheating either, because it's "none of my business," they said they think that people cheats to get good grades and to obtain better results. *Cheating is a very controversial subject. Some people think it's very wrong to cheat, and indeed, they are cheaters.* Others think it could be a benefit to cheat some ways. What do you think about cheating?

This was a very difficult question in terms of both gathering information and summarizing it. The analytical skills of students in discussing whether cheating was right or wrong, and under what conditions it could be either right or wrong, led this student to conclude that a lot of people, including adults, thought cheating was wrong, and yet they themselves were cheaters. Some students were not satisfied with the analysis done so far, and requested time to think and re-write their piece. Their questions and uncertainty showed that they were troubled. The subject of the composition was not a simple writing exercise; it dealt with an important moral issue faced every day in school and at home. Therefore, in attempting to distinguish circumstances in which it was all right to "cheat," they had to deal with difficult negotiations for meaning and language nuances. Here is an example of both the writing and thinking skills demonstrated by one of the students:

> I believe that cheating may be right or fair. It may be wrong and unfair too. I think that cheating may be right when you need good grades, like in a very important test. It can be good, too, when you are lazy and do not want to study, it's very easy to copy some one else's work. But you might get caught when you do this, and it can be a lot worse than studying. It may be right in an emergency, like when you are in a hurry for some very important reason, like your mother is in the hospital, and you have just been informed about it, and you get caught in a traffic jam. It may be right when the rules are not fair, or you are not guilty for something some one said you did, it may be helpful to cheat. I believe that cheating may be right some times, but not always. Cheating it's dangerous too. You can get in real trouble with law, the teacher, or your family. And cheating it's not honest, not either for you or others. *You will never learn if you cheat in school work. You can cause trouble not only to yourself, but to others. I believe cheating should be left to our own responsibility.* It can help a lot sometimes and there are emergencies too. But it can be very harmful for everyone, too. Think twice before cheating, no matter what situation.

This statement represents a mature analysis of the complexity of cheating, and an excellent concluding suggestion to leave cheating to each person's own responsibility, but to think twice before resorting to cheating.

Conclusion

Previous research has noted that some students are socialized to fail or to miscommunicate in schools (McDermott 1977, McDermott & Gospodinoff, 1981; Carrasco, 1981), and that micropolitical situations in the school and classroom place them at such a disadvantage that they refuse to learn in order to dramatize their political resistance to schools. This thought is summarized by Erickson (1984):

> Resistance theory points out that non-elite students cooperate in this situation of unfair competition [i.e., a situation in which cultural and social elites hand on advantages to their own only, from generation to genera-

tion] by disadvantaging themselves still further by refusing to learn. Failure to learn simple tasks of literacy and numeracy, from this point of view, is seen not as evidence of innate disability in the student, but as political resistance. *In self-defeating attempts to fight back the student resists being defined by the school as a person of less worth than others. The child's defiance provides a more acceptable self-image than does agreement with the schools definition.* (1984, p. 538)

These reflections bring into perspective the contrast between traditional schooling, in which the instructional process is based on the social and cultural capital of elite students, and the type of instruction generated by the knowledge and experience nonelite students bring.

Sociologists and psychologists dealing with the school failures of language minority students, especially with the failure to acquire literacy, often agree that nonschool factors seem to determine the outcomes. Thus, for example, Cole and Griffin (1983) argue that social-historical contexts determine the nature of instruction and the production of school failure. They feel that "educational failure is not done in the classroom, it is done at home, it is done on the way from the classroom to home, it is done in the workplace, it is done everywhere. It is systemic" (1983, p. 71). Ogbu (1978, 1980, 1984), among others, argues also that the failure of minority students is the result of complex social, economic, and political factors.

While these and other theories seem to account for the failure of language minority students, they do not account for their success, limited as it may be. Researchers must explain why and how some students, in the worst of circumstances, in socially and culturally marginal and isolated learning environments typically recognized as environments of students who are academically unmotivated and most likely to fail, have successfully and rapidly acquired writing and thinking skills to the surprise of their own teachers.

We must also reflect on the dual stand we seem to take regarding academic failure of minorities. We insist that there is nothing the school can do to remedy the social and cultural isolation ultimately causing failure. And yet we look back to the teachers with the secret expectation that they will resolve these problems and will work miracles in transmitting and developing basic literacy skills. It is not easy. Teachers themselves must go through very comprehensive periods of observation and reflection before they can adapt their teaching methods to the new knowledge and expectations obtained through intensive training and experimentation (such as the one described here). This brief study has attempted to show some of the ways in which teachers can in fact help nonelite students discover the joy of learning to engage in effective written communication in English (their second language), and thus to compete successfully in school.

References

Anderson, A. B., & Stokes, S. (1984). Social and institutional influences on the development and practice of literacy. In H. Goelman, A. Oberg, &'F. Smith (Eds.), *Awakening to Literacy* (pp. 24-36). Exeter, NH: Heinemann Educational Books.

Applebee, A. N. (1984). Writing and reasoning. *Review of Educational Research, 54(4)*, 577-592.

Au, K., & Jordan, C. (1981). Teaching reading to Hawaiian children: Finding a culturally appropriate solution. In H. Trueba, G. Guthrie, & K. Au (Eds.), *Culture and the bilingual classroom: Studies in classroom ethnography* (pp. 139-152). Rowley, MA: Newbury House.

Carrasco, R. (1981). Expanded awareness of student performance: A case study in applied ethnographic monitoring in a bilingual classroom. In H. Trueba, G. Guthrie, & K. Au (Eds.), *Culture and the bilingual classroom: Studies in classroom ethnography* (pp. 153-177). Rowley, MA: Newbury House.

Clifford, G. N. (1984). Buch und Lesen: Historical perspectives on literacy and schooling. *Review of Educational Research, 54(4)*, 472-496.

Cole, M. & Griffin P. (1983). A socio-historical approach to re-mediation. *The Quarterly Newsletter of the Laboratory of Comparative Human Cognition, 5(4)*, 69-74.

Erickson, F. (1984). School literacy, reasoning, and civility: An anthropologist's perspective. *Review of Educational Research, 54(4)*, 525-544.

Jacob, E. (1984). Learning literacy through play: Puerto Rican kindergarten children. In H. Goelman, A. Oberg, & F. Smith (Eds.), *Awakening to Literacy* (pp. 73-83). Exeter, NH: Heinemann Educational Books.

Leichter, H. J. (1984) Families as environments for literacy. In H. Goelman, A. Oberg, & F. Smith (Eds.), *Awakening to Literacy* (pp. 38-48). Exeter, NH: Heinemann Educational Books.

McDermott, R. (1974). Achieving school failure: An anthropological approach to illiteracy and social stratification. In G. Spindler (Ed.), *Education and cultural process* (pp. 82-117). New York: Holt, Rinehart and Winston.

McDermott, R. (1977). School relations as context for learning in school. *Harvard Educational Review, 47*, 298-313.

McDermott, R., & Roth, D. (1978). The social organization of behavior: Interactional approaches. *Annual Review of Anthropology, 7*, 321-345.

McDermott, R. & Gospodinoff, K. (1981). Social contexts for ethnic borders and school failure. In H. T. Trueba, G. Guthrie, & K. Au (Eds.), *Culture and the bilingual classroom* (pp. 212-230). Rowley, MA: Newbury House.

McDermott, R. & Hood, L. (1982). Institutionalized psychology and the ethnography of schooling. In P. Gilmore & A. Glatthorn (Eds.), *Children in and out of school: Ethnography and education* (pp. 232-249). Language and Ethnography Series/2. Washington, DC: Center for Applied Linguistics.

Michaels, S., & Collins, J. (1984). Oral discourse styles: Classroom interaction and the acquisition of literacy. In D. Tannen (Ed.), *Coherence in spoken and written discourse* (pp. 219-244). Norwood, NJ: Ablex.

Moll, L. C., & Diaz, E. (1982). *Bilingual communications in classroom texts*. Final Report, National Institute of Education.

Ogbu, J. (1978). *Minority education and caste: The American system in cross-cultural perspective*. New York: Academic Press.
Ogbu, J. (1980). *Literacy in subordinate cultures: The case of Black Americans*. Paper presented at the Literacy Conference, Library of Congress, Washington, D.C.
Ogbu, J. (1984). *Understanding community forces affecting minority students' academic effort*. Unpublished manuscript for the Achievement Council. Mills College, Oakland, CA.
Trueba, H. T. (1984). The forms, functions and values of literacy: Reading for survival in a barrio as a student. *NABE, IX* (1), 21–38.
Trueba, H., Moll, L., Diaz, S., & Diaz, R. (1984). *Improving the functional writing of bilingual secondary school students*. Final report submitted to the National Institute of Education, Contract No. 400-81- 0023.

Author Index

A

Abelson, R., 49, *55*, 72, *104*, 159, *185*
Acosta, L., 11, *31*
Adams, M.J., 85, *101*
Airasian, P.W., 76, *101*
Allington, R.L., 73, 74, *101*
Amastae, J., 181, *184*
Ammon, M.S., 2, *8*, 77, 81, *105*
Ammon, P., 2, *8*, 81, *105*
Anderson, A.B., 47, *52*, 236, *251*
Andersson, T., 128, 130, *151*
Applebee, A.N., 75, *101*, 235, 236, *251*
Armbruster, B.B., 75, 76, *101*
Au, K., 10, *29*, 47, 48, *52*, 124, *125*, 205, *231*, 236, *251*

B

Baca, L., 127, *151*
Bailey, D., 127, *151*
Baker, C., 63, *70*
Baker, E.L., 76, 88, 100, *101*
Baker, K., 211, *228*
Baker, L., 107, 108, *125*
Baratz, J., *52*

Barrera, R.B., 132, 146, 147, *151*
Barron, R.W., 74, *101*
Bates, E., 190, *202*
Bernal, E.M., 127, *151*
Bernal, H.H., 10, *30*
Bernstein, M., 190, *203*
Berreman, G.D., 12, *29*
Blair, P.M., 13, *30*
Bloome, D., 1, 4, *7*, 72, *101*
Bock, J.K., 66, *69*
Boggs, S.T., 124, *125*
Bolinger, D., 73, *101*
Bossert, S., 213, *228*
Bottein, J., 12, *30*
Bourdieu, P., 12, *30*
Boyer, M., 128, 130, *151*
Bransford, J., 188, *202*
Brewer, W.F., 66, *69*, 72, *104*
Brophy, J.E., 211, *229*
Brown, A.L., 85, 100, *101*, 188, *203*
Brown, J.S., 76, *101*
Brown, T.L., 66, *69*
Bruce, B.C., 72, *104*
Bryan, T.H., 128, 129, *152*

Bryen, D.N., 128, *151*
Burke, C.L., 99, *102*, 132, *151*
Burton, R.B., 76, *101*
Butler, L., 190, *203*

C

Calfee, R.C., 88, *102*
Campione, J., 75, 76, *101*, 188, *202*
Carpenter, P.A., 72, *103*
Carr, T., 60, *69*
Carranza, M.A., 36, *55*
Carrasco, R., 236, 249, *251*
Carter, T., 10, *30*, 36, *52*, 128, 130, *151*
Cazden, C.B., 1, 4, *7*, 205, 206, *228*
Cervantes, R., 10, 11, *30*
Chall, J.S., 108, *125*
Chapa, J., 11, *30*
Chapman, J.P., 75, *101*
Chapman, L.J., 75, *101*
Cherry, L., 187, 190, *203*, 211, *228*
Chiang-Chi-Pang, 187, 188, 189, 190, *202*, *203*
Chinn, P.C., 127, *151*
Chomsky, N., 4, *7*, 208, *228*
Cicourel, A., 46, *52*, 216, *228*
Clark, E., 188, *202*
Clark, R., 10, *30*
Clifford, G.N., 236, *251*
Cole, M., 10, *30*, *31*, 51, 52, *52*, *53*, 129, *151*, 214, 215, *228*, 230, 250, *251*
Coleman, J.S., 10, *30*
Collins, A., 81, 85, *101*
Collins, J., 47, *53*, 73, *101*, 236, *251*
Conway, B., 190, *203*
Cook, L.K., 88, *102*
Cook-Gumperz, J., 10, *30*, 47, *53*
Crowell, D., 47, *52*
Cummins, J., 35, *53*, 124, *125*, 128–130, 132, 149, *151*, 156, 160, 179, *184*
Curtis, J.K., 168, *184*
Cziko, G.A., 61, *69*

D

Danks, J.H., 72, *102*
De Avila, E., 35, *53*, 128, *151*
de Beaugrande, R., 71, 72, 73, *101*
dekanter, A., 211, *228*
Delucchi, K., 2, *8*, 81, *105*
DeStefano, J.S., 4, *7*, 73, *102*
deVilliers, J., 190, *203*
deVilliers, P., 190, *203*
Dew, N., 129, *151*

Diaz, E., *55*, 148, *152*, 211, *231*, 236, *251*
Diaz, R., 35, 47, *54*, 243–246, *252*
Diaz, S., 10, *31*, 243–247, *252*
Dominguez, D., 156, *185*
Dore, J., 208, 214, 215, *228*
Dornic, S., 35, *53*
Downley, G., 214, 215, *228*
Drum, P.A., 88, *102*
Duffy, J.B., 127, *151*
Duncan, S., 35, *53*, 128, *151*
Duŕan, R.P., 10, *30*, 35, 41, 43, 47, 49, 50, *52*, *53*, 54, 220, *228*

E

Eaton, A.J., 132, *151*
Edelsky, C., 46, *54*, 158, 173, 182, *184*
Eder, D., 4, *7*, 226, *228*
Elette, E., 47, *55*
Elmandjra, M., 12, *30*
Enright, D.S., 218, *229*
Enright, M., 41, 43, *53*
Erickson, F., 208, 211, *229*, 230, 236, 249, *251*
Ervin-Tripp, S., 187, *203*, 207, 208, *229*
Estrada, E., 47, *55*, 211, *231*

F

Fanshel, D., 208, *230*
Fasold, R.A., 182, *185*
Ferguson, C., 33, *54*
Fernandez, R., 37, 41, *54*, *55*
Ferrara, R., 188, *202*
Ferreiro, E., 157, 168, *184*
Fillmore, C.J., 80, 100, *102*, 159, *184*
Flanders, N.A., 207, *229*
Fleming, J.S., 128, *151*
Frederiksen, C., 72, *102*
Frederiksen, J., 72, *102*
Freedle, R., 49, *54*
Freire, P., 9, 11, 29, *30*
Fuentes, E.J., 212, *229*

G

Gaardner, B., 130, 149, *151*
Garcia, J., 128, *152*
Gardner, E., 79, 82, 85, *103*
Garrod, S.C., 159, *185*
Garvey, C., 187, 189, *203*
Gay, J.K., 51, *52*
Gearhart, M., 214, 215, *228*
Geertz, C., 12, *30*
Gibson, E., 64, *69*

Gill, N., 10, *31*
Ginsburg, H., 131, *152*
Glaser, B., 221, *229*
Glaser, R., 73, 76, *102*
Gleitman, H., 188, *203*
Gleitman, L., 188, *203*
Glenn, C.G., 108, *126*
Glick, S., 51, *52*
Goldman, S.R., 35, *54*, 60, *70*, 108, 113, *125*
Goldschmindt, W., 12, *30*
Golinkoff, R.M., 73–75, 85, *102*
Good, T.L., 211, *229*
Goodman, K.S., 51, *54*, 62, *69*, 72, *102*, 131, *152*, 158, 159, *184*
Goodman, Y.M., 51, *54*, 99, *102*, 132, 140, 147, *151*, 158, 159, *184*
Gospodinoff, K., 236, 249, *251*
Gough, P.B., 72, *102*
Grebler, L., 12, *30*
Green, J., 1, 4, *7*, 72, 73, *101*, *102*, 205, 217, *229*
Grice, H.P., 210, *229*
Griffin, P., 10, *30*, 129, *151*, 250, *251*
Guerra, E., 49, *53*
Gumperz, J., 10, *30*, 34, 47, *53*, *54*, 160, *184*, 206, 220, 222, *229*
Guthrie, G.P., 205, 208, 211, *231*
Guthrie, L.F., 206, 208, 209, 211, 215, *229*, *230*
Guthrie, J.T., 63, *69*
Guzman, R., 12, *30*

H

Hakuta, K., 35, *54*
Hall, J.W., 75, *102*, 206, *228*
Hall, W.S., 209, 214, 215, *230*
Hallahan, D.P., 128, 129, *152*
Halliday, M.A.K., 128, *152*
Harbin, G.L., 127, *151*
Harker, J.O., 73, *102*, 217, *229*
Harnisch, D., 76, 85, 89, *103*
Harris, A.J., 177, *184*
Hatch, E., 61, *69*
Hayes-Bautista, D., 11, *30*
Haynes, M., 66, *69*
Heap, J., 73, *103*
Heath, S., 10, *31*, *54*, 160, *184*, 206, *230*
Herman, J.L., 76, 88, *101*
Hernandez-Chavez, E., 34, *54*, 168, *184*, 220, *229*
Hindle, D., 162, 164, 168, *184*

Hirsh-Pasek, K., 188, *203*
Hogaboam, T.W., 60, *70*
Holland, A.L., 127, 129, *152*
Holtzman, W., 156, *185*
Hood, L., 236, *251*
Hoover, W., 156, *185*
Hornby, P.A., 73, *103*
Hresko, W.P., 127, 129, *153*
Hudelson-Lopez, S.J., 132, 146, 147, *152*
Humphrey, M.A., 73, *103*
Humphreys, M.S., 75, *102*
Hunt, K.W., 164, *184*
Hymes, D., 10, *31*, *32*, 34, *54*, 205–208, *228*, *230*

J

Jacob, E., 236, *251*
Jacobs, J., 211, 218, *229*
Jacobson, M.D., 177, *184*
Jencks, C., 12, *31*
Jensen, J., 2, *8*, 81, *105*
John, V., 205, *228*
Johnson, K.R., 12, *31*
Johnson, N.S., 108, *126*
Johnston, G.A., 61, *69*
Johnston, P.H., 99, *103*
Jordan, C., 10, *29*, 47, *52*, 124, *125*, 236, *251*
Just, M.A., 72, *103*

K

Kamil, M.L., 72, 74, 85, *104*
Karlsen, B., 79, 82, 85, *103*
Kay, P., 80, 100, *102*, 159, *184*
Keith, R., 11, *31*
Kernan, K., 189, *203*
Ketron, J., 190, *203*
Kintsch, W., 72, *103*, 159, *184*
Kleiman, G.M., 72–75, *103*, *104*
Klein, T., 47, *52*
Kloss, H., 34, *54*
Koford, K., 12, *31*
Krashen, S.D., 149, *152*
Kroch, A., 162, 164, 168, *184*

L

LaBerge, D., 60, *69*, 72, *103*, 116, *125*
Labov, W., 163, *185*, 207–209, *230*
Lambert, W., 35, *54*, 130, 150, *152*, 179, *185*
Langdon, H.W., 128, *152*
Laosa, L., 34, *54*

Larkin, K.M., 85, *101*
Lave, J., 51, *55*
Lawlor, J., 181, *185*
Legarreta, D., 207, *230*
Legarreta-Marcaida, D., 149, *152*, 207, 210, *230*
Leichter, H.J., 236, *251*
Lesgold, A.M., 60, *70*
Levin, H., 64, *69*
Liebman, E., 130, *152*
Linn, R.L., 76, *103*
Lopan, W., 193, *203*
Lope Branch, J.M., 176, *185*
Lopes, L., 211, *231*
Lopez, L.M., 47, *55*
Luria, A.R., 51, *54*

M

Mace-Matluck, B.J., 156, *185*
Macias, R., 34, *54*
Madaus, G.F., 76, *101*
Madden, R., 79, 82, 85, *103*
Magoon, J., 128, *152*
Mandler, J.M., 108, *126*
Margolis, S., 11, *31*
Maritza, M., 12, *30*
Matute-Bianchi, M., 36, *55*
McClure, E., 220, *230*
McDermott, R., 73, *103*, 211, 226, *230*, 236, 249, *251*
McLaughlin, B., 2, *8*, 57, 58, 62, 63, *69*, *70*, 81, *105*
McLeod, B., 58, 62, *70*
Mead, G.H., 130, 131, *152*
Mehan, H., 46, 52, 208, *230*
Meichenbaum, D., 190, *203*
Mercer, J., 128, *152*
Meyer, B.F., 72, *103*, 120, *126*
Michaels, S., 47, 53, 73, *103*, 160, *185*, 236, *251*
Milk, R., 210, *230*
Minicucci, C., 11, *31*
Mitchell-Kernam, C., 189, *203*, 207, 208, *229*
Mohatt, G., 211, *230*
Moll, L., 10, *31*, 47, *55*, 148, *152*, 181, *185*, 211, *231*, 236, 243–247, *251*, *252*
More, J.W., 12, *30*
Morrison, F.J., 72, *103*
Mosenthal, P., 121, *126*
Mosteller, F., 197, *203*
Myers, A., 72, 73, 75, 76, 85, *104*

N

Na, T.J., 121, *126*
Neale, D.C., 10, *31*
Netting, R., 12, *31*
Newman, D., 214, 215, *228*
Nielsen, F., 37, 41, *54*, *55*
Norman, D.A., 68, *70*

O

Ochs, E., 162, *185*
Ogbu, J.U., 2, *7*, 9–12, 29, *31*, 36, *55*, 250, *252*
Olson, D.R., 10, *31*, 160, *185*
Opper, S., 131, *152*
Orasanu, J., 72, *103*
Ortiz, A., 129, *152*

P

Padilla, A.M., 130, *152*
Parsons, T., 131, *152*
Part, S., 61, *69*
Pepinsky, H.B., 4, *7*, 73, *102*
Perfetti, C.A., 60, *70*
Pfifer, A., 11, *31*
Philips, S., 47, *55*
Polin, P., 61, *69*
Pung Guthrie, G., *231*

R

Ramirez, A., 36, *55*, 211, 218, *229*
Read, B., 187, *203*
Read, C., 157, 173, *185*
Rees, N.S., 127, 128, 129, *152*
Reid, D.K., 127, 129, *153*
Resnick, L.B., 73, *103*
Reyes, M., 35, *54*, 107, 108, 113, *125*, *126*
Rist, R., 211, *231*
Rivas, G., 128, *153*
Rock, D., 41, 43, *53*
Rodriguez-Brown, F.W., 147, *153*
Rogoff, B., 51, *55*
Rossman, T., 58, *70*
Roth, D., 236, *251*
Rubin, A., *103*, 109, 112, *126*
Rumelhart, D.E., 68, *70*, 72, *104*
Ryan, E.B., 36, *55*

S

Salvia, J., 127, 128, 151, *153*
Samuels, S.J., 60, *69*, 72, 74, 85, *103*, 104, 116, *125*
Sanders, T.S., 4, *7*, 73, *102*

Sanford, A.J., 159, *185*
SantaCruz, R., 129, *153*
Sato, T., 85, *104*
Saville-Troike, M., 130, *153*
Schachter, J., 172, *185*
Scanlon, D.M., 59, *70*
Schallert, D.L., 73, *104*
Schank, R., 49, *55*, 72, *104*, 159, *185*
Schmidt, F.H., 12, *31*
Schnick, W., 11, *30*
Schneider, W., 58, 59, *70*
Schultz, J., 208, *229*
Scollon, R., 47, *55*
Scollon, S.B.K., 47, *55*
Scribner, S., 1, 2, *8*, 10, *31*, 51, *55*
Segura, R., 10, *30*, 36, *52*, 128, 130, *151*
Sharp, D.W., 51, *52*
Shiffrin, R.M., 58, 59, *70*
Shipley, E., 188, *203*
Shuy, R., 128, *153*, 182, *185*
Skutnabb-Kangas, T., 179, *185*
Sloat, C., 47, *52*
Smith, E., 81, *101*
Smith, 62, *70*, 72, *104*, 131, *153*
Smith, J.K., 81, 88, *104*
Speidel, G.L., 47, *52*
Spencer, M., 128, *153*
Spencer, P.L., 131, *153*
Spinell, F., 187–190, 202, *203*
Spiro, R.J., 72, 73, 75, 76, 85, *104*, 107, 108, 109, *126*
Stanovich, K., 67, *70*, 72, 86, *104*
Stein, N., 107, 108, *125*, *126*
Sternberg, R.J., 1, *8*, 75, 76, 99, *104*, 190, *203*
Stokes, S.J., *47*, *52*, 236, *251*
Strauss, A., 221, *229*
Strong, M., 2, *8*, 81, *105*

T

Tannen, D., 162, *185*
Tatsuoko, K.K., 76, *104*
Tatsuoko, M.M., 76, *104*
Taylor, M., 107, 108, 109, *126*
Tempes, F., 132, *153*
Tharp, R., 47, 48, *52*, 55, 124, *125*
Thonis, E.W., 130, 147, 149, *153*

Tikunoff, W., 207, *231*
Tismer, W., 10, *31*
Torrance, N., 160, *185*
Toukomaa, P., 179, *185*
Trueba, H., 10, *31*, 128, *153*, 205, *231*, 239, 243–247, *252*
Troike, R.C., 130, *153*
Tucker, G.R., 130, *153*, 179, *185*
Tucker, J., 127, *151*, 197, *203*

U

Ulibarri, D.M., 128, *151*, *153*

V

Valdes-Fallis, G., 220, *231*
Van Dijk, T.A., 159, *184*
Van Kleeck, A., 188, *203*
Varnhagen, C.K., 35, *54*, 108, 113, *125*
Vellutino, F.R., 59, *70*, 72, 74, *104*
Vygotsky, L., 130, 131, *153*, 157, *185*

W

Wald, B., 33, *55*, 183, *185*
Wallat, C., 205, *229*
Warner, L.W., 12, *32*
Wilkinson, A., 187, 188, 189, 190, 202, *203*
Wilkinson, L.C., 187–190, 202, *203*, 205, *231*
Wilson, J., 208, *229*
Winograd, P.N., 73, *103*
Wisenbaker, J.M., 212, *229*
Wong Fillmore, L., 2, *8*, 77, 78, 81, 86, *104*, *105*, 149, *153*, *229*
Woods, E.C., 10, *32*
Woods, W.A., 72, 100, *105*
Wright, P., 129, *153*

Y

Yates, J.R., 129, *152*
Yirchott, L.S., 147, *153*
Ysseldyke, J., 127, 128, *151*, *153*

W

Wagner, R.K., 75, 76, *104*

Z

Zintz, M.V., 10, *32*

Subject Index

A
Alphabet, 158
Assessment, 75–76, 79, 98–100, 127–128, 131, 148

B
Bilingual
  children, 67
  East Los Angeles community, 155
  employment, 21
  instructional program, 133, 110–111, 212
  readers, 1, 65, 89–98
  Spanish readers, 110
  students, 64, 109, 121
Bilingualism, 33–35, 46
  additive, 35–36, 49
  subtractive, 35–36, 49

C
Cognitive anthropology, 51
Communicative competence, 207, 211
Comprehension
  content area, 107, 115
  discourse, 66
  expository, 108
  inferential, 85
  literal, 85
  metacomprehension, 190
  of informational material, 107–109
  questions, 117
  reading, 80–85, 100, 107–110, 158–159
  strategy, 92, 94
Conversational acts, 214–217
Critical thinking, 244, 247
Cultural
  capital, 12
  congruence, 211
  constraints, 209
  ecological theory, 9, 11, 15
  schemata, 66
  sociocultural environment, 237
  values, 22

D
Diglossia, 34
Discourse
  expository, 108

SUBJECT INDEX 259

features, 209
genres of, 163
informational, 109
narrative, 108, 163, 168–169, 183
strategies, 50–51
structure, 120
units, 162
Discriminant function analysis, 196, 198
Drawing, 157

E
Education
  aspirations, 37–41
  attainment, 36
  comparative research, 36
  outcomes, 37–41, 48
Ethnographic
  analysis, 243
  of speaking, 208
  research, 45–52

F
Factor analysis, 142

H
High School and Beyond Survey, 37–41

I
Immersion, 179
Information processing, 58
  accretion, 68
  automatic, 58–60, 62–63
  controlled, 58–60, 63
  restructuring, 68–69
  tuning, 68
  types of learning, 68
Interdependence hypothesis, 156, 167
Item difficulty, 82, 86

K
Kamehameha Early Education Program, 47–49
Knowledge
  background, 99
  deficiencies in, 99

L
Language
  and development, 130
  assessment, 79

attitudes, 36
dependent writing skills, 156
formal, 110, 112
independent writing skills, 156–157, 168
informal, 110, 112
input/output, 113
knowledge of, 196
lexical knowledge, 88
linguistic structures, 246
multiple functions of, 208, 210
natural, in context, 207
oral, 110, 212, 214
pragmatics, 187
preference, 34
proficiency, 38–40, 149, 220
reflective, 236
relationship between L1 & L2, 117
syntactic constraints, 88
transition to English, 146, 149
use in classrooms, 206–210
written, 110, 235
Learning disabilities, 127
  assessment, 148
  determination of, 146
Learning style, 78, 86
Literacy, 1, 9, 11, 22, 29, 237
  acquisition of English, 45–52, 236
  adult project, 3
  conventionalization principle, 158
  cross-language skills, 180
  development of, 157–159
  events, 47–52
  formal steps to, 225
  forms at home, 22
  functional, 2, 238
  language independent principle, 158, 181
  phonetic principle, 158
  read first theory, 179–180
  skills, 17, 19, 21, 157
  speak first theory, 179–180

M
Metalinguistic awareness, 187
  development of, 188–189
Mexican-Americans, 190
Mexican immigrants, 9, 28
Miscues, 51, 131, 159
  grammatical, 139
  graphic, 139
  sound, 139

O
Observation, 207–209

P
Paralinguistic cues, 161
Parental support, 27–28, 241
Participation structures, 47–48, 208, 216
Pragmatics
  development of, 187
  request functions, 188–189

Q
Qualitative data, 193
  analysis, 77, 82

R
Reading
  acquisition, 74–76
  adult learners, 60
  as information processing, 59–60
  child learners, 63
  comprehension, 66, 80, 85, 100, 107–110, 158–159
  constructivist models, 72
  content-area, 115
  decoding, 85
  development, 74–76
  diagnosis, 79, 100
  disabilities, 74
  English reading, 116, 127
  first language, 129
  good, 63–65, 69, 132
  interactive processes in, 66
  lessons, 213, 216, 225
  oral, 49–51, 80, 129
  oral miscues, 74, 80, 129–131, 139–141
  performance patterns, 89–98
  poor, 63–65, 69, 74, 89–98
  restructuring processes, 57, 62, 67–68
  second language, 71, 129, 132
  Spanish reading, 115, 127, 149
  strategies, 61, 146–147, 159
  symbol sound correspondence, 59, 67
  transfer, 127, 147
  transition to English, 111
  versus listening, 119
  word decoding, 59–60, 62, 67
Reasoning, 51

Recall of text, 115, 120–121
Requests
  embedded forms, 198
  functions, 188–189

S
Schooling
  language of, 206
  value of, 19
Scripts, 49–50
Second language
  acquisition, 3
  as information processing, 58
  English, 61
  ESL, 61–62, 134
  input, 108
  instruction, 134
  learning, 3, 4
  proficiency, 206
  readers, 127
  strategies, 63
Self-report, 207
Sentence complexity, 164–168
  index, 165, 167
  Spanish, 166
  subordination, 165–166
Social interaction, 121
Sociocultural environment, 237
Socioeconomic
  opportunities, 15
  status, 37–41
Special education, 131
Speech events, 49, 208, 216
Story schema, 96, 108
Strategies, 61, 146–147
  discourse, 50–51
  in reading, 61, 63, 86, 91, 94, 159
  inversion, 170
  matching words, 85
  metacognitive, 95
  schema-based, 95
  spelling, 177–178
  transfer, 147
Students
  adolescents, 162
  bilingual, 64, 109, 115, 124
  Chinese, 71, 211–212
  fluent English proficient (FEP), 111
  high school, 155
  Hispanic, 37–45, 71, 109, 127, 132, 162

SUBJECT INDEX 261

Hispanic college, 41–45
junior high school, 163
limited English proficient, 109–110, 128, 130
linguistic minority, 128
Mexican American, 190
monolingual English readers, 111
Spanish readers, 115

T

Teachers, 239, 241
   expectations, 211
   language use, 210–212, 217
Teaching styles, 239
Tests
   achievement scores, 38, 41, 46
   CTBS, 64–65, 111
   Gates-McGinitie vocabulary, 64–65
   Houghton-Mifflin Basal-word, 65
   Reading miscue inventory, 129, 135
   Scholastic Aptitude, 41–45
   Stanford Diagnostic Reading, 79
   Test of standard written English, 44
Text structure, 120
Threshold hypothesis, 124
Translation, 215, 221, 225
Turn taking, 207, 218, 226–228

V

Vocabulary, 92

W

Writing, 155, 235
   alphabets, 158
   and critical thinking, 247–249
   and speech, 159, 162
   context reduced, 160
   conventionalization, 158, 160
   English, 162, 239
   explicitness in, 160–161, 169–171
   instruction, 238, 243
   inversion, 164, 170
   language dependent, 156
   language independent, 156, 168
   meaning in, 235
   mechanics of, 173–179
   modules, 242
   motivation, 240–241
   organization in, 162
   pre-writing, 240–241
   punctuation, 164–165, 173
   sentence complexity, 164
   skills, 155, 157, 237
   Spanish, 162
   spelling, 164–165, 173, 176–177
   subject position, 168–169